THE ANGEL

THE ANGEL

The Egyptian Spy Who Saved Israel

URI BAR-JOSEPH

Translated from the Hebrew-language edition by David Hazony

HARPER

An Imprint of HarperCollins*Publishers*

HarperCollins books may be purchased for educational, business, or sales promotional use. For information, please e-mail the Special Markets Department at SPsales@harpercollins.com.

Originally published as *Hamal'ach* in Israel in 2010, 2011 by Kinneret Zmora-Bitan.

FIRST U.S. EDITION

Designed by Chris Welch

Library of Congress Cataloging-in-Publication Data

Bar-Joseph, Uri, author; Hazony, David, translator.
[ha-Mal'akh. English]
The angel : the Egyptian spy who saved Israel / Uri Bar-Joseph; translated from the Hebrew-language edition by David Hazony.
ISBN 978-0-06-242010-7
1. Marw'an, Ashraf, 1944–2007. 2. Politicians—Egypt—Biography.
3. Spies—Israel—Biography. 4. Spies—Egypt—Biography. 5. Israel. Mosad le-modi'in ve-taf'kidim meyu'hadim. 6. Israel-Arab War, 1973—Military intelligence—Israel.
DT107.828.M375 B3713   2016
327.125694062092—dc23   2015042832

16 17 18 19 20 OV/RRD 10 9 8 7 6 5 4 3 2

Contents

Cast of Characters

ASHRAF MARWAN, AKA "THE ANGEL": President Nasser's son-in-law, President Sadat's close adviser, and a spy for the Mossad (Israel's intelligence service)

MONA MARWAN: Daughter of President Nasser and the wife of Ashraf Marwan

GAMAL ABDEL NASSER: President of Egypt, 1952–1970

TAHIA GAMAL ABDEL NASSER: Wife of Gamal Abdel Nasser

SAMI SHARAF: Nasser's chief of staff and the strongman of the Mukhabarat (Egypt's intelligence service) until his arrest in 1971

MOHAMED HASSANEIN HEIKAL: Editor in chief of *Al-Ahram*, the most widely circulated Egyptian newspaper, from 1957 to 1974, and one of Nasser's closest friends

ANWAR SADAT: President of Egypt, 1970–1981

JEHAN SADAT: Wife of Anwar Sadat

SAAD EL-SHAZLY: The Egyptian army's chief of staff during the Yom Kippur War

MOHAMED ABDEL GHANI EL-GAMASY: The Egyptian army's chief of operations during the Yom Kippur War

HOSNI MUBARAK: President of Egypt, 1981–2011

ISRAEL

DUBI, AKA "ALEX" AND "DR. LORD" (FAMILY NAME STILL WITHHELD): Mossad operative and Marwan's handler from 1970 to 1998

MAJ. GEN. (RET.) ZVI "ZVIKA" ZAMIR: Chief of the Mossad from 1968 to 1974

FREDDY EINI: Zvi Zamir's chief of staff

SHMUEL GOREN: Head of Mossad operations in Europe, 1968–1974

GOLDA MEIR: Prime minister of Israel, 1969–1974

MOSHE DAYAN: Minister of defense, 1967–1974

YISRAEL GALILI: Minister without portfolio, and Prime Minister Meir's close adviser

LT. GEN. DAVID ELAZAR: Israel Defense Force (IDF) chief of staff, 1972–1974

MAJ. GEN. ELI ZEIRA: Director of Military Intelligence (MI), 1972–1974

BRIG. GEN. ARIEH SHALEV: Head of the MI Research Department, 1967–1974

LT. COL. MEIR MEIR: Head of Branch 6 (in charge of Egypt) in the MI Research Department, 1969–1972

LT. COL. YONAH BANDMAN: Head of Branch 6 in MI's Research Department, 1972–1974

AHRON BREGMAN: Israeli historian living in London

RONEN BERGMAN: Israeli journalist who wrote about Marwan

OTHERS

KAMAL ADHAM: Nephew of Saudi Arabia's King Faisal bin Abdulaziz, founder of the Saudi intelligence service, and Marwan's counterpart in maintaining relations between Sadat and King Faisal

MUAMMAR GADDAFI: Libya's leader, 1969–2011

ABDESSALAM JALLOUD: Gaddafi's number two, 1969–1977, and Marwan's counterpart in maintaining Egyptian-Libyan relations

ABDULLAH AL-MUBARAK AL-SABAH: Kuwaiti sheikh, billionaire, and a friend of Ashraf and Mona Marwan

SOUAD AL-SABAH: Wife of Abdullah al-Sabah, and also a friend of the Marwans

HAFEZ AL-ASSAD: President of Syria, 1970–2000

ROLAND "TINY" ROWLAND: British tycoon and Marwan's business partner in London since the early 1980s

MOHAMED AL-FAYED: London businessman and a rival of Rowland and Marwan

CHRIS BLACKHURST: British journalist who covered Marwan's activity in London in the 1980s

THE ANGEL

Prologue

THE FUNERAL AND THE MYSTERY

July is a hot month in Cairo, and July 1, 2007, was no exception. The narrow streets were crowded with millions of sweaty pedestrians, the crowds swelling with children on their summer vacation. The Khan al-Khalili bazaar was flooded with housewives who hurried to make their daily shopping and with tourists who came to watch the magic of the famous oriental market. And Cairo's eighty thousand taxi drivers honked and honked as they struggled to cut a path through the city's congested streets.

Very little of this mess penetrated the Mosque of Omar bin Abdul Aziz in the city's modern suburb of Heliopolis. The hundreds of mourners attending a funeral being held in the mosque wore unusually formal suits and ties or military uniforms. They were the elite of Egypt's political, security, and business establishments. And they all had come to pay their last respects to a man who was one of them—a family member, friend, colleague, and business partner for many years: Dr. Ashraf Marwan.

Marwan died four days earlier, when he mysteriously fell from the balcony of his fifth-floor luxury apartment not far from Piccadilly Circus in London. In 1966 he married President Gamal Abdel Nasser's daughter Mona. Joining the presidential family paved his way to the top echelon of Egyptian politics: first as an official in Nasser's presidential office; and later, after Nasser's death, as a close adviser to President Anwar el-Sadat. After he left public service he used his contacts in the Arab world in order to build a shady business career and had been living in London since 1981.

Marwan's body arrived in Cairo a day earlier. Dr. Zakaria Azmi, the head of the office of President Hosni Mubarak, and Ahmed Shafik, the minister of civil aviation, waited at the airport for the coffin. Now, at the mosque, Gamal ("Jimmy") Mubarak, the president's son and heir apparent, was comforting Marwan's widow and her two sons. This was not merely an official gesture but a personal one as well: Gamal was a close friend of Ashraf Marwan's son, and the two frequently visited each other's homes. The Marwans attended Gamal Mubarak's spectacular wedding at Sharm el-Sheik at the southern tip of the Sinai Peninsula that had taken place less than two months earlier.

President Mubarak himself was participating in an African summit in Accra, Ghana, and could not attend the funeral. But he released an official statement describing Marwan as "a true patriot of his country." Mubarak added that he was personally aware of the great service that the departed had rendered for his country. General Omar Suleiman, the strongman of Egypt's intelligence and military establishment, who attended the funeral, provided the official authorization to the presidential declaration of Marwan's unquestionable patriotism.

The legislative branch was represented by the Speaker of the Egyptian Parliament and the head of the upper house. Senior generals of the armed forces stood next to business tycoons, and academicians including the president of Cairo University were seen talking with senior journalists such as the head of *Al-Ahram*, Egypt's leading daily.

Dr. Muhammad Sayyid Tantawy, the former grand mufti of

Egypt who in 1996 was nominated by Mubarak to be the grand imam of Al-Azhar University, the oldest institute of its kind in the Muslim world, led the religious ceremonies. Close by were Marwan's family members: The widow, Mona, was dressed in a dark, elegant dress, her head covered by a veil; the firstborn son, Gamal— who like many members of his generation was given Nasser's first name—stood next to her, and next to him stood her younger son, Hani. Hani was married to the daughter of Amr Moussa, Egypt's former minister of foreign affairs and, in 2007, the secretary of the Arab League. Moussa himself was not seen at the ceremony.

Despite a well-known animosity between Mona and the rest of Nasser's family, her brothers and sister came to pay their last respects. None of Anwar Sadat's family was present, however. This was quite a surprise, as some of Cairo's journalists noted, since prior to his assassination in October 1981, Sadat and his wife, Jehan, were known to be close friends of Ashraf and Mona Marwan.

Relatively speaking, however, the absence of Jehan Sadat and her daughters from the funeral was inconsequential. As some of the mourners surely sensed, the honor paid to their former colleague was no more than a facade covering up a very painful truth: that despite all the official recognition, the man they were burying was in fact no Egyptian patriot at all. He was, rather, the worst traitor in their nation's history.

SINCE THE EARLY 1990s, it had been known that the Israeli Mossad had "a miraculous source" at the heart of Egypt's strategic nervous system in the years that led up to the 1973 October war—the most intensive war in the history of the Arab-Israeli conflict. Some people—such as Maj. Gen. Eli Zeira, chief of Israel's Military Intelligence who published his war memoirs in 1993—claimed that the source was actually a double agent who betrayed the Mossad at the most critical moment, thus enabling the Arab armies to surprise

Israel on Yom Kippur, the most sacred Jewish holiday. But there were others, with firsthand knowledge of the events no less reliable than Zeira, who dismissed the double agent theory and firmly believed that without the source's last-minute warning, Israel would likely have lost the war.

As time passed, additional details concerning the identity of the spy and his activities had become known. In 2001 he was identified as being exceptionally close to both President Nasser and President Sadat and as the one who was allegedly nicknamed by the few Israelis who knew who he was, "the son-in-law." Egyptian journalists actually asked Marwan if he was the famous spy. When Marwan denied the claim, Ahron Bregman, an Israeli historian at King's College in London who played a major role in exposing his identity, confirmed to an Egyptian journalist that "the miraculous Mossad source" was, indeed, Marwan.

Marwan himself kept denying the accusations. But in the wake of a court ruling in Tel Aviv on June 7, 2007, that affirmed that he was, indeed, the famous spy, Marwan began to feel the rope tightening around his neck. Three weeks later, he was dead.

At least a few who attended the funeral, such as Gen. Omar Suleiman, knew very well who gave the order to get rid of Marwan and why. After all, the violent death of Marwan saved the Egyptian leadership the embarrassment that would have been involved in putting him on trial and publicly admitting that a prominent member of the Egyptian ruling elite—a man whose wife was a daughter of the legendary Nasser, whose first son was a good friend and business partner of the likely heir of President Mubarak, and whose second son was married to the daughter of Amr Moussa— had been a Mossad spy at the height of the Egyptian-Israeli conflict.

Following the fall of the Mubarak regime in early 2011, the question of who gave the order to liquidate Marwan was answered as well. According to the Egyptian magazine *Rose al-Yusuf*, it was none other than Mubarak himself, the man who, following Marwan's mysterious death, told reporters, "I do not doubt his loyalty."

ON MAY 10, 2009, CBS's *60 Minutes* investigated the rise and fall of Ashraf Marwan and the controversy surrounding his death. At the very end of the episode, titled "The Perfect Spy," CBS's Steve Kroft summed up by posing the toughest question this way: "So in the end, who did Ashraf Marwan really betray? And who finally killed him? If the truth wasn't buried with him, it is most likely buried somewhere in a top-secret vault."

This book unveils the truth. And in order to get to it, we have to go back to Cairo and to the year 1944, when it all began.

Chapter 1

CAIRO, 1944–1970: BEGINNINGS

Mohammed Ashraf Abu al-Wafa Marwan, known simply as Ashraf Marwan, was born on February 2, 1944, in the home of his family at 5 Al-Hakma'a Street in Cairo's Manshiyat al-Bakri district. It was then, and remains today, a middle-class neighborhood in the new section of the capital. Marwan's family came from the best Egyptian stock. On his mother's side, he was part of the Al-Fayyad clan, which owned property in the village of Sa el-Hajar in Gharbia Province, an agricultural district in the Nile delta north of Cairo. His father's family came from the village of Sohagha, in Minya Province, about 150 miles south of Cairo. The Marwan family was one of the most honorable clans in the region; many of its members continue to live there today.

It was Ashraf Marwan's grandfather, Muhammad Ahmed Marwan, who moved his branch of the family to Cairo. A graduate of Al-Azhar University, the oldest and most important school of Islamic law and theology in the Arab world, he rose to become the chief of the Sharia courts in Egypt. Ashraf Marwan's father, Abu al-Wafa Marwan, was a career officer in the Egyptian military. He started out as a junior-level officer in the army of King Farouk and worked his way up the military ladder until retiring, during the

1970s, with the rank of major general. In his final posting, he served as deputy commander of the Egyptian Republican Guard, an army division mostly responsible for internal security. Despite the fact that Ashraf Marwan and his family were in Cairo, they remained in contact with the village of their origins and would travel there for visits and family celebrations. According to villagers, it was Ashraf himself who ensured, during the 1970s, that Sohagha became the first village in the area to be connected to the electrical grid. For this, and for the warmth and support that Marwan's family gave the village over the years, they are grateful to this day.[1]

THERE WAS NOTHING especially unusual about Marwan's upbringing. Together with his brother, Hani, and two younger sisters, Mona and Azza, he grew up in a typical middle-class home in Cairo. In July 1952, when he was eight years old, Egypt witnessed the revolution of the Free Officers Movement, which brought to power Gamal Abdel Nasser—the man who, in a few short years, would become the most revered leader in the Arab world. Though Marwan's father was a senior officer, he was in no way connected to the coup. But the family grew close to the new leadership nonetheless, because many of its leading figures came to live in their neighborhood shortly after coming to power. Nasser and his family had already lived in Manshiyat al-Bakri for a few years, and quite a few of the Free Officers now moved there as well. It quickly became known as the nerve center of political power in the new regime.

Throughout his childhood, Marwan attended schools in the same neighborhood: six years at the Manshiyat al-Bakri elementary school, three at the Alhalfaa middle school, and finally at Kubri al-Quba High School, where he majored in science. As was the norm in Egypt, schools were tuition-free, but the family had to pay for schoolbooks, as well as other expenses, such as health insurance. His high school studies were intensive: seven or eight hours per day, including seven weekly class hours of math, five of English, four of French, and three each of chemistry, biology, and a third scientific discipline of his choosing.

Already at this stage many of Marwan's outstanding qualities became evident, especially the sparkling intellect that earned him notably high grades—grades that gained him admission into the army's elite academic reserve. That program allowed him to defer his military service and to enroll in a bachelor's degree program in chemistry at Cairo University in Giza. His studies included a special officer's training program, which he completed with the rank of second lieutenant. In 1965 he finished his degree and began serving as an officer and chemical engineer in the Egyptian military industry.

Despite his intensive course of study, Marwan found time to read prodigiously about subjects far outside his field—particularly economics, banking, and finance. People who remember him from that period describe him as tall, attractive, and friendly, someone who knew how to get the most out of life. Two close friends from his college days, Mohammed Fakhri and Essam Siam, studied with him in the academic reserves. Siam chose a military career and eventually attained the rank of major general. He also built a successful career as a soccer commentator and referee on the international level, and served for years on the soccer federations of Egypt and Africa. During their time together in the mid-1960s, the three regularly enjoyed the nightlife of Cairo; on Fridays, when there were no classes, they often traveled together to Alexandria, where they tanned on the beach, swam in the sea, and strolled the promenade.

Ashraf Marwan's best energies, however, were spent on the tennis court. He was an enthusiastic member of the Heliopolis Sporting Club, just half a mile from his parents' home. It was here, at the age of twenty-one, that he met the woman who would be both his wife and his springboard up the Egyptian hierarchy.[2]

MONA ABDEL NASSER was the president's daughter. She was born in January 1947, two years after her parents were married and a year after the birth of their first daughter, Hoda. Hoda's name, which is related to the Arabic word *hadiya* or "gift," was given by her mother, Tahia, to express their gratitude for the baby despite the fact that they had wanted a son. After Mona, the Nassers went on to have three sons: Khaled, who would one day enter politics and be accused of conspiring to assassinate Israeli and American diplomats; Abdel Hakim; and Abdel Hamid. Mona was eighteen years old, studying at the American University in Cairo and still living with her parents, when she first met Ashraf Marwan.

Life in the Nasser household was far from simple. In the mid-1950s, when the Egyptian leader first blazed his way onto the political stage, he quickly became a kind of messianic figure for the masses who saw him as one of them and, simultaneously, as a wondrously talented leader who would take them out of their collective squalor and lead them into a new era of national pride and prosperity. His impressive early achievements—evicting the British from the Suez Canal in 1954; cutting a major arms deal with the Soviet Union in 1955; nationalizing the canal in 1956; and standing strong in the face of the "tripartite aggression" of the Israelis, French, and British during the Suez Crisis a few months after that—confirmed and entrenched his status at home and abroad. His agrarian reforms, begun shortly after he took office, as well as other initiatives suggesting a more equitable distribution of wealth, testified to his radical political worldview and gave his regime, beginning around 1960, a socialist overtone never before heard in the Arab world. Graced with a personal charm that appealed to leaders and ordinary folk alike, and guided by a pan-Arabist worldview coupled with his own impressive political and diplomatic insights that enabled him to deftly overcome both internal and external challenges, Mona's father turned himself, in just a few years, from an unknown Egyptian army officer into the greatest Arab leader since Saladin. (The fact that the historical Saladin was not actually an Arab but a Kurd mattered little.)

WE CANNOT KNOW just how much of Nasser's legendary status affected his family life or how it affected the way he raised his children. As opposed to other Arab rulers, especially his predecessor King Farouk, Nasser never took advantage of his status for personal gain. His family continued living in the same house they bought in Manshiyat al-Bakri immediately after he married Tahia in 1944, and Tahia continued to run the household on her husband's relatively modest government salary. The family continued driving the same little Austin that Nasser bought when he was still a teacher at the military academy. In 1954, when the car was on its last legs, they replaced it with a Ford they bought on installments.

In a society where graft was the grease that made the whole machine run, Nasser was a paragon of probity. At the same time, he clearly knew that his colleagues in the Egyptian leadership, especially his good friend Abdel Hakim Amer, had their hands in the till, and he saw their corruption as a weakness that he could take advantage of for his own ends. Nasser, moreover, felt a sincere revulsion toward the very wealthy. He once paid a visit to the al-Jezira Sporting Club, a preferred hangout for Egyptian aristocrats, but the atmosphere there was so repugnant to him that he refused ever to return. He also was unwilling to give his children any unusual privileges, and he always reminded them of their origins in the village of Beni Mur on the banks of the Nile. "I am very proud that I come from a poor villager family," he told them, "and history will bear witness to the fact that Nasser was born to a poor family, and I promise that he will live and die as a poor man." His elder daughter recalls that her life was "an ordinary life of an Egyptian girl of her generation." His son Khaled insisted that he never received any special consideration in his own political career.[3]

Of course, there can be no doubt that Nasser's children were acutely aware of their changed status when their father came to power. True, they continued to attend the Kawmeya school in Giza, where children of the new elites went, and to play with the same friends. But because Nasser preferred working at home and receiving foreign dignitaries there rather than at the palaces of Cairo, life in their house was anything but normal. They built additions to the house more than once, both to make room for their growing family and to make it easier for foreign leaders and their staffs to work effectively. The house soon gained a tennis court, a library, and more. On occasion, when the guests were especially interesting, Nasser's children met them as well. One photograph showing Khaled with the world boxing champion, Muhammad Ali, offers a snapshot of their life. Obviously their father's status had some impact on the children's lives, but clearly the impact was limited and varied from child to child. That emerges most clearly in the different experiences of Mona, Marwan's beloved, and her older sister, Hoda.

Hoda was, by all accounts, the more serious and intelligent of the two. Her schoolteachers, who on Nasser's orders denied her any preferential treatment, later recalled her innate smarts, dedication, and work ethic, which enabled her to finish at the top of her class. Hoda's life story took what must have appeared to many as its most natural course: a bachelor's degree in economics and political science, and then a doctorate in political science, from Cairo University. During her studies, she and her husband, Hatem Sadeq, started working at the Center for Strategic Studies established at the *Al-Ahram* newspaper in 1968. Her family ties clearly helped her get the job, but her personal achievements justified it as well. Because she was so talented, and because of the career path she chose, many saw her as a natural successor to her father—an Egyptian answer to Indira Gandhi. But Hoda, it turned out, had other plans: She preferred the academic life, and her political potential was never realized.

Mona, on the other hand, was not as bright as her older sister, and a few people who knew her during that period remember her as a frivolous girl who, more than anything else, enjoyed a good party. She showed little interest in politics or anything requiring intellectual effort. As opposed to her sister, whose grades in high school cut her path to an academic career at the top university in Egypt, Mona's grades were mediocre. Nevertheless, after high school, she wished to join her sister and study economics and political science at Cairo University but did not have the required grades. Although the minister of higher education and the university's authorities agreed to accept Mona, Nasser rejected any favors for his daughter and sent her to study at the American University in Cairo.[4] He had little choice: During the 1960s, it was a private institution with a relatively poor reputation, and the students who enrolled there were those with parents of means but who lacked the grades needed to get into Cairo University. Nasser himself, so he claimed, had trouble covering Mona's tuition. Mona's habits changed little when she got to college. Friends of hers from that period recall that she spent at least as much time at the Heliopolis Sporting Club's tennis courts and in coffee shops as she did in class.

In the summer of 1965, after completing her first year of college, she met Ashraf Marwan. Within a year, they were married.[5]

IT WAS NOT a chance encounter. Marwan's younger sister Azza, with whom he was very close, was Mona's age and a good friend of hers, and she made the introduction after telling Mona all about her handsome and talented brother. According to the memoirs of Tahia, Mona's mother, they first met at the Heliopolis Sporting Club, which at the time was one of the most trendy meeting spots for Egyptian youths from good families.[6] According to Mona

herself, however, she met Marwan on the beach, apparently in
Alexandria.[7] Wherever it was, two things are clear. First, Mona
fell in love with Marwan right then and there. The girl's heart
was swept away by his tall and trim figure, his fine features, and
his expensive clothes.[8] Second, what attracted the handsome and
ambitious young man was not Mona's looks, her wit, or any other
personal qualities. It was, simply, her family. He was twenty-one
years old, hungry and ambitious, and had set his sights on great-
ness. A marriage to the daughter of Nasser would put him directly
on course to fulfill his destiny.[9] Yet while most of our sources see
this as his main reason for dating Mona, there are those, however,
who insist that Marwan genuinely fell in love with her.[10]

Mona told her father about her new boyfriend not long after
they started dating. She apparently did not hide her desire to marry
and start a family with him. Nasser received by this stage many
requests for the hands of his daughters from the sons of rich and
noble persons. He refused them all.[11] He suspected anyone who
showed romantic interest in Mona, and he wanted to hear more.
She told him about Marwan, about how he came from a "Saidi"
family (that is, from the best Egyptian lineage), and that his father,
Abu al-Wafa Marwan, was an army colonel.

Nasser had heard enough. He immediately ordered a comprehensive inquiry into Ashraf Marwan.[12] The man responsible was
Sami Sharaf, Nasser's chief of staff and one of the most powerful
men in Egypt—and who, in years to come, would play a crucial
role in Marwan's story.

The report Sharaf sent to Nasser was not flattering. It emphasized Marwan's ambitiousness and his love for the high life, while
doubting the sincerity of his feelings for Mona. For Nasser, a puri-
tan in his personal life who was already worried about his daughter's lifestyle, this sort of suitor was not a positive choice, to say the
least. Nasser was about to marry Hoda off to a serious, learned,

modest gentleman, and her groom was clearly a better model for the kind of man he would want Mona to marry as well.[13] Having received Sharaf's report, Nasser sat Mona down for a heart-to-heart talk, with the aim of convincing her not to marry Ashraf Marwan.

Mona refused to listen. She had made up her mind and insisted that Nasser enter into negotiations with Marwan's father over the terms of their engagement. Nasser rebuffed her repeated requests, but in the end, the greatest Arab leader since Saladin was bested by his even more stubborn daughter. He agreed to meet Ashraf Marwan's father.[14]

THE ENGAGEMENT AGREEMENT reached between the two families did not strictly follow tradition. The groom's family would pay a dowry of 1,000 Egyptian pounds (about $100), but no amount was set to be paid in the event of a divorce. Neither did the groom's family buy jewelry for the bride, as tradition would have it. Instead, Marwan gave Mona a diamond ring that had previously belonged to his mother, and to her mother before her.[15]

The wedding was held in July 1966 in the Nassers' home. As opposed to other family events, this was a grand affair. Years later Mona recalled that her father had felt a need to host a large event because Hoda's wedding the previous year had been more modest, with many important people left off the invitation list. This time, invitations were extended not only to close family members but also to classmates of the bride and groom, as well as the entire top political echelon of Egypt, including members of the Revolutionary Council. The marriage contract was written by the *madhun* (the official who handles marriages and divorces) of Cairo, who in 1944 had officiated at the wedding of Mona's parents. War Minister Abdel Hakim Amer, an old friend of Nasser's, signed as a witness to the marriage contract, as did

Prime Minister Zakaria Mohieddin, who was one of the leaders
of the Free Officers Movement.

Photos and movies from the ceremony show Nasser sitting with
his wife to his right, his son Khaled to his left, and Khaled's younger
brother Abdel Hakim to Khaled's left. Ashraf and Mona sat opposite
her parents, next to Hoda and her husband. After hearing the rec-
itation of the first sura of the Quran and a few other texts, Nasser
gave his blessing to the young couple. Marwan, in his dapper gray
suit, sky-blue tie, and white shirt, stood up and embraced his new
father-in-law. But not everything was rosy: In the middle of the
ceremony, Mona suddenly turned to her father and demanded a
pair of earrings as a wedding gift. When Nasser balked, Field Marshal Amer took matters into his own hands, tracked down a pair of
earrings, and handed them to the beaming bride.[16]

The entertainment was world-class, with performances by two
of the Arab world's top singers, Abdel Halim Hafez and Umm Kulthum. Hafez was a movie star at the peak of his career, and very
close with Nasser's chief of staff, Sami Sharaf. Hafez would often
visit the President's Office just to take in the revolutionary air—
which he would then weave into his patriotic songs.[17] Among his
other hits, he sang "The Wanderer" ("al-Sawah"), which was one
of Nasser's favorites.

Umm Kulthum was the greatest female Arab vocalist of the
twentieth century. She had known Nasser for years. A few days
after the coup of July 1952, Nasser called her on the phone and
promised her that if until then she had been the voice of Egypt,
now she would become the voice of the whole Arab world. He
also told her that he had deliberately scheduled the Revolutionary
Council's secret meetings to coincide with live broadcasts of her
concerts on Egyptian radio because he knew that the whole country was listening to her, and the council could meet without in-
terruption.[18] Nasser's words had filled her with pride. And indeed,

Kulthum's concerts, broadcast on the first Thursday of every month across the Arab world via the Voice of Cairo, were a cultural event of the first order, stopping the entire Arab Middle East in its tracks as millions of listeners, from the poorest *fallah* to the wealthiest sheikh, were glued to radio sets at home or transistors on the street corners, listening to her magical voice. Kulthum's repertoire included nationalistic songs as well as love songs. She sang "The New Dawn" in praise of the short-lived United Arab Republic, which joined Egypt with Syria from 1958 to 1961; her song "Baghdad, the Lions' Fortress" was written after the overthrow of Iraq's monarchy in 1958. But at a wedding in Nasser's own home, she sang none of these. At Mona's request, she sang "You Are the Love" ("Ant Al-Hub"), which she first sang in 1965 and had become one of her greatest hits ever.[19]

Radio Cairo reported on the wedding, stressing the joyful atmosphere and the loving glances that the couple and their parents exchanged, in the best romantic tradition of Egyptian movies of that time. Newspapers ran photographs of the event as well, showing Ashraf Marwan, dressed to the nines, standing with his young bride in her traditional wedding gown, as she held her father's hand.

Needless to say, not a word was mentioned about Nasser's dissatisfaction with his daughter's choice, even though the president was far from alone in his suspicions. One of Marwan's friends recalled, years later, that his "marriage to Mona did not surprise anyone who knew him, and testified to his lofty ambitions."[20]

THE NEWLYWEDS MOVED into a small apartment purchased for them in Cairo. Nasser, who had married off two daughters in less than a year, wanted to buy both of them apartments. He knew little about the real estate market in Cairo, however, and had never paid much attention to his own finances, so he had no idea that he didn't have anything close to the necessary funds. A number of his friends got together and paid a major part of the cost, without Nasser's ever finding out.[21] Just as he helped Hoda and her husband get jobs with the *Al-Ahram* newspaper conglomerate, so did Nasser help Mona. But while Hoda and Hatem were talented enough to work at the paper's prestigious strategic studies center, Mona worked at the children's books division.[22] Some people saw their jobs as a fitting expression of the difference between the abilities and talents of the two sisters.[23]

Ashraf Marwan's own life went through changes then as well. His marriage to Mona dramatically improved his status and brought him closer to the main centers of power in Egypt, much as he had hoped. He was soon transferred from the chemical plants of the Egyptian military industry to the Republican Guards, a military division whose main purpose was to protect sensitive facilities on the home front. Yet while Marwan probably viewed the transfer as a step up, it was also a sign of Nasser's fragile faith in his son-in-law. He wanted to keep him close.

It wasn't close enough. Additional information concerning Marwan's ambitions that reached the Egyptian leader convinced him that another move was needed. In 1968, Ashraf Marwan was transferred to work in the President's Office, under the direct supervision of the chief of staff, Sami Sharaf.[24]

SHARAF WAS WIDELY known as a consummate schemer and one of the most ambitious men in Nasser's entourage. He was one of those shadowy types who wend their way into the corridors of power in every dictatorial regime. Born in Heliopolis to a doctor of means, Sharaf finished his studies with honors at the military academy in 1949 and joined the artillery corps. After the revolution, rumors surfaced that he was plotting against the new regime, together with other officers. At a certain point, he turned on the other conspirators, handing them over to Interior Minister Zakaria Mohieddin, who oversaw the internal security apparatus (Mukhabarat). Mohieddin was impressed with the young officer's talents and took him on board at his intelligence unit. The interior minister would eventually cool to Sharaf, however, and when Nasser asked him in 1961 to find him a new presidential chief of staff, Mohieddin sent Sharaf to the President's Office.

In this new post, the former artillery officer brought out his biggest guns. He quickly assembled a whole new intelligence operation. The agency's main task was to collect both secret and public information on every senior member of the regime. Sharaf became Nasser's eyes and ears in the top levels of Egyptian society.[25]

Under Sharaf's direction, the President's Office became the nerve center of Egypt, as well as the filter through which information reached the president. Anything of diplomatic, political, or military significance, even ordinary gossip collected by the security agencies, went through him, and he personally edited the intelligence reports written exclusively for Nasser. At around the same time, the Egyptian leader began cutting himself off, avoiding direct meetings with top figures in the regime. It wasn't long before there remained only a small number of people—such as his close friend Mohamed Hassannein Heikal, editor of *Al-Ahram*—who could meet Nasser without the chief of staff's prior approval. Sharaf made sure not only to isolate Nasser but also to sully the reputations of various individuals as the need arose. Anyone who had lost favor with Nasser quickly found themselves out of a job, and sometimes in prison. Sharaf quickly amassed immense power, becoming one of the most feared men in Egypt.[26]

When Ashraf Marwan was transferred to the President's Office, he was not unknown to Sami Sharaf. By this point, Sharaf must have had a thick dossier on Nasser's new son-in-law.

Marwan began working at the President's Office soon after the birth of his first son—Nasser's first grandson—Gamal. The president dedicated some of his extremely limited free time to his grandson, as well as to his new granddaughter that Hoda had given him at around the same time. Ashraf Marwan, however, felt neglected. Fully aware of his father-in-law's mistrust, he failed to develop any significant relationship with him. Instead of mitigating the sense of distance and hesitation coming from Nasser, time had only made things worse. People who overheard exchanges between the two recall a young Marwan standing tense before his father-in-law, sometimes even quaking in his presence, stammering when he had to speak with him directly.[27]

This was not what Marwan had in mind when he married Mona. Proximity to the core of power in Egypt certainly advanced his personal and political goals, but life in the shadow of a father-in-law who had no trust in him, and under a manipulative and aggressive boss who was constantly watching over him, was oppressive. Given that Marwan knew full well what kind of fate awaited people who crossed Sami Sharaf, he may have actually been afraid as well. The close supervision also prevented the young couple from enjoying life the way they had in college. Marwan's salary was a pittance. Abdel Majid Farid, who worked with him in the President's Office and wrote an important book about Nasser's final years, writes that Marwan earned 70 Egyptian pounds per month—the lowest salary of anyone in the office.[28] According to another source, he was a "level-6 employee," with a salary of 32 pounds per month. Either way, his minuscule pay reflected his inconsequential position. According to the same source, Mona, while working in the children's books division of *Al-Ahram*, earned 35 pounds per month.[29] While the couple's income was reasonable for a middle-class family, it didn't match their expectations for a better life. What was more, Cairo in the years after the defeat in the 1967 Six-Day War was not the hopping town it had once been, with a much greater focus on the growing conflict with Israel, including a military buildup that would allow Egypt to restore what had been lost (namely, honor and the Sinai Peninsula); there was also a focus on correcting fundamental weaknesses such as the poor quality of the army's manpower as well as corruption at all levels, including the level of the minister of war, that the war had laid bare.

So whether it was because he really wanted to go back to school, or just to get out from under the eyes of his father-in-law, Ashraf Marwan decided to put in a request to study abroad. To justify it, he cited the poor level of educational institutions in Egypt. Even Cairo University, where he had completed his bachelor's degree, and which was considered the best in the Arab world, didn't meet his profession's standards. Criticisms of Egypt's higher education system, especially in the sciences, were even voiced in public.[30] Without a doubt, life outside Egypt looked more promising. In 1968, the Marwans relocated to London, where he was to undertake a master's degree program in chemistry.

Nasser gave his approval.

IN LATE 1968, Ashraf and Mona Marwan arrived in one of the most dynamic and stimulating cities on earth. The music and fashion mecca, the ultimate playground for the beautiful and the wealthy—this was London of the Beatles and Rolling Stones, boutiques on Carnaby Street, fashion realms of Chelsea and Knightsbridge. The reigning designer was Mary Quant, inventor of the miniskirt and hot pants; and the supermodel was Twiggy, who gave new, diminutive dimensions to feminine beauty. London had become the setting for countless movies and novels, the global capital of the new world culture, the premier destination for anyone fashionable and young.

It fit Ashraf Marwan like a glove.

The couple quickly settled in. Nasser had arranged a modest allowance for them, and Marwan added to it his salary as a junior employee at the Egyptian embassy in London. He also began his studies, and Mona took care of the home and raised their boy, Gamal. Their relationship was a good one. Mona loved Ashraf, even revered him. And Marwan, even if he didn't love her in the same way, at least remained faithful. London, however, was a city of infinite temptations, and Ashraf Marwan was easily tempted. Soon after their arrival, he was spotted at the card tables of the Playboy Club, the most grandiose casino in the city, which, since its opening in 1965, had become a magnet for those wealthy enough to play there. Marwan wasn't among them, but he somehow managed to get the most out of what London offered, and to feed his fondness for gambling.

But he was careless, and soon his behavior caught the attention, and fierce disapproval, of Nasser. With his own two hands, Ashraf Marwan precipitated the greatest crisis that ever took place between them—and he nearly lost everything he had gained.

Soon after arriving in London, the Marwans befriended a couple who themselves had only recently arrived: Sheikh Abdullah al-Mubarak al-Sabah and his second wife, Souad, daughter of Muhammad al-Sabah. The sheikh was the youngest child of the founder of modern Kuwait, Mubarak al-Kabir. In 1954 he became commander of the Kuwaiti armed forces, and he served for a few years as deputy prime minister until his resignation and retirement from political life in 1961. He spent the 1960s outside of Kuwait, mostly in London, until he returned to his home country in the mid-1970s. In 1960 he married Souad, who was nearly thirty years younger, and who would give birth to five of his six children. But Souad al-Sabah was also an important personality in her own right. At age thirty-one she finished her bachelor's degree at the University of Cairo with honors, and she would later receive her doctorate in economics from the University of Surrey in Great Britain. She was also a poet, publishing three collections in 1960.

Later she published additional books, including academic works. She was also something of a social activist, speaking out on the status of women, education, and culture.

The sheikh, who was a pan-Arabist and ideologically anti-British, first met Nasser in 1956 and was immediately enraptured, counting himself as one of the Egyptian leader's most ardent followers. So was his wife, who gradually became the model of an educated, modern Arab woman. By Nasser's invitation, they moved to Egypt in 1965 and built a web of relationships there. The sheikh took part in various official ceremonies, such as the opening of parliamentary sessions, Revolution Day celebrations, and visits from foreign leaders. The couple became close friends of the Nassers and were invited to Mona and Ashraf's wedding.[31]

So it was only natural that upon the Marwans' arrival in London, the Al-Sabahs took them under their wing, showing them the city and taking them out for nights on the town. And when Ashraf Marwan's gambling habit got him in trouble, Souad even covered his debts. We have no reason to suspect any romantic link between Souad and Marwan. He may have been handsome and charismatic, and she was only two years his elder while her husband was much older, but still there is no evidence of an affair. And indeed, the 1995 biography she wrote about her husband is a paean to the man with whom she shared a rich, long life. Nor is it reasonable to assume that Marwan cheated on his wife so soon after his marriage— not just out of fear of his father-in-law but also because infidelity was not known to be among his weaknesses. The explanation that Souad gave after the fact was compelling: She believed it was simply unthinkable that the daughter of the greatest leader in the Arab world, mother to Nasser's grandson, should live in poverty. Since she had the means to prevent it, she acted accordingly. This also fit the Kuwaiti couple's pattern of financial generosity: In early 1963 the sheikh donated twenty-five jeeps to the Egyptian army, and twice, just before the 1967 and 1973 wars, he gave $1 million to help defray Egypt's military expenses. In 1966 he personally gave Nasser $1 million to do with as he pleased. Nasser donated the money to education in Egypt.[32] So it was clear that the Al-Sabahs, who had enjoyed the fruits of Kuwaiti oil, saw it as completely natural to support projects they thought were dear to Nasser's heart, or the hearts of his family.

However, it is difficult to discern what Ashraf Marwan was thinking when he went into debt and accepted the money. As someone who had worked under Sami Sharaf, he knew what kind of scrutiny faced anyone connected to the Egyptian regime. That was why he went to London in the first place. Marwan was well aware that Nasser strongly opposed any effort to translate the reverence people felt for him into gifts to his family. So he must have known what kind of tightrope he was walking when he took the money, and what kind of crisis it might cause if it were discovered. But Ashraf Marwan apparently enjoyed taking risks. He had tremendous self-confidence, in part because he had succeeded in becoming part of the presidential family in Egypt, and this confidence stayed with him so long as he didn't come into daily contact with Nasser himself. He clearly didn't see anything wrong with taking the money. In his view—a view grounded firmly in the norms of the society he grew up in—both giving and taking bribes were an inextricable part of life. In this case one couldn't even call it a bribe. Ashraf Marwan had nothing he could give the Al-Sabahs in return, other than a feeling of intimacy with the president's family.

Under the circumstances, a major clash with Nasser was only a matter of time.

The Marwans' deepening friendship with the Al-Sabahs did not go unnoticed at the Egyptian embassy in London, which had been given a standing order to keep an eye on the president's son-in-law. Shortly after the two couples began spending time together, Sami

Sharaf started getting reports. And when money changed hands, he heard about it immediately. The distance from Sharaf's office to Nasser's ear was not far. The damning evidence was on the president's desk within hours, and his reaction was swift and explosive. He ordered the embassy to put Marwan on the first flight to Cairo. Upon his arrival, Marwan was taken directly to Nasser, who demanded an explanation. Not that anything Marwan said would have made a difference. He tried to argue that London's high cost of living put him in a position where he had to take the money. Nasser, however, had heard about the couple's lifestyle in the city, their nights out, and Ashraf's gambling. He demanded that his daughter return to Egypt, and when she did, he insisted that she divorce Marwan.

But Mona, who loved Ashraf with all her heart, refused.

Just as in their dispute over the marriage itself, this time, too, it emerged that in the struggle between the peeved father and his implacable daughter, Mona had a leg up. Nasser capitulated. He summoned Marwan's father to meet him, and the two worked out an agreement that would allow the marriage to continue without the risk that the president of Egypt would gain a reputation as someone whose family is supported by a Kuwaiti sheikh.[33] First, Marwan would return the money he received from Souad al-Sabah. Second, Ashraf and Mona would move back to Egypt. Ashraf would go back to working for Sami Sharaf; he would continue his studies in London but he would go to England only for a few days at a time to submit papers or take exams. The rest of the time he would remain under Sharaf's watchful eye. And so, Ashraf Marwan went back to the life he had so desperately wanted to escape.[34]

Although Marwan's standing in Nasser's eyes was certainly fragile, the president would at times make use of his diplomatic skills. Possibly the most important case involved Saad el-Shazly, who later became chief of staff of Egypt's armed forces during the 1973 war. In his memoirs, Shazly recounts how, in March 1969, he quit his post as commander of the special forces because of Nasser's decision to appoint Ahmad Ismail to the position of army chief of staff, replacing Abdel Munim Riad, who had been killed by an Israeli mortar attack. Shazly and Ismail had been bitter rivals since 1960, and in Egyptian military circles everybody knew about the punch that Shazly had landed on Ismail's jaw during one of their disagreements.

Attempts to convince Shazly to withdraw his resignation had little effect. Finally, three days after Shazly resigned, Nasser sent Marwan, carrying a personal letter from the president, who wrote that he saw the resignation as a personal criticism of himself. Shazly denied this, insisting that his decision was solely a function of his poor relations with the designated chief of staff. Marwan relayed the message back to Nasser. Finally, Shazly agreed to return to his post only after Nasser—again, using Marwan as a go-between—promised not to allow Ismail to impinge upon his authority.[35]

From the public confidence Nasser placed in his son-in-law in the Shazly affair, it seems reasonable to conclude that, notwithstanding the deepening tensions between the two, Marwan was never fully sidelined. To be sure, part of what made him the right man to solve the Shazly crisis were his family ties; symbolically he embodied the personal will of the president. At the same time, the fact that Nasser relied on him for the job suggests that he also recognized Marwan's specific talents, talents that could advance Nasser's interests in the situation at hand. Marwan apparently had good access to senior figures of the military; they saw him as reliable and, in some cases, even one of them.

This, however, was not enough for Ashraf Marwan.

IN THE SUMMER of 1970, he was just twenty-six years old, a chemical engineer and an officer in the Egyptian army. As the son from a good family, Ashraf Marwan succeeded, through his marriage to Mona, to tie himself to the center of power, dining at the table of the greatest leader in the Arab world. Neither he nor his family had ever been neglected or threatened by the state.

On the face of things, he was the archetypal Egyptian patriot.

In truth, however, he was about to undertake the single greatest act of treason in his country's history. Precisely why he chose to risk his life and career in order to help his country's most despised enemy, in the middle of an ongoing violent conflict that daily spilled the blood of his country's best youths, is a difficult question to answer.

In recent years, an entire field of research has emerged to help us understand what drives people in the middle of successful careers in military, intelligence, or public affairs to hand over their nation's most highly guarded secrets to the enemy. Until recently, it was widely believed that there were five main causes: ideology, money, ego, extortion, and sexual temptation. Recent studies have suggested an additional motive, that of dual loyalty with a country of origin or strong ethnic affiliation. The case of Jonathan Pollard, a naval intelligence officer who passed classified information to Israel because of his ardent Zionism, is the best-known example; Muslim Americans working for Al-Qaeda or Hezbollah have created an enormous challenge for federal enforcement agencies since 2001.

Another fact that emerges from these studies is that the main motivations behind treason tend to change over time. From the 1930s to the 1960s, for example, betrayal was heavily ideological, usually by committed Communists who chose to assist the Soviet Union. The ring known as the "Cambridge Five," men who attended Cambridge University together and were recruited by the KGB in the 1930s, were typical of their time. Ideology weighed heavily, too, for many of the Manhattan Project scientists who, after having helped the United States develop an atom bomb during

World War II, then passed their secrets on to the Soviets. Most of them had escaped Europe and either identified with the Soviet Union, which had taken the lion's share of the burden in defeating the Nazis, or believed that the cause of peace dictated that Americans not be the only ones with the bomb. Sometimes ideological considerations worked in the opposite direction as well: Col. Oleg Penkovsky, who was considered the most important Western spy in the Soviet Union at the height of the Cold War, passed his country's secrets to Great Britain and the United States out of a deep concern for Russia's future under Nikita Khrushchev.

Disillusionment with communism after the de-Stalinization of the 1950s and 1960s brought about a relative rise in the importance of the second major motive to commit treason: money. Aldrich Ames, a counterespionage officer for the Central Intelligence Agency, handed the Soviets names of dozens of American agents working in the Soviet Union during the 1980s, in exchange for $4.6 million. For the Federal Bureau of Investigation's Robert Hanssen, the betrayal was just as serious, though his fee of $1.4 million was smaller. For Hanssen, money was not the only motive: Studies about his case suggest a whole web of complex and clashing personality issues, such as a tendency toward risk-taking, bizarre sexual inclinations, and a fractured ego, all of which combined to create a powerful impetus to betray his homeland.

By itself, however, greed is rarely enough of a motive to undertake something so morally problematic and personally dangerous as betraying one's country. Studies have suggested that such behavior is connected to specific personality patterns. One of the most striking is the tendency to divide one's loyalties, including an inclination to extramarital affairs. Another is a tendency toward narcissism and egocentrism—often expressed in a dysfunctional relationship with one's employer or spouse, and a sense of being unappreciated in their talents or achievements. Further studies, covering cases of deserters and traitors during the Cold War, have noted that many suffered from the untimely loss of, or a problematic relationship with, their fathers. The sense of loss, these studies suggest, is channeled into action and motivation to offer their service to the enemy.[36]

All this research can help us understand why Ashraf Marwan decided to offer his services to Israeli intelligence. Two factors seem especially pertinent. One was financial. Marwan yearned for the good life, and his time in London made it especially clear to him what that might entail. His entry into the presidential family brought him into contact with a wide range of wealthy people in Egypt and abroad—but paradoxically it also reduced his chances of becoming wealthy himself because of the Spartan ethic that Nasser imposed on his family. If Marwan thought he might be able to work around the problem through his newfound friends, his clash with Nasser over the assistance from the Al-Sabahs disabused him of the thought. If he wanted to fulfill his dreams, he now understood, he would need a source of income that even Nasser's intelligence couldn't discover.

The second motive was ego. This is the best explanation for why, of all the intelligence agencies he could have turned to, Marwan chose the Mossad. Having married the president's daughter and joined the circle of power in Egypt, this good-looking, talented, ambitious young man had succeeded beyond the wildest dreams of any other Egyptian his age. But Ashraf Marwan's ambitions went further. Carrying the burden of infinite self-confidence, he yearned for the power and influence he felt he deserved. Not only did he fail to receive these from his surroundings; what he got from his father-in-law was very much the opposite. Marwan's salary was paltry, and his stature was barely noticeable compared with many others around him who were not married to the president's daughter. The feeling that he was suspected, his every move scrutinized, followed him wherever he went. Nasser, he must have already understood, had little faith in him or his marriage to Mona. The pressure the president put on her to divorce Marwan was only the most blatant expression of it, a permanent reminder of the possibility that one day he would be evicted from the family. For Marwan, this looming threat was also a source of shame. Nor did he have any reason to think things might improve in the near future. His advanced state of egoism so dramatically clashed with the lack of credit he received that it apparently created in him a need to extract a price from the world around him, the world that stood in his way. He would have to show them.

The best way to show them was to give his loyalty to Nasser's greatest enemy of all, the enemy that, just three years before, had handed Egypt its most humiliating defeat, shaming the president and hurting him in a way that nothing and no one had ever done before. Whether Marwan was conscious of it or not, disloyalty to Nasser offered him the most effective solution to both his financial and psychological crises.

But Marwan's issues went beyond getting back at Nasser. His narcissism expressed itself in an infinite craving for honor, power, and influence, and the insistence that people follow his advice. In this he closely resembled Col. Oleg Penkovsky of the Soviet Military Intelligence. Penkovsky believed that Khrushchev's policies endangered the nation's very existence and saw himself as somebody who could save the country. Both his behavior and his thinking patterns suggest a man convinced that he can and should change the course of history. Marwan, as we will see, displayed similar tendencies. His Mossad handlers recognized these qualities in him and knew how to use them. The decision, for example, to introduce him to the chief of the Mossad, Zvi Zamir, was partially made out of the belief that this young man needed to be shown that only the Israelis really understood his true worth.

Ideology, in the way it is normally understood, was less of a factor. Ashraf Marwan was no closet Zionist. But there were what we may call ideational qualities, aspects of his worldview that led him to conclude that he should be on the Israeli side. Israel's impressive victory in the Six-Day War may have flipped a switch in his mind. He was not a man to take the humiliation of his country lightly. Such a feeling was felt throughout Egypt and certainly had its greatest impact on those closest to Nasser. By switching his inner loyalty to the Israeli side and putting himself on the side of the victor, he found a way out of the agony of defeat. The Israelis who spoke with him saw that he had a deep emotional need to be on whichever side had the upper hand in the Arab-Israeli conflict. As we will see, the results of the Yom Kippur War, and especially the restoration of Egypt's wounded pride, ended up having an opposite effect on Marwan, undermining his motivation to continue working for the Mossad.

It is also possible that the Six-Day War had another effect, as well. One of Nasser's greatest achievements before 1967 had been his ability to infuse in Arabs in general, and Egyptians in particular, a belief that under his leadership, they were returning to the center stage of world history after having been sidelined for centuries by European powers. A whole generation grew up in an atmosphere of excitement, accompanied by slogans coined by Nasser: *Brother, raise your head! The days of your humiliation have passed.* The Six-Day War, however, took the wind out of Nasser's sails. He had failed to lead Egypt into the kind of modernity that was meant to prevent exactly this sort of humiliation. The national disappointment was channeled, after the war, in two main directions: One was Islamism, reflecting a search for new sources of faith. The other was a kind of nihilism, the abandonment of faith in any national, religious, or social ideology, looking instead for fast wealth as the key to a personal self-fulfillment detached from the fate of the collective. It could well be that Marwan was pushed into the latter channel.

Finally, we should not forget that Marwan was no ordinary man. One of the Mossad operatives who knew his case from up close described him as "very complicated," having "acute complexes." His behavior included a need for stimulus, which often drives people to take risks, whether physical or emotional. Some people take up rock climbing, skydiving, or bungee jumping. But Marwan was not drawn to the sporting life; instead, he indulged both in gambling and, later, in unsavory business deals; or in taking needless risks in his contacts with the Israelis. It is therefore fair to assume that alongside his inflated ego, his frustrated relationship with Nasser, and his need for money, the act of betrayal itself gave Marwan a sense of adventure that his stormy psyche desperately needed.

All of this came to a head with his decision, in the summer of 1970, to place a call to the Israeli embassy in London.

Chapter 2

LONDON, 1970: CONTACT[1]

Ashraf Marwan began his path to the Israeli Mossad in one of those iconic red phone booths that used to mark London. He had come to London in connection with his studies, as allowed for in the agreement between Nasser and his father. Although some people would later claim that he just showed up one day at the Israeli embassy demanding to speak with the intelligence officer, this is inaccurate. Marwan may have been reckless at times in dealing with the Israelis, but his first contact actually involved a great deal of forethought.

Finding the address and phone number of the embassy did not require high-level espionage skills. They were in the phone book. When the switchboard operator answered, Marwan asked to speak with someone from the Mukhabarat—the intelligence agency. For him, such a request was only natural, not just because he was offering himself to Israeli intelligence but because in Marwan's world, the man in charge of the Mukhabarat was always the most powerful person around.

The operator may not have known Marwan's world. But she did know the protocol. This wasn't the first time she had fielded a phone call from someone with an Arab accent asking to speak with

the embassy's intelligence officer or a defense official. The procedures were clear. She transferred the call to the office of the Israel
Defense Forces military attaché.

The attaché picked up the phone and responded politely. Ashraf
Marwan identified himself by name and asked to speak with the
embassy's intelligence officer. Like the switchboard operator, the
attaché followed protocol. The name meant nothing to him, and
Nasser's son-in-law did not elaborate. The attaché told him that he
could not transfer him directly to the intelligence officer but suggested that Marwan leave a message; he promised he would pass it
on to the relevant authorities. Marwan repeated his name, adding
that he wanted to offer his services to Israeli intelligence. The attaché asked him to spell his name again. Marwan refused to leave
a phone number where he could be reached, so the attaché asked
that he call back again. The call ended.

The attaché took the slip of paper where he'd written down
Marwan's name and details and put it in the outbox on his desk. There
it remained. The IDF attaché in London was not, at that moment,
on especially good terms with the Mossad's local representatives.

ABOUT FIVE MONTHS after his initial contact, late in 1970, Marwan
returned to London and decided to try again. But between his
first attempt and the second, a major development had taken place:
His father-in-law, the greatest Arab leader since Saladin, died after
suffering a major heart attack. Nasser's death had a huge impact on
the course of Egypt's history as well as that of the Arab world and
of the Arab-Israeli conflict. It also brought changes in Ashraf Marwan's life. But what didn't change was Marwan's determination to
work for the Mossad.

Again Marwan called the embassy and was again transferred to
the IDF attaché—a different one. Maj. Gen. Shmuel Eyal, a longtime senior officer who had held a number of top army positions,

including directing the IDF's Human Resources Branch, had just been rotated to London following new orders arising from the targeting of Israeli embassies in Europe. Again Marwan asked to speak with the intelligence officer, only this time he left a number where he could be reached. Eyal, however, explained to him that he would have to come to the embassy in person. Marwan explained that he was a public personality and could not do that. Eyal stood his ground, and a few days went by without any progress. Like his predecessor, Eyal, too, had troubled relations with the local Mossad officials, and he also failed to pass Marwan's message along.

It is hard to imagine what history would have looked like had fate not intervened—and not for the last time. In mid-December, two senior Mossad officials arrived in London on unrelated business. One was Rehaviah Vardi, the head of Tzomet ("Crossroads"), the Mossad's Human Intelligence (Humint) wing. Forty-seven years old and balding, Vardi was known as a superb professional with excellent instincts and wide experience. His intelligence career had begun before the founding of the State of Israel in 1948, when he was an intelligence officer in the pre-state Haganah defense force, handling Arab operatives in the Sharon region. After statehood he worked for the IDF's Military Intelligence wing, and in 1950 he took command of MI's Humint division. Later he was given responsibility for all of MI's intelligence-gathering operations; there he learned about technological surveillance (Sigint) as well. In 1963, the chief of MI, Maj. Gen. Meir Amit, was appointed to take charge of the Mossad, and he took Vardi with him to run the Mossad's Humint operations. In that context, Vardi also took responsibility for special projects, the most famous of which was getting an Iraqi pilot to defect to Israel in 1966, bringing his advanced Soviet aircraft with him.

Traveling with Vardi in London was Shmuel Goren, director of the Mossad's European operations. Twice wounded in Israel's War of Independence while serving under Moshe Dayan's command, Goren joined MI after the war and launched a career in handling agents. After filling a string of posts that involved close cooperation with the Mossad, Goren was appointed deputy IDF attaché in Israel's embassy in Washington in 1968. Before he took the post, the incoming director of the Mossad, Zvi Zamir, asked him to join his organization; Goren deferred the request. A year later, Zamir turned to him again, this time with a concrete offer to head up the Mossad's European division, which in practice meant Western Europe. The ambassador in Washington, Yitzhak Rabin, and MI chief Aharon Yariv gave their consent, and Goren agreed as well. By late 1970, he had gained vital experience with the agency.

Soon after arriving in London, the two Mossad officials met up with Eyal and the local Mossad station chief, and the four agreed to drive together to Heathrow Airport, where the MI chief was scheduled for a brief layover on his way to the United States. In the car, Eyal mentioned the Arab fellow who had been calling for a few days to offer his services, but who refused to come to the embassy in person. When they asked his name, Eyal said that he called himself Ashraf Marwan.

Vardi, Goren, and the station chief all looked at one another. They knew the name well.

Marwan had been in the Mossad's sights for some time. The London station, which always looked for new sources from the Arab side, had kept tabs on Nasser's son-in-law from the moment he had first arrived in London. They knew he was strapped for cash, even if they didn't know the details, and they knew he had been forced to return to Egypt. They knew, in other words, that money could be a decisive factor in motivating Marwan to sell his country's secrets. His closeness to Nasser and access to materials that passed through his office would make Marwan a source of extreme value—but until now, these same factors also made it hard to believe that he would ever work for the Mossad. What Eyal now had said almost in passing, however, completely changed the picture.

The fear that Marwan would again leave London without successfully making contact now set the pace of events. With no idea how much time they had to work with, they would have to improvise, bending the rules regarding meetings with agents. A message about Marwan's call did make its way immediately to Mossad headquarters in Tel Aviv, but Goren, acting in his capacity as director of Mossad operations in Western Europe, didn't wait for the analysts back home to examine the situation from every angle and approve contact with the prospect. The fact that he and Vardi, two top Mossad officials, were in on the decision made it easier. This, too, was a matter of luck being on Israel's side: The London station chief would not have made such a decision on his own, even if he had gotten the message from the attaché. And any delay could easily have meant losing track of Marwan.

And yet, engaging Marwan was still not an easy decision. Marwan was what intelligence people call a "walk-in"—someone from the enemy's side who just shows up one day offering his services. Intelligence agencies generally steer clear of such volunteers, mostly because of the high likelihood that they represent some kind of trap. The CIA, for example, had discovered how complicated working with such volunteers could be in 1962, when a KGB officer named Yuri Nosenko offered his services to the CIA, and then defected to the United States two years later. James Jesus Angleton, the agency's head of counterespionage, soon became convinced that Nosenko was a double agent, having been sent by the KGB to quell suspicions that Lee Harvey Oswald had been trained and sent by the Soviets to assassinate President Kennedy. Others in the CIA and the broader American intelligence community rejected Angleton's theory, seeing Nosenko as a genuine defector whose information

should be considered reliable. The flap went on for years, disrupt-
ing a major part of the agency's operations in the Soviet Union in
the late 1960s.[2]

The Mossad knew all about the Nosenko affair. Angleton was,
after all, not only in charge of counterespionage but also the point
man on Israel for the entire American intelligence community.
Both Mossad and CIA officials saw him as Israel's best friend at the
agency, and there can be little doubt that in the ongoing conversations between Angleton and Mossad representatives in Washington,
Nosenko was a major topic of discussion. Goren, we may assume,
was thoroughly versed in the affair as well. While Egyptian intelligence agencies were not nearly as sophisticated as the KGB, there
was still room to wonder whether they were setting a trap. The last
thing Goren and Vardi needed was for the British MI5 to discover
Mossad operations taking place in central London after being
tipped off by Egyptian intelligence. Even worse was the possibility
that an Arab intelligence agency or Palestinian terror group would
try to kill Mossad agents who showed up at a meeting with someone claiming to be Ashraf Marwan. But against these fears stood a
heavy countervailing consideration: The prize was so enormous,
the potential intelligence boon so great, that it pushed aside other
considerations.

All these questions resolved into a single quick decision as the
four men made their way to Heathrow. They stopped the car, and
the Mossad station chief got out and headed back to the embassy.

It was not long before the telephone at the number Marwan had
left was ringing. He was told that a meeting would be arranged
soon and was given a number in London to call whenever he
wanted to make contact with Israeli intelligence. He was asked to
stand by near his phone until he received a call with details of the
rendezvous. Meanwhile the Mossad team in London got to work
setting it up.

The hour had grown late, and they decided to push the meeting off to the next day. It would take place in the lobby of a major hotel in central London. If everything went as planned, Marwan and his handler would talk in the lobby for a few minutes and then head up to a room that had been reserved on one of the upper floors, where they could speak openly.

The short notice put significant pressure on those charged with securing the location, but the London Mossad station quickly pulled together the necessary arrangements. All that was left was to decide who, exactly, would attend the meeting. In a brief conversation between Goren and the station chief, they settled on a man named Dubi (his last name remains an official secret). He was the London station's number two man and had been gathering intelligence in London for a few years. In his midthirties, a native Israeli whose grandparents had arrived in Palestine from Europe at the turn of the century, Dubi looked European but spoke fluent Arabic. This was an important consideration for the simple reason that nobody in the Mossad's London station could say how well Marwan spoke English.

The meeting was set for the evening hours. London-based Mossad operatives took up positions outside the hotel to make sure it wasn't a trap. Goren sat on a couch in the lobby, pretending to read a newspaper as he kept his eye on the entrance. The paper hid from view a photograph he was holding of Ashraf Marwan. Dubi stood off to one side, keeping eye contact with Goren.

They didn't wait long. At precisely the time they had set with Marwan, he entered the lobby, carrying a black briefcase. Dubi immediately recognized him from the description he'd received: tall, slim, dark. Goren thought he recognized him as well but wanted to be sure. He glanced at the photo and back at the man. The photograph was from Ashraf and Mona's wedding four years earlier and was clipped from an Egyptian newspaper. Goren hesitated. Another look at the photo, and then again at the man who stood in the lobby, and that was enough. He looked at Dubi and nodded slightly. Marwan stood tense as Dubi walked up to him, extending his hand and smiling.

"MR. MARWAN," HE said to him quietly in Arabic. "It is a pleasure to meet you. My name is Alex."

The young Egyptian was visibly surprised by the Arabic. He, too, worried that a trap had been set by the Egyptian Mukhabarat. He replied in English, "Are you Israeli?"

Dubi switched into English as well, confirmed that he was Israeli, and tried to calm the fellow's nerves. They exchanged a few more words, and Dubi suggested that they go up to a room where they could talk. Marwan nodded his assent. Goren, who was not far from them, took a deep breath of relief when he saw them walk toward the elevator. The initial contact had gone off without a hitch.

Up in the room, Marwan felt considerably more at ease and led the conversation. He asked Dubi if he knew who he was. Dubi had been around long enough to know that he didn't need to reveal everything he knew. Marwan began describing himself at length, his public stature, his marriage to Mona, his relationship with Nasser and Sadat, and the fact that he worked in the information bureau in the President's Office under Sami Sharaf. Dubi tried to commit every detail to memory.

Marwan explained his role at work, slightly overstating his importance. For Dubi, the more interesting question was not Marwan's status or his relationship with Nasser's successor, but what kind of information crossed his desk. He raised the point carefully and politely. Marwan smiled, almost boastfully. He explained that the most important information in all of Egypt was concentrated in the hands of Sami Sharaf. Dubi asked him to be more specific. Was it political information? Military or diplomatic? Relations with the Soviets? Marwan had been waiting for the question. Picking up his suitcase, he produced a number of pages of handwritten Arabic and told Dubi that he was handing over, as a kind of down payment, something of great interest to Israel. He began reading aloud. Dubi, who had some understanding of military affairs, realized that Marwan was giving over details from a top-secret memorandum cataloging the Order of Battle (OB) of the entire Egyptian military. Dubi began quickly writing down the details of units, their location, commanders, and equipment at their disposal. Occasionally he would stop to ask Marwan to clarify one point or another. When Marwan finished reading, the Mossad officer looked over the list. It was incredible.

Marwan's willingness to pass along information so sensitive about Egypt's military capabilities encouraged Dubi to ask more specific questions. For years, the Mossad had worried about whether Egypt would try to develop unconventional weapons. In the early 1960s, the agency had launched a controversial campaign to stop the operations of German scientists working with the Egyptians to develop biological and chemical weapons. In the mid-1960s, Egyptian forces used these chemical weapons in the civil war in Yemen. For Israelis, fresh memories of German gas chambers made the issue of chemical weapons being used against civilians especially sensitive. Thus, information about Egyptian chemical weapons development continued to be a high priority for the Mossad. They knew Marwan had a degree in chemistry and had served in the army as a chemist, and they wanted to know anything he could tell them about it. So Dubi asked. Specifically, he asked about activities taking place at Abu Za'abel, northeast of Cairo, an area where civilian and military chemical facilities stood side by side.

Marwan was surprised by the line of questioning. He failed to understand why the Israelis were so worried about this particular field. Though he had never worked at Abu Za'abel, he was able to give remarkably accurate information about the work being done there. Dubi continued writing everything down. When he was done, Marwan handed him a manila envelope containing one final document. Dubi placed it in his briefcase without opening it. Marwan nodded his approval. To this day, no one recalls, or is willing to divulge, what exactly was in the envelope.

During the entire meeting, Marwan did not once raise the issue of payment. In the way of gentlemen, he and Dubi left such unpleasantries for another time. Yet clearly the Egyptian was not working for the Mossad on a volunteer basis. From his end, Marwan wanted to demonstrate the value of his contribution before raising the matter of a fee. Indeed, it was wise on Dubi's part not to risk spoiling the atmosphere. The two had quickly developed a sense of mutual trust. Dubi recognized Marwan's charisma, his good nature, his sense of humor. Marwan found in Dubi a cultured conversationalist, serious and believable. It is well known that the early relationship between a handler and his agent can have a huge impact on the source's long-term ability to contribute. In this sense, the Mossad's first encounter with the son-in-law of the former president of Egypt was a stellar success.

At the end of the meeting, Dubi reconfirmed that Marwan had the proper contact information to stay in touch by phone or mail. Marwan estimated that within a few weeks he would be back in London and promised to make contact when he arrived. He asked that at the next meeting, only "Alex" would attend. Dubi promised.

Marwan left the room first, took the elevator down to the lobby, and walked out of the hotel. Mossad agents watched as he hailed a cab and rode off. Dubi made sure he had all the materials in his case and followed a few minutes later. He took a taxi as well, giving the driver an address near, but not exactly at, the Israeli embassy.

When he reached his office, he found Shmuel Goren waiting for him. When Rehaviah Vardi and the Mossad bureau chief joined them, they were already plowing through the pages Marwan had given Dubi. Goren looked up from the document he held in his hands and said, "Material like this, from a source like this—it's something that happens only once in a thousand years."

THE REPORT MADE its way to Tel Aviv the next day via diplomatic mail, landing on the desk of Zvi Zamir, chief of the Mossad. It described how Marwan contacted the embassy in London, the fortuitous way his message had reached the attention of senior Mossad officials heading to Heathrow, the meeting between Marwan and Dubi in the hotel, and Dubi's detailed account of the conversation. Mossad officials in London had translated into Hebrew most of the documents that Marwan had given Dubi, enclosing it in the same encoded communiqué.

By the time Zamir finished reading the report, he fully understood the potential Marwan held as an Israeli agent. By themselves, the original documents were invaluable. He called a meeting of relevant individuals, including Shmuel Goren, who was summoned from Brussels, and Rehaviah Vardi, who had returned from London.

It really did not trouble Zamir that the officers had made contact with Marwan without waiting for authorization. In 1968, when he first came to the Mossad despite lacking any background in intelligence, Vardi had been his mentor, teaching him everything he knew about working with human sources. Now Zamir had been in charge for over two years, and he saw Vardi as a man he could rely on. The situation was similar with Goren, whom Zamir had handpicked to head up operations in Western Europe. He knew them both well and had tremendous faith in their professional judgment about how best to take advantage of an enormous opportunity. Moreover, responsibility taking and improvisation had always been pillars of the agency's ethos. So the question of whether they had been authorized to initiate the meeting with Marwan didn't even come up. The central concern in this meeting was what the next steps ought to be. The chief of the Mossad led the discussion.

ZVI ZAMIR WAS born in 1925. Until he joined the Mossad in 1968, his entire adult life had been spent in the military. When he was seventeen, he volunteered for the Palmach, the elite fighting force of the pre-state Jewish community in Palestine; by the end of the British Mandate he had spent ten months in a detention camp for illegally smuggling Jewish immigrants into Palestine across the Syrian border. During Israel's War of Independence in 1948, at the age of twenty-three, he was chosen to command the 6th Battalion of the Harel Brigade, which was tasked with keeping the route open from the coastal plain to besieged Jerusalem. After the war, he filled a number of senior positions in the newly created Israel Defense Forces, including chief of the training division and commander of the Southern Command. In 1966 he was appointed military attaché in Great Britain and the Scandinavian countries. In 1968, Prime Minister Levi Eshkol surprised him with the request that he replace Meir Amit as chief of the Mossad. The appointment came against the backdrop of Eshkol's increasing frustration with Amit, who, despite being formally under the direct command of the prime minister, had been showing an increasing loyalty to Defense Minister Moshe Dayan, with whom Amit had worked closely in the IDF. Eshkol wanted a Mossad chief who was less politically invested and was referred to Zamir, who was considered more independent and politically impartial.

When Zamir started out at the Mossad, senior agency officials raised concerns that he had been brought in mainly to pave the way for the appointment of another man, Yosef Yariv, to the same position. Beginning in 1957, Yariv had been commander of the IDF's Military Intelligence unit 188, which was focused on running operatives deep in enemy territory. In 1963, when Meir Amit, who served as the MI chief, was appointed to simultaneously head up the Mossad, MI's unit 188 was shifted into the Mossad, and Yariv went with it. When Zamir reached the Mossad in 1968, Yariv was the head of the Caesarea branch, the Mossad's main operations division that included both unit 188 and another unit headed by the future prime minister Yitzhak Shamir. Yariv saw himself as a candidate to head up the entire agency; his friendship with IDF chief of staff Chaim Bar-Lev and Deputy Prime Minister Yigal Allon meant that he had a serious shot at it. But other senior Mossad officials did not think he was right for the job and came to believe that Zamir, an IDF major general and a friend of Bar-Lev and Allon, had been brought in in order to calm the opposition to Yariv and make it easier for him to become a Mossad chief later. Some of them, including Rehaviah Vardi, made it clear that they would leave the Mossad if that happened.

Zamir moved quickly to dispel the suspicions. As opposed to his predecessors, he did not appoint a deputy, a decision that reflected less a political calculus than his understanding of the job. The main purpose of a deputy, he felt, was to take over if something happened to the director. But as he explained to anyone who asked, the head of the Mossad was not at the front lines and therefore not at serious risk of assassination. So there was no need for a deputy who could complicate his own job by becoming a buffer between the director and his operational units.

Zamir spent much of his first year on the job systematically studying the central areas of the Mossad's activity. He spent hours going over the dossier of every Mossad operative, held ongoing consultations with Vardi and the heads of Tzomet branches, learned all about how sources were valued, recruited, and handled, their potential maximized, and more. He also went over the files of operatives who had stopped working with the agency and, in at least one case, convinced the people in Tzomet to reengage an agent, resulting in some very

high-value intelligence for Israel. Along the way, Zamir learned just
how fragile the relationship between a handler and his operative
could be, and how crucial was the handler's ability to recognize and
meet the agent's psychological needs in determining the fate of their
relationship. Money was, of course, a central motive for most of the
agents who worked for the Mossad, but it was far from being the
only one.

Zamir also ordered a shift in the Mossad's intelligence-gathering
priorities. He wanted the agency to work harder on supporting the
operational needs of the IDF. When he was IDF Southern Commander in the early 1960s, he felt that the Mossad had offered him
no support whatsoever. Now with the War of Attrition heating up,
the agency would dedicate its best efforts to helping the IDF, especially in getting reliable advance warning of attacks and gathering
whatever intelligence would help the IDF take timely defensive
action. In 1968, when Zamir first took the post, the question of
a sneak attack was less urgent because the Arab armies, especially
Egypt's, were still licking their wounds from the Six-Day War. The
question became much more acute after the War of Attrition ended
in 1970 and Sadat started publicly threatening to restart hostilities.
MI estimated that this time the Egyptians wouldn't make do with a
static war of attrition but would instead try to cross the Suez Canal
and advance into Sinai.

A second major change in priorities concerned intelligence
gathering from technological sources (Signal Intelligence, or Sigint)
rather than just human ones (Human Intelligence, or Humint).
From its inception, the Mossad had been created solely as a web
of human intelligence sources. Under the direction of Meir Amit,
the agency began employing various forms of technological surveillance, such as wiretapping and bugging. Now Zamir decided to
take the emphasis on Sigint much further, including the creation
of a division called Keshet ("Bow"). Even though this was, in es-

sence, encroaching on areas that until now had been handled exclusively by MI, the close friendship between Zamir, IDF chief of staff Chaim Bar-Lev, and MI chief Aharon Yariv kept the relations among the intelligence branches on a healthy footing.

Before Zamir's arrival, successive Mossad chiefs had suffered from complicated relationships with Israel's prime ministers. Isser Harel was one of David Ben-Gurion's greatest admirers but he found himself clashing with Ben-Gurion and ultimately resigning his post in the wake of the affair of the German scientists in Egypt in 1963. In the years that followed, relations between Prime Minister Levi Eshkol and Mossad chief Meir Amit were tense as well. The Mossad's problematic involvement, apparently without Eshkol's knowledge, in the kidnapping and killing of the leader of the opposition in Morocco, Mehdi Ben Barka, in 1965 made things even more difficult. With the establishment of Ben-Gurion's Rafi Party as Eshkol's greatest political rival, and the prime minister's concern that the Mossad chief was in cahoots with Ben-Gurion, Amit had little choice but to step aside.

As opposed to his predecessors, Zamir lacked any serious political entanglements. As a former Palmach officer, he did keep close ties to his brothers-in-arms from pre-statehood days, but both in his IDF career and in his position as Mossad chief, he cut himself off from party politics. Eshkol had met him a few times in a work context but could not have known from these alone that Zamir would be an especially comfortable Mossad chief for him. He had, however, been highly impressed by a report Zamir had written when he was the IDF's military attaché in Great Britain, in which he recommended cutting back on staff at the office there. When Eshkol, who was also serving as defense minister, saw the report, he held it up as an example of how a military attaché is supposed to function.

But Zamir scarcely had a chance to work with Eshkol, who

died in February 1969. His more serious relationship was with Eshkol's successor, Golda Meir. Meir scarcely knew Zamir before taking office, but he quickly won her confidence and effectively became her mentor in intelligence affairs. "It's very easy to work with Zvika [Zamir]," she once quipped, "as long as you're willing to do what he wants."[3] At the same time, in broader security issues she relied almost exclusively on the judgment of her defense minister, Moshe Dayan.

This was not a problem, so long as Dayan was getting his intelligence assessments from MI chief Aharon Yariv, with whom Zamir worked well. But in October 1972, Yariv was replaced by Maj. Gen. Eli Zeira, and the differences between the intelligence estimates of the two agencies grew. Dayan tended to rely on Zeira's assessments, and Golda Meir wasn't willing to challenge him on it. Zamir grew increasingly frustrated. It was his belief, based on a variety of sources of whom Ashraf Marwan was the most important, that Egypt was headed for war. Military Intelligence, and especially Zeira himself, saw things very differently. But since Dayan relied heavily on Zeira, and Golda Meir relied heavily on Dayan, Zamir was boxed out, and knew it.

Later on we will see just how devastating such a constellation was for Israel as a whole. For now, suffice it to say that by the end of 1970, Zvi Zamir had gained enough experience to lead the Mossad's discussions about whether or not to pursue the services of Ashraf Marwan.

A SMALL YET highly experienced group took part in the discussions that followed Dubi's first meeting with Marwan. Zamir, Vardi, and Goren were joined by Shlomo Cohen Abrabanel, a senior Tzomet official who had become deputy director of the Mossad, and Nahik Navot, Zamir's chief of staff. During the discussions, a consensus was reached on two central points.

First, it was agreed that Marwan's offer represented an unprecedented opportunity to cultivate a source with access to the highest
levels of Egyptian decision making. The documents Marwan gave
Dubi were, it seemed, just a taste of what the man could produce.
In their conversation, Marwan had suggested that in his position,
he could put his hands on the majority of the materials that crossed
the president's desk. The participants in the discussion accepted
Marwan's description of both his status and his access. After all,
in the top echelons of Egyptian political life, wouldn't the door
always be open to Nasser's own son-in-law?

The second point of agreement concerned the question of
whether Marwan had been sent by Egyptian intelligence. After examining the problem from every angle, the group concluded that
the chances were low that Marwan was other than what he seemed.
There were three main reasons. First, because only the most sophisticated spy agencies knew how to operate double agents successfully over time. The British were the best at it, especially during
World War II. The Soviets were pretty good as well, though not
as good as the British. The Mossad understood the difficulties involved and refrained from deploying double agents entirely. The
only Israeli agency that used them was the Shin Bet, and their
experience was limited. The Egyptian Mukhabarat was not known
for being especially sophisticated. Their efforts to infiltrate Israel
with spies had made them out to be a fairly amateur organization
whose best successes were in crushing opposition within Egypt
itself. The Mossad officers were hesitant to underestimate their
enemies, but they had difficulty giving the Egyptians credit that,
according to their own professional opinions, they didn't deserve.
On this basis, they concluded that the likelihood that Marwan had
been put up to it by Egyptian intelligence was very low.

The second reason had to do with Marwan's family ties. It was
one thing to send an ordinary operative on a mission as dangerous

as double agency, another thing altogether to send Nasser's son-in-law. In their own assessment of risks and benefits, the Egyptians would have to allow for the possibility that in the struggle between rival intelligence agencies, the Israelis might have the upper hand—and that Marwan could be killed or imprisoned. For Egypt the cost would be intolerably high, in part because Marwan knew a great many state secrets, including about the private lives of senior Egyptian figures, all of which he could give over to the Israelis.

The final thing that made the double agency hypothesis seem implausible was the quality of information that Marwan had already given Dubi in their first meeting. In the play between a double agent and his supposed handlers, an agent will often hand over real information, but only of the sort that either becomes dated quickly or that the recipients are likely to already know. True, one has to reveal some real information in order to establish the credibility of the agent—information that the British, who turned it into an art form during the war, called "chicken feed." Perhaps the most important example of this was on the eve of the invasion of Normandy in June 1944. Juan Pujol García, a double agent operated by Britain under the code name Garbo, warned the Germans of the coming invasion just hours before it happened. As the invasion began to unfold exactly as he had warned, his credibility and importance rose in German estimation. Three days later, he sent another warning, saying that the Normandy attack was a diversion meant to draw forces away from the more massive intended landing area in Pas de Calais. German intelligence believed Pujol, and the Germans continued to maintain the bulk of their ground forces in Pas de Calais through the end of June. When they realized they had been duped, it was too late. The Allies had established their bridgehead at Normandy and driven deep into France.[4]

The Mossad men knew about Pujol and similar affairs, and thoroughly went through the documents and other information that Marwan gave Dubi. This, they concluded, was no chicken feed. It was not only reliable but exceptionally valuable. This made it seem even less likely that Marwan had been sent by Egyptian intelligence. And no less important, the officials concluded that even if he were a double agent, they would have the means to discover it in a timely fashion. They would need to constantly double-check both the accuracy and the style of information he passed along. They also set up two committees to oversee his handling: one just of Mossad officials, the other a joint committee with Military Intelligence. The latter was the product of a strong tradition in the Israeli intelligence community, which held that at least some of the people evaluating new operatives needed to be completely disconnected from their recruitment and handling.

The consensus that emerged concerning these two initial questions enabled Zamir, Vardi, Goren, and the others to turn the discussion to more practical matters. The first concerned payment. Marwan did not mention any specific figure he expected to receive, but everyone knew it wouldn't be small. More than four years earlier, in August 1966, the Mossad had paid $50,000 to Munir Redfa, an Iraqi pilot, to take his advanced MiG-21 fighter and land it safely at the Hatzor Air Force Base in Israel. This dramatic operation, painstakingly planned and executed, allowed Israeli pilots to study up close the dominant warplane in the Egyptian and Syrian arsenals, and contributed significantly to Israel's air superiority in the Six-Day War. Israel then let experts from the US Air Force examine the aircraft, helping boost Israel's security ties with the Americans, for whom the MiG-21 had been a mystery. To convince Redfa to defect, then Mossad chief Meir Amit had been willing to pay twice as much, but Redfa accepted the first sum offered him. That, however, was a one-off. Marwan, they figured, would want to be paid for every meeting in which he handed over secret information. At this point there was little choice but to wait and hear his price.

This, however, raised another problem. From everything they

knew about Marwan, it was clear that an infusion of cash could translate into a suddenly profligate lifestyle—raising questions about whether he was selling state secrets. The Mossad had faced this problem in the past, but the amounts were always small and the agents extremely careful. The recruitment of Ashraf Marwan now raised the problem to a whole new dimension. The Israelis, however, were familiar with the behavioral norms of upper-crust Egyptian society and concluded that Marwan would be able to find a plausible explanation for his sudden change in standard of living. As he would himself later tell his handlers, in a country like Egypt, where bribe taking was the rule rather than the exception, you don't have to explain why Nasser's son-in-law might have money. The answers were so clear that the questions didn't need asking.

The final question concerned who would be Marwan's handler. The problem was complex. A successful handler combined a variety of outstanding skills and traits. John le Carré, who served in British intelligence, once described the successful handler as offering his operative an "image of mentor, shepherd, parent and befriender, as prop and marriage counselor, as pardoner, entertainer, and protector. . . ."[5] Such was the prevailing attitude in the Mossad as well, especially when thinking about how to handle a young man as complex as Ashraf Marwan. The handler ought to be someone of unassailable authority, a shoulder to lean on, who could help him function while leading a dangerous double life. Someone older, experienced, wise, and cautious.

Dubi did not exactly fit the bill. He had been chosen to meet Marwan in London mainly because no one else could be found in the narrow time frame. But he was not a natural choice. His experience with operatives was relatively limited. A number of names were raised in the discussions that now took place. And yet, Dubi had proven himself amply since arriving at the London bureau and had earned a reputation of being responsible and professional, accurate and a stickler for rules, someone who wrote reports that described things as they were, without embellishment. This last quality was especially valued in a handler. Agents like Marwan were often willing to work with only one person, which meant that the handler was the agency's only source of information about what was happening on the ground. Dubi had other advantages as well. He had charm, grace, and the ability to generate chemistry. All these created the potential for a high-quality relationship with Ashraf Marwan.

What ultimately tipped the scales in Dubi's favor were the specific circumstances at hand. His one meeting with Marwan had clearly gone well. From his restrained report it was clear that a bond had been forged. But because of the personal risk involved, Marwan had insisted that he would not meet with anyone other than "Alex." At this stage, the main concern of Zamir and the others was that Marwan would not renew contact the next time he came to London, and they were unwilling to take any chances. Replacing Dubi might have led Marwan to feel that the Mossad was not taking his needs seriously, and the new prospect could easily be lost. Thus it was decided, after considerable deliberation, that Dubi would continue to handle Marwan for the time being. As opposed to other operatives, however, Marwan's handling would be conducted in direct consultation with headquarters in Tel Aviv. This reflected Marwan's unusual significance. In effect, it put both Vardi and Zamir in the circle directly involved in handling Marwan.

With this they concluded their discussions about the recruitment of Ashraf Marwan. All that was left were a number of bureaucratic procedures involved in any new agent's recruitment. One was assigning a code name to protect his identity. This was the responsibility of a subunit of Tzomet. Names were taken from prepared lists and were assigned at random. Ashraf Marwan's early code names included "Packti" and "Atmos." The one that stuck, however, was "the Angel." The officer who had come up with it was a fan of the 1960s TV series starring Roger Moore, *The Saint*. Because of the original title's Christian resonance, the show was sold in Israel under the title *Hamal'ach*—"The Angel."

Years later, after the Yom Kippur War, it would become clear just how apt the code name really was.

Chapter 3

APRIL 1971: ENTER MILITARY INTELLIGENCE

The first meeting with Ashraf Marwan took place about four months after an August 7, 1970, cease-fire agreement brought an end to the War of Attrition between Egypt and Israel. The outcome of that war had not given the Egyptian government any reason to believe it was in a position to launch another round of hostilities, especially one aimed at crossing the Suez Canal and taking back the Sinai Peninsula. True, the war had proven the Egyptians' resolve to roll back the losses of the Six-Day War—but it had also proven their abiding military inferiority.

The Egyptian strategy behind the War of Attrition had been to wear down Israel's will to fight through the steady letting of IDF soldiers' blood. Egypt took advantage of its superior artillery, constantly shelling the line of Israeli fortifications along the canal known as the Bar-Lev Line, as well as the roads connecting them, while occasionally launching commando raids aimed at killing Israeli soldiers. The cost to Israel was high but not insufferable. In the seventeen months of fighting, 260 IDF soldiers lost their lives—less than half the number of highway fatalities tallied in Israel in 1970. Nor is it clear exactly how many Egyptians died in the war. One American source estimated no fewer than 5,000, while Israeli sources put the number around 15,000. Not only was the kill ratio intolerable for the Egyptians, but it was an ongoing reminder that on every battlefield, in the air or on the land, Israel had the upper hand.

This was most pronounced in air warfare. The ratio of planes shot down was seven to one in Israel's favor—compared, for example, to American major aircraft losses in the Vietnam War of up to fifteen F-105s for every North Vietnamese MiG-21. By late 1969, IAF raids had eviscerated Egypt's antiaircraft batteries, leaving the country completely open to air attack. In early 1970, Israel began launching bombing raids deep in Egyptian territory, attacking military installations in the suburbs of Cairo, Alexandria, and elsewhere. These raids aimed not only to weaken Egypt militarily but also to destabilize Nasser's regime and force him into a cease-fire. But then the Soviets came to Egypt's rescue, sending a whole antiaircraft division, including more than seventy batteries of SA-2 and SA-3 surface-to-air missiles and seventy MiG-21 fighter planes—a major deployment that put an end to Israel's deep-bombing raids and, to some extent, evened the playing field in the sky. Hostilities escalated, reaching their peak on July 30, 1970, in a direct Israeli-Soviet air battle in which five Soviet warplanes were shot down and just one Israeli aircraft damaged. After the battle, the sides agreed to a cease-fire.

In July, when Marwan first called the Israeli embassy in London, the War of Attrition was at its peak. By mid-December, when he finally met Dubi, the sides had signed a ninety-day cease-fire agreement that had already lapsed. Although an extension was signed for another ninety days, it was clear that without significant diplomatic progress, including an Israeli commitment to withdraw from the Suez Canal, the resumption of fire was just a matter of time. The Angel quickly became a crucial source for the Israelis as they tried to understand Egyptian intentions regarding war, and this question dominated his intelligence-gathering assignments.

The question, of course, was seriously complicated by the death of Nasser in September 1970 and his succession by Anwar Sadat. In a series of meetings between Dubi and Marwan, a picture emerged of the new Egyptian leader as a man facing an impossible dilemma. On the one hand, the more Sadat explored the options for taking Israel on militarily, the more he realized how few and futile they were. With the end of the War of Attrition, some generals had insisted they knew how to take back the Sinai; Sadat, however, did not believe his army capable of even crossing the Suez Canal. Instead he was more interested in launching a limited military assault aimed at forcing Israel back to the negotiating table. At the same time, even that was dangerous; the Israelis had warned explicitly that if Egypt restarted hostilities, Israel would make sure they did not remain static. Sadat's biggest problem was the IAF's overwhelming air superiority, which had rendered the Egyptian home front extremely vulnerable. The only way for Egypt to keep Israel from using the full weight of its air force was if the Soviets were to give Egypt some serious "weapons of deterrence"—namely, long-range warplanes that could attack the IAF bases in Israel and missiles that could reach Israeli population centers. Yet the Soviets, for fear of another Egyptian defeat and in order to maintain detente with the United States, were not forthcoming. And so, in early 1971, Sadat did not believe he really had a military option.

At the same time, the diplomatic door seemed locked as well. True, Israeli defense minister Moshe Dayan advocated cutting a deal in which the IDF would pull back from the bank of the Suez Canal, but Egyptian forces would not enter the territory vacated, in order to enable the reopening of the canal and create a buffer that would make it a lot harder for Egypt to retake the Sinai by force. But Prime Minister Golda Meir opposed any diplomatic initiatives with Egypt at this stage and forbade Dayan from making any moves in that direction. When Sadat made a similar proposal in February 1971, about two months after Ashraf Marwan began feeding information to Israel, she dismissed it out of hand.

In a meeting with Dubi early in 1971, Marwan described the dead end Sadat felt he had reached, adding that even if the current president was more open to a diplomatic accord than was his predecessor, the best one could hope for was a broad armistice rather than a peace agreement. Marwan also presented the new Egyptian offensive battle concept developed by Minister of War Mohamed Fawzi and the fruitless talks with the Soviets about supplying "weapons of deterrence." From all this, the Israelis came to understand just how unrealistic the military option for Egypt was—lending significant support to those in the Israeli government, especially Golda Meir, who opposed any diplomatic initiative.

Marwan's compensation for all this was relatively modest. Just as in his first meeting with Dubi, Marwan did not raise the issue of payment in their second meeting, either, allowing the matter to simmer while the Israelis learned to appreciate his full value. When the subject finally came up, it was agreed that he would receive payments of $10,000 from time to time. This was not a small sum, but it was reasonable given the quality of his intelligence, especially the top-secret documents from the President's Office that began finding their way to the desks of Israeli leaders at a startling pace.

This was a promising beginning, to say the least. Yet despite the ease with which "Alex" and the Angel established their relationship, efforts were already under way to have Dubi replaced as Marwan's handler. The driving force behind them was Shmuel Goren, head of operations in Western Europe. He knew from experience that a too-close relationship between a handler and his operative could get in the way, for example, of pressuring the agent to hand over the most urgently needed information. Dubi, for all his merits, was still pretty new at the job, and Goren wanted someone more experienced. Goren may have had ulterior motives, however. His relationship with the station chief in London was tense, and he wanted direct authority over an operation that was turning into a stellar success. His candidate for the job was a veteran intelligence officer born in Aleppo in Syria. Goren pressed Zvi Zamir, who promised to consider it but in the end decided not to make the change. This was not the last time the subject of replacing Dubi would come up.

As Marwan's importance became more evident, however, it became clear that he ought to be introduced to officials from different parts of Israeli intelligence, people who could bring their own experience into the dialogue. This was not unusual. According to the accepted division of labor in the Israeli intelligence community at the time, the agency responsible for formulating national intelligence assessments was IDF Military Intelligence (MI); the Mossad, on the other hand, was formally under the command of the prime minister and charged with running operatives in Arab states and other relevant places. Information gathered by the Mossad was then sent to the IDF MI's Research Division, which was the Mossad's main consumer of intelligence; there it was analyzed along with materials from the Shin Bet and MI itself. MI-Research would then formulate the priorities for intelligence gathering, including specific questions that the IDF wanted answers to. MI's Unit 11 was in charge of relations with the Mossad, preparing the questions and sending them to the Tzomet operations branch of the Mossad, which would then pass them on to the relevant handlers. This is how Marwan was handled from the very first meeting with him, until the early spring of 1971. Dubi would ask him the questions that Intelligence Unit 11 had sent, writing down the answers and sending them back to MI-Research and Air Force Intelligence.

Cooperation between the two agencies included another practice, however, in which high-quality agents would meet not only with their Mossad handler but also with different experts in the

specific areas being discussed, usually from MI-Research. Marwan
had quickly positioned himself as Israel's top-ranked operative in
the entire Arab world. The heads of the Mossad and MI decided
that in light of the importance of air battles in any conflict with
Egypt, and Marwan's access to crucial materials in that area, it
might help if an analyst from Israeli Air Force Intelligence met
him. But the man who they believed could best take advantage of
a direct meeting was the chief of MI-Research's Branch 6 (Egypt),
Lt. Col. Meir Meir.

IN 1971, MEIR MEIR had been head of MI-Research Branch 6 for
almost two years. But he had been in intelligence much longer
than that. In the 1948 War of Independence, he had been seriously
wounded in defense of Kibbutz Negba, a grueling battle that had
slowed the advance of Egyptian forces into the Israeli heartland.
After recovering from his injuries, Meir joined the IDF's nascent
Military Intelligence branch, where he gained an expertise in field
intelligence, and in preparation for the 1956 war he was chosen
to assemble the field book for the Sinai Peninsula, which would
serve as the IDF's main reference during the war. The book, which
benefited from the input of the country's experts in geology, hy-
drology, oil drilling, and more, proved to be exceedingly accurate,
an irreplaceable aid for the troops conquering the peninsula. After
the war, Meir took up a series of posts in MI, including assistant
intelligence officer for the chief of the Northern Command and
chief of staff under MI commander Meir Amit. During the crisis
leading up to the 1967 Six-Day War, he served as the personal assistant to MI commander Aharon Yariv. But when Nasser closed
the Straits of Tiran, cutting off all maritime traffic to Israel's southern port of Eilat and making war with Egypt all but imminent,
Meir tried to get transferred to something more combat-oriented.
During the war, he served as intelligence officer for the 84th Ar-

mored Division—the force responsible for destroying the bulk of the Egyptian forces in northern Sinai—under Maj. Gen. Israel Tal. After the war, Meir took part in the interrogations of captured Egyptian officers and was later appointed deputy military attaché in Paris, his final position before becoming the IDF's top intelligence expert on Egypt.

In the late 1960s, Branch 6 (Egypt) was the most important branch of MI-Research. As commander, Meir Meir brought together some of the most talented intelligence minds in the country. The head of his military section, Maj. Zusia Kaniazer, was a superb intelligence man. The head of the political section was Shimshon Yitzhaki, who later wrote a book about Arab perceptions of the Six-Day War based on his MI service. He was soon replaced by a civilian named Albert Sudai, who was one of the country's foremost experts on Egypt. Under Kaniazer and Sudai there emerged an entire class of young officers with tremendous knowledge of the Egyptian military and political regimes. As opposed to MI-Research's other divisions, Branch 6 was so large that it couldn't be housed in a single space. Meir and the military section worked on the same floor as the chief of Military Intelligence, Maj. Gen. Aharon Yariv; the political section, as well as other officers connected with various North African states, sat with the commander of MI-Research, Brig. Gen. Arieh Shalev, on a different floor at IDF headquarters.

Early in April 1971, Meir was summoned to Yariv's office. There he found Yariv seated along with Shalev, as well as the commander of Air Force Intelligence, Col. Shmuel Shefer. Yariv wasted no time. He gave Meir some general background about a new source that the Mossad had found in Egypt, describing how he had been engaged. Yariv did not reveal the source's name, but Meir understood from the materials he had delivered that it was an exceptionally high-quality source, someone with top-level access to

highly classified information on both the military and diplomatic
fronts, including intelligence on Egyptian-Soviet relations. Yariv
added that the reliability of the source's information had yet to be
determined and told Meir that the Mossad had given its consent
for a representative of MI to join the next meeting with the operative. From the presence of the chief of IAF Intelligence, Meir
understood that someone from the air force would be joining the
meeting as well.

Yariv concluded by ordering Meir to head straight for Mossad
headquarters, where he would receive a briefing in advance of his
flight to London the next morning. Beyond the goal of making
the dialogue with the agent more productive from MI's point of
view, the main purpose of the meeting was to take advantage of
Meir's expertise in Egypt in order to answer two key questions:
first, whether the source was in fact real and not a trap; and second,
whether he really had the access that he claimed to have. In order
to answer these, Meir would have to prepare a detailed list of questions before taking off for London.

Meir was not terribly surprised by all this. Since taking up the
post, he had gone abroad a number of times to meet Egyptians
offering their services to Israeli intelligence. The greatest fear was
always that these walk-ins were really double agents; the best way
to check them out was to send an expert who would have a long,
detailed conversation with them, in which it would become clear
whether their information matched what was already known, and
whether the volunteers' description of themselves and reasons for
betraying their country sounded plausible. Moreover, such a conversation enabled the expert to create his own direct impression of
the potential value that the source offered.

And yet, despite Meir's experience with Egyptian walk-ins,
something about this one felt different. The urgency, the personal
involvement of the MI chief, and the quality of the intelligence

that the source had already provided—all this pointed to someone in a whole different league.

And then, alongside all these professional questions, there was one other pressing matter that Meir just couldn't get out of his mind: Passover. The Seder was just a week away, and his wife, Gita, would never forgive him if he wasn't home to run it. But he had to put the thought out of his mind, because now the chief of IAF Intelligence was talking. He told Meir that because a large part of the information delivered by the source concerned the Egyptian air force and related to procurement requests to the Soviet Union, a representative of IAF Intelligence would join him.

The path from Yariv's office to Mossad headquarters was one that Meir had walked countless times since joining MI-Research. He left IDF headquarters and headed north until he reached the guard booth at the campus exit, at the corner of King Saul Boulevard in Tel Aviv. He then turned right, and within five minutes he reached the corner of King Saul and Dafna. The gray office building on the corner was, at the time, one of the tallest buildings in Tel Aviv. Known as the Hadar-Dafna Building, very few people knew it housed the Mossad headquarters. Meir went around to the right side of the building, down a few steps, and then pressed the button on the intercom. The guard knew him, and in any event had been warned he was coming. The chief of MI-Research Branch 6 left his officer's ID at security, took a visitor's tag in exchange, and entered the narrow elevator that took him up to Zamir's office.

There were four people sitting in the Mossad chief's office. Meir knew Zamir from the time he'd spent as an intelligence officer in the IDF Southern Command, when Zamir was its commander. During the early 1960s, relations among officers in the command were close and informal, and Meir and his wife had been hosted more than once in Zamir's home. The second man, Rehaviah Vardi, was known to him as well; Meir had served under Vardi's command in the intelligence-gathering division of Military Intelligence. Capt. Yoav Dayagi was a research officer in IAF Intelligence, responsible for the Egyptian air force, and Meir worked with him on a daily basis. The fourth man was Nahik Navot, Zvi Zamir's chief of staff.

After a few pleasantries, Vardi began briefing the two military men, Meir and Dayagi. He didn't reveal everything, but from what little he told it was clear that this new source was incredibly well placed. He told them about how the Angel had contacted the Israeli embassy, how the opportunity had been very nearly lost, and how the meeting with Dubi went down in the London hotel. Vardi hesitated. "This is not an ordinary source," he added cautiously. "It's not an army officer or a diplomat. We've had those in the past, and will have them again in the future. This source sits very close to the president, both because of his position and because of his family connections." He would not elaborate further, but he assured them that prior to meeting the Angel, Dubi would let them in on the details, including his identity. The IDF men completely understood Vardi's behavior. It was a basic principle in both MI and the Mossad that information was given on a strict need-to-know basis. They were about to operate in a foreign country, and, even if it was an ally, the possibility of their being arrested and interrogated was always there. The less they knew, the less damage would result.

Zamir concluded the meeting with a few operative instructions. They would leave on the Monday-morning El Al flight to Heathrow. On Navot's desk outside, there waited an envelope for each of them, containing a passport, plane tickets, and cash for expenses in London. The meeting was expected to take place shortly after they arrived, but there could be last-minute changes. If their stay was extended and they needed more cash, they would get it from the Mossad's London station.

This last bit didn't sit well with Meir. In the past, trips to London to meet Mossad sources required a stay of two or three days at most. This time felt different, and Passover loomed. When he was about to leave, he turned to Zamir. "Zvika," he said, "if I'm not back for the Seder, Gita will have my head."

"You take care of the Angel," Zamir said, smiling. "I'll take care of Gita."

Meir and Dayagi headed back to their respective offices and shut themselves in. Each of them now had to plow through the thick dossiers they had received, which included countless pieces of intelligence collected from both human and technical sources, copied documents, and intelligence reports from allied governments. On the basis of all these, they put together their lists of questions to ask the Angel. Although they were very pressed for time, their task was made much simpler by their own considerable familiarity with the subject and the fact that in the archives of MI-Research Branch 6 and IAF Intelligence there were numerous folders filled with concrete questions for other sources and for other intelligence agencies that the Israeli intelligence community had cooperated with for many years.

Meir reached his home in Holon in the evening hours. He packed a small suitcase, hoping he wouldn't be gone for more than a few days. He shared that hope with his wife. The next morning a Mossad car picked him up from his home. Dayagi was already in the car. Two hours later they had taken their seats aboard a Boeing 707 bound for London.

HEATHROW AIRPORT WAS relatively empty at midday on a Monday, and the line at immigration was not long. Meir Meir had an uncomfortable feeling when he presented his passport to the officer. It was the fourth time he had entered Britain with a doctored, Mossad-provided passport, and every time he worried that the immigrations officer might start asking questions. But British immigrations officers at the time were generally polite and unsuspecting;

international terrorism had yet to strike the United Kingdom. The officer stamped the passport. Two minutes later, Meir was through. Dayagi was waiting for him, and the two picked up their bags and headed for the airport's message board. Before there were cell phones and pagers, many airports offered large boards where people could leave messages. They scanned the board, which was arranged according to the last name of the intended recipient, and saw the message bearing the name that appeared in Meir's passport. A Mossad agent had been there not long before and had left a handwritten note. Following its instructions, they found a cab that took them to an address in central London. The ride took less than an hour. They paid the fare, walked two hundred yards, and knocked on the door.

A tall man in his mid-thirties answered. Good-looking, slim, with brown hair and blue eyes, soft-spoken. Dubi had been expecting them. He invited them in and immediately got to work making coffee. Once the men had mugs in their hands, he started telling the story of the Angel in riveting detail.

Meir had never heard of Ashraf Marwan, or of his father, the high-ranking officer. Later on he would explain that although he had carefully studied the names and details of most of the senior officers in the Egyptian military, including division commanders, the Republican Guard had simply never interested him. The top priority for Branch 6 was to know about the Egyptian fighting forces that the IDF might face in the next war. But the Republican Guards were assigned to protect sensitive facilities in Cairo and the regime as a whole, and to provide security for the president's travels, and these were of little interest to Military Intelligence. Nor were the private lives of Nasser and Sadat of much interest to Meir, who saw them as little more than the subject of gossip. He was much more eager to know what Nasser had thought of the Soviets than of his son-in-law. And yet, Meir knew enough about Egyptian culture and norms to appreciate the importance of someone like Marwan. Even if his official position in the President's Office was a relatively minor one, he would still be able to get his hands on documents that no other source in Egypt would dream of seeing. Meir was very impressed indeed.

At the same time, Marwan's sudden approach to the Mossad made Meir cautious. The idea that an Egyptian so well connected, at home in the corridors of power with his whole life ahead of him, would take so dramatic a step as calling the embassy and trying to get a meeting with the Israeli Mukhabarat—all this was a little hard to swallow. True, he had seen a few cases like this over the years, but Marwan's profile was different. True, the Mossad had thoroughly checked out the new source. And yet, as the senior professional who would work with him, he felt duty-bound to verify his reliability—with a microscope, if necessary. He had already met with other potential Mossad recruits and had experience with verification, and he knew Egypt well. He thought himself up to the task.

He was less excited about Dubi's next piece of news. First of all, the meeting with Marwan wasn't set for the following day, as originally planned. The man had indeed arrived in London, Dubi explained, but then he had suddenly gone off to Rome for a few days. "We do not have good control over his actions," he added. "He knows that we will do everything necessary to keep him on board. So we can't tell him what to do." To this he added another problem. Marwan had informed him the day before that under no circumstances was he willing to meet with any Israeli other than his own handler. Dubi explained that it would take some time and effort to build Marwan's full confidence in the Mossad's willingness to protect his safety. He was constantly afraid for his life, and every additional Israeli he revealed himself to could potentially turn him over to the Egyptians. So when Dubi had told him that in the next meeting they would be joined by two Israeli experts on the Egyptian army and air force, he had flatly refused.

This was not a new problem. Marwan's refusal to meet anyone other than Dubi was just the latest in a string of determined refusals facing handlers across the Mossad, and for any operatives already suspected of being double agents, it only increased the suspicion. Marwan knew that the Israelis had no alternative, that he held some very good cards in his hand. He played them not just to increase his payments but also to maximize his own safety.

In this delicate game between handler and operative, however, the Mossad held a few cards of its own. Dubi had already won Marwan's trust. As with many agents and handlers, theirs was a relationship in which the agent had no choice but to put full faith in the handler; Marwan was, in a crucial sense, entirely dependent on Dubi's judgment. Moreover, the Mossad had paid Marwan handsomely. The customer had every right to make demands in exchange for his payments. Finally, from the moment Marwan had begun selling his country's secrets to Israeli intelligence, he knew he couldn't afford to seem less than fully useful to the only people on earth who knew what he was up to. Despite all this, however, Dubi still had to emphasize to Meir and Dayagi that if Marwan didn't budge, Dubi would have to continue meeting with him alone—and the IDF would have to deal with it. The Angel was too valuable an asset to risk losing.

This was a big problem, and the solution was still not in the offing. But again, Meir had a different problem on his mind. The orders from Israel, Dubi informed them, were for Dayagi and Meir to stay in London until Marwan returned. The chance that this would happen before Passover was slim and fading. Though this was upsetting, there was an upside. For as long as they were in London, Dubi said, they could do what they wanted, within the budgets at their disposal. Their only obligation was to check in by telephone twice a day, at 9:00 a.m. and at 5:00 p.m., using a public phone. The person answering their call would let them know if anything had changed.

And so, Lt. Col. Meir Meir and Capt. Yoav Dayagi spent the next two weeks in London, waiting. They studied the footpaths of Hyde Park and St. James Park, the quiet cul-de-sacs of Mayfair and Belgravia, the nightclubs cropping up just then at Kings Road and the Chinese restaurants in Soho near Piccadilly Circus. The guards at the British Museum and the Tate Gallery knew their faces well. Every morning and every afternoon they would call the number Dubi had given them and discover that nothing had changed. Every few days they would call home from a pay phone and exchange a few hurried words with their loved ones. That was all they could afford. Friday arrived, and so did Passover. True to his word, Zvi Zamir called Gita to tell her that all was well with her husband but that he would not be home for the Seder.

And then, early in the third week of April, the voice at the other end of the line had something different to say. "The meeting is on. Today."

DUBI HAD MET with Marwan the night before. The Egyptian had just come back from Rome, where he'd met with senior members of the Libyan regime of Col. Muammar Gaddafi. In Rome they discussed the creation of a company that would enable Egypt to circumvent the arms embargo that the United States and Britain had slapped on Libya. Dubi now told him that the two Israeli intelligence officers were in London and waiting to meet him. Marwan's response, predictably, was again categorical refusal. As it was, he explained, he was very concerned that Egyptian intelligence would soon be on to him; widening the circle would only increase the risk. But Dubi held firm, employing every maneuver he had learned to pressure Marwan. In the end, they reached a compromise. Marwan would meet one, but not both, of the offi-cers. The obvious choice was Meir Meir, the senior of the two, and whose responsibilities were far broader. Dayagi, and with him IAF Intelligence, were left out of the intimate circle of Israelis who would meet Marwan.

The next day Dubi sat with Meir, walking him through the plan for the evening. He was to go to an upscale building in the Mayfair district. He would tell the guard there his name—the one on the passport the Mossad had supplied. The guard would hand him a key. To the left he would see an elevator, which he would take to the fourth floor, and then find the apartment matching the number on the key. Once inside, he was to wait in the bedroom. Dubi and Marwan would arrive together and talk in the living room. When the time was right, Dubi would invite Meir to join them.

Everything went as planned, much to Meir's relief. The guard was expecting him, and the key worked. The apartment was im-pressive. But Meir didn't spend too much time studying it. He headed for the bedroom, closed the door behind him, and sat on a chair by the bed. Half an hour later, he heard the front door open. He recognized Dubi's voice; there was another man with him. Dubi poured his guest a drink. Meir couldn't hear their words, but he could tell they were speaking English. A few minutes went by, and Dubi knocked on the bedroom door, asking Meir to join them.

MEIR ALREADY KNEW what Marwan looked like from his photo-graphs. But there was something the photos hadn't really captured. His first impression of Marwan was that he was young and arro-gant. He sat back, stretched out languorously on the armchair, a lit cigarette in one hand and a scotch in the other. When Meir extended his hand and offered his best English "How do you do?" Marwan deigned to shake it but didn't think of getting up. Meir would later recall that Marwan had acted as if a very large roach had wandered into the room. But Meir was a veteran intelligence officer. Unfazed, he sat down in the armchair next to Marwan's. Dubi, who until that moment had been standing, took a seat by the dining-room table, pulled out a writing tablet and pen, and waited for Marwan and Meir to speak. During the entire conversation, he scarcely opened his mouth, instead just writing down everything that was exchanged between the two.

The commander of MI-Research Branch 6 had decided in advance that he would start in with the heaviest, highest-priority questions. He did this for two reasons: first, to maximize the efficiency of the meeting, extracting the best, most detailed information possible; and second, to give Marwan the impression that his questioner was an expert who knew Egypt well and understood military affairs, and who therefore should be taken seriously. The most pressing question facing Israel at that moment concerned the possibility that Egypt would shift from a static posture of attrition to an active, aggressive assault. From everything they knew about Egypt's war plans, the attrition had been meant as an initial phase of war, "softening" Israel's defenses to create the best conditions for Egypt to cross the canal and try to take back the Sinai. Meir's first question to Marwan, therefore, concerned Egypt's war aims. Marwan answered confidently, but his answer echoed what was already being said in the Egyptian media: that the goal was to retake the Sinai. When Meir asked how Egypt planned to do so, Marwan answered, "We will build bridges and pontoons across the canal, and we'll cross."

"And how," Meir asked, "will you fight in the desert when we have air superiority?" Marwan answered with what he had clearly heard from the generals. Egypt would get attack aircraft and surface-to-surface missiles to attack and neutralize Israeli air bases in the Sinai. Meir pressed the point: How would Egypt neutralize the air bases located in Israel proper, out of the missiles' range? Marwan hesitated and then repeated what Meir had heard from countless other sources: If Egypt failed to neutralize the IAF's bases, the Soviets would provide advanced antiaircraft weaponry that would allow the Egyptians to cross the canal under their umbrella. Then, after the first strip of land on the east bank of the canal was taken, they would move the antiaircraft missiles across the canal into Sinai, extending the umbrella eastward, allowing the ground forces to push farther in.

Meir had received no instructions about how to proceed, but he had enough experience with Mossad operatives to decide, on his intuition, to move the conversation toward something more productive. Over and over he tried, carefully, gingerly, to make it clear to Marwan that what he was describing with respect to the Egyptian plans for conquering Sinai made no sense or that he had heard it before. He asked again how the Egyptian generals planned on overcoming Israel's superiority in both air and armor, but all he kept hearing were slogans rather than plans. It became clear to Meir that Marwan actually had no idea how the Egyptians could retake the Sinai, not that he didn't know such plans existed or that he couldn't get his hands on them. Instead, Meir realized, Marwan's non-answers reflected what was actually being said in Egypt. The generals themselves had not yet found a way to overcome Israel's air and armor dominance.

While trying to extract whatever he could about Egypt's battle plans, Meir also kept trying to assess Marwan's reliability. Occasionally he would throw in a question to which he already knew the answer. Who is the commander of the 21st Armored Division, and where are its headquarters? Who commands the Cairo-West airfield, and what planes are stationed there? Marwan never failed. In most cases his answers matched what Meir already knew. In others, when he didn't know, he said as much and promised to have the answers by the next meeting. As the session progressed, the mood in the room began to change. Marwan dropped much of his pose and began to look at the intelligence officer before him as someone who understood military affairs in general and the Egyptian military in particular every bit as thoroughly as Marwan himself did. His arrogant tone gave way to a more careful choosing of words. From time to time, when Meir's questions became more specific and professional, Marwan was forced to concede that he didn't know the answers.

This had been Meir Meir's goal all along.

Now the conversation turned to a subject that especially troubled the Israeli leadership. Since the middle of March 1970, when the Israelis first espied Soviet military personnel manning anti-aircraft units in Egypt, Israeli decision makers had been worried that in the next war, the IDF might have to clash directly with Red Army troops. When Meir asked about the subject, Marwan revealed his loathing for the Soviet units stationed in Egypt, and for the Soviet Union as a whole. He repeated his belief that the Soviets were trying to take over Egypt and its army. Here he revealed a sincere, potent nationalist sentiment. But given the fact that the Soviets were effectively helping Egypt defend itself at an especially difficult time, while Marwan was selling his nation's most closely guarded secrets to its gravest enemy, there was something pathetic, even perverse, about his patriotism. It reflected the bizarre duality of his mind-set, the contradictions of his soul.

The meeting lasted three full hours. Near the end, Meir gave Marwan his assignment for the next meeting. He was to bring with him the Egyptian army's plans for crossing the Suez Canal, as well as the order of battle for the entire Egyptian military. These were the top priority for Branch 6—and also the kind of materials that would lay any suspicions of his double agency to rest.

Dubi escorted Marwan out of the apartment. Meir sat at the

heavy dining-room table and started writing, wanting to get it all down while it was still fresh. The hardest part of these meetings, he thought to himself, was making sure nothing was forgotten or distorted. Fortunately he was not alone. Dubi came back a few minutes later, and the two compared notes, checking every detail and resolving inconsistencies. Finally, they wrote up a four-page communiqué that included everything Marwan had told them. They sent it the next morning from the Mossad's London station to headquarters in Tel Aviv.

Meir and Dayagi went back to Israel the day after the meeting, as well. The car that picked them up at the airport took them straight to Mossad headquarters. They returned their fake passports and went to accounting to submit the receipts for their expenses. They both were sternly advised not to divulge the purpose of their trip to anyone. Meir was asked to go over the report that the Mossad had produced based on that morning's communiqué from London. A few hours later, the report went out, under the code name Khotel, to exactly three people: Prime Minister Golda Meir, Defense Minister Moshe Dayan, and IDF chief of staff Chaim Bar-Lev. Over the next few years, this unusual way of disseminating raw intelligence directly to the top leadership, without going through MI's process of compilation and analysis, would become routine for reporting about meetings with the Angel.

Golda Meir and Moshe Dayan would become totally dependent on these Khotel reports.

THE NEXT MEETING between Meir Meir and Ashraf Marwan took place about four months later. Sadat had declared that 1971 would be the year of decision between the diplomatic and military roads to restoring the Sinai to Egypt. In the absence of any diplomatic progress, the option for war gained ground. But Egypt's military preparedness had not improved dramatically. Sadat knew that his army wasn't ready to take on the IDF.

Indeed, the question of whether and when hostilities might be renewed was the central focus of Meir's line of questioning in their second meeting, and the answers Marwan gave did not fully satisfy. But that didn't matter once he pulled out the documents he'd brought with him. Meir now held in his hands both the plans for crossing the Suez Canal and the order of battle for the entire Egyptian army—exactly what he had asked for. If Meir still had any doubts about Marwan's intentions, they were now gone.

In the months that had passed since their last meeting, Egypt had undergone a number of internal changes in the wake of Nasser's death. A new cadre of leaders now occupied most of the top positions in Egypt. One of them was Ashraf Marwan.

Chapter 4

MAY 1971: LIFTOFF

From the day he first ascended to the world stage, Gamal Abdel Nasser was seen by Israeli leaders as potentially the most dangerous enemy they had ever faced, a man who could one day unite the entire Arab world in a war to destroy the Jewish state. A number of developments seemed to confirm these fears. In 1955, Nasser dramatically upgraded Egypt's military posture by cutting a huge arms deal with the Eastern Bloc countries; in 1958, he initiated the formal unification with Syria to create the United Arab Republic (a union that dissolved three years later); and in 1967, he precipitated a massive crisis with Israel that triggered the Six-Day War.

The arms deal was seen by the Israelis as an unparalleled menace; once it was completed, they believed, Israel would no longer be able to defeat Egypt in war. To ward off the threat, Prime Minister David Ben-Gurion launched the Sinai Campaign in 1956, in order to destroy the Egyptian army before it became a major threat. The plan was effective but short-lived, with Israel soon pulling out of Sinai under intense international pressure. Egypt's unification with Syria, together with the fall of the monarchy in Iraq and efforts to overthrow King Hussein in Jordan and the ruling Christians in Lebanon, combined to give Israelis the sensation of a vast geopolitical noose tightening around their country's neck. The Israeli intelligence community believed that the conditions were ripening for Nasser to launch a full-blown war against Israel.

And then, in May 1967, Nasser ordered the UN peacekeepers stationed in Sinai since 1956 to leave, and he began amassing his forces in the peninsula. Overplaying his hand, he then ordered the closure of the Straits of Tiran (a narrow water passage separating Sinai from Saudi Arabia) to Israeli ships, cutting off Israel's southern port of Eilat to all maritime traffic. This constituted a casus belli by any standard. This was no longer just rising tensions; it was a full crisis, with Egypt now leading a broad coalition of Arab armies and triggering what many Israelis saw as their first existential crisis since independence in 1948. Even after Israel's overwhelming victory in six days in June 1967 put the crisis behind them, many Israelis remained traumatized long afterward from the weeks of tension that had led up to it.

That victory was probably what ended up doing Nasser in. "Those who knew Nasser," Sadat wrote later in his memoirs, "realized that he did not die on September 28, 1970, but on June 5, 1967, exactly one hour after the war broke out."[1] Nasser genuinely felt that the policy of brinksmanship with which he had led his country prior to the war had precipitated the worst catastrophe in Egypt's modern history, and this may well have contributed to the deterioration of his health.

Nasser had suffered from health problems, especially diabetes and ulcers, for years, however. That is why he always had food specially prepared for him, even at state dinners. His intense lifestyle didn't help matters; since 1961, he had been taking painkillers on a regular basis. After the 1967 war, things got worse. His insufferable pain led to hormone therapy, which triggered stress and nervous attacks. His diabetes worsened, and he saw the first signs of heart problems. He retained a personal physician, Dr. Al-Sawy Habib—a cardiologist by training. In his memoir, Habib wrote that Nasser suffered his first heart attack in December 1969. After recovering, he refused Habib's advice to slow the pace of his life. In early July 1970, while on a visit to Moscow, he was hospitalized and underwent a series of tests, in which it was discovered that he suffered from arterial sclerosis and heart disease. The doctors again counseled rest, but his workload won out.

A month later, just a few days before the armistice was reached ending the War of Attrition with Israel, tests revealed that his condition had not improved, and Habib again urged him to rest. The end of the war allowed him a brief hiatus from the stress on him, but then, just weeks later, fighting erupted between Jordan and the Palestinian groups operating in its midst—the bloodshed that became known as Black September. On September 28, 1970, just hours after seeing off Arab leaders who had convened for a grand summit in which Nasser had successfully brokered a deal between Jordan's King Hussein and PLO leader Yasser Arafat that would end the violence, Nasser suffered another heart attack. A few hours later, surrounded by his close relatives, friends, and physicians, the greatest Arab leader since Saladin was dead.[2]

Reports about Nasser's ill health had appeared in Western media from time to time, but his sudden death shocked the entire world—all the more so the Arab world, and still more so Egypt itself. The sight of millions of Egyptians weeping in the streets of Cairo, the funeral procession joined by more than two million people, which spun out of control when inconsolable mourners turned hysterical near the coffin, newspaper headlines declaring that one hundred million Arabs were now orphaned—all of these expressed the sincere, immeasurable pain, the vacuum left behind.

Nasser's passing had huge implications for the future of Egyptian and Arab history, as well as for the Israeli-Arab conflict. It triggered a fierce battle for power among Egyptian elites and a shifting of alliances in the Arab world in the short run, as well as a major change in Egypt's relations to the Cold War powers in the long run.

Nasser's death also had immense implications for the Mossad's greatest spy. Eight months after the leader's fatal heart attack, his relatively obscure son-in-law would, under dramatic circumstances, become a close aide to the new president. Marwan's access to the most closely guarded secrets of the Egyptian regime was now almost unlimited. Nasser's death, in other words, took the greatest source of intelligence Israel had ever had and made him suddenly far, far better.

FOR ASHRAF MARWAN, the death of his father-in-law presented both new dangers and new opportunities. The greatest danger was that he would lose whatever privilege he had gained from being a member of the president's family. This threat quickly abated. If anything, Nasser's status only grew after his death, and the family he left behind would gain a patina of royalty both under Anwar Sadat and, later, under the regime of Hosni Mubarak. At the same time, Ashraf Marwan had always been something of a black sheep. There were more than a few people among the ruling elites who knew exactly what Nasser had thought of his son-in-law. They knew that less than a year before his death, the president had demanded that his daughter divorce Marwan, and that only Mona's stubbornness prevented this from happening. With Nasser's death Marwan knew there was some chance that the new regime would feel less impressed by Mona's passion than her father was, and would cast Marwan out.

At the same time, Marwan had reason to feel immense relief. Although he assumed that regime officials like Sami Sharaf would continue keeping tabs on him, none of them would hold him to Nasser's standard, according to which members of the family were forbidden from taking advantage of their status. On the contrary, for these officials, profiting from one's status was perfectly normal. Suddenly, the chances of Marwan triggering a scandal like the one involving Souad al-Sabah had shrunk dramatically. Nasser's death cleared the way for Marwan to significantly improve his financial situation.

Much harder to tell, however, is whether the president's passing had any impact on Marwan's motivation to work for Israel. Nasser was still alive when Marwan made his first moves. But we have no reason to think anything changed when Nasser died. The financial impetus might have become less of a factor, in light of all the new opportunities that now would present themselves. His need to get back at Nasser for slights to his honor might have lost some of their edge once Nasser was dead. But the fact is that Marwan never displayed any hesitation in helping Israel whatsoever, neither before nor after the president's death. Once he had crossed the line of making that first phone call to the embassy in July 1970, calling again the following December seemed that much easier.

Nasser's successor was his deputy, Anwar el-Sadat, one of the less noteworthy members of the Egyptian leadership following the Free Officers revolution in 1952. Most people in the know, both in the Arab world and in Israel, believed Sadat would not hold power for long. But over the next few months, he solidified his position, outmaneuvering his opponents and keeping his nose above water. The period between Nasser's death in September 1970 and the climactic purge of pro-Nasserite elements that Sadat undertook the following May, which he called the "Corrective Revolution," proved his mettle as a political survivor and impressed observers around the world. Marwan's own political gymnastics over the same few months drew far less attention—except among Israel's intelligence chiefs. Like Sadat, Marwan displayed a breathtaking ability to seize opportunities while deflecting threats to his position. A close alliance emerged between Sadat and Nasser's young and ambitious son-in-law—an alliance that came about through no small amount of luck. The end result was that by May 1971, when Sadat had finally stabilized his rule over Egypt, Ashraf Marwan enjoyed a meteoric rise in the Egyptian hierarchy.

And thus Egypt became an open book for Israeli intelligence.

ANWAR EL-SADAT WAS fifty-two years old when he was chosen, because of his position as vice president of Egypt, to succeed Gamal Abdel Nasser as president. He was born on December 25, 1918, in the isolated village of Mit Abu al-Kum in the Nile delta. In 1938 he completed the officers' academy and quickly became known as a nationalist fiercely opposed to British influence in Egypt. He achieved renown during World War II when he was arrested by the British on charges of spying for Germany. Later he was charged in the murder of a senior minister in the Wafd Party–led regime in Egypt, which was considered a puppet of the British government—but was then acquitted due to lack of evidence. Sadat was a member of the Free Officers Movement that carried out the coup in 1952, overthrowing King Farouk and installing a new republican regime led nominally by Muhammad Naguib, the republic's first president, but more substantially by Nasser, who ousted Naguib and assumed the presidency in 1954. Sadat's coconspirators remembered him principally for his delay, of several crucial hours, in joining the revolutionary movement as it was trying to overthrow King Farouk, because he had been at the movies with his wife. The Egyptian public, however, remembered Sadat on more positive terms, as the officer who declared the overthrow of the king via Egyptian radio.

Yet despite his high profile, Sadat was not a prominent figure in the Free Officers Movement. The positions he held tended to be more ceremonial than executive. Nasser and the others held him in low regard. "Give him a car and vouchers for gas," Nasser used to say of Sadat, "and he'll be happy." Sadat, it was believed, lacked political ambition and could be bought for a fairly low price. And when he did attain positions of consequence, his performance was substandard at best. One example was his unique contribution to the Egyptian war in Yemen. In 1962, when the Yemenite monarchy was partially toppled by a military coup, a civil war erupted between the new republican regime supported by Egypt and the loyalist forces supported by Saudi Arabia and Western states. Nasser sent Sadat to Yemen to see whether it made sense for Egypt to intervene. When he came back, he announced before the entire National Assembly that helping the republicans win the war would be "like a picnic by the Red Sea." Basing his decision heavily on Sadat's opinion, Nasser sent his army to Yemen. The war quickly became a quagmire, occupying fully a third of Egypt's forces, dragging on for years, and offering little hope of ending. Sadat's hasty, arrogant assessment resulted in one of Nasser's greatest international failures.

The image of Sadat that began to form among Israeli decision makers was not so different from the one held by his peers. The historian Shimon Shamir, who served as a reserve officer in MI-Research Branch 6 (Egypt) at the time, was called to duty immediately when word arrived of Nasser's death. He was given dossiers of three possible candidates and was asked to give his opinion on each. One was Ali Sabri, considered the most powerful man in the regime after Nasser; there was also Shaarawy Gomaa, the interior minister in charge of internal security; and finally Anwar Sadat. In a memorandum dated October 6, 1970, Shamir concluded that Sabri and Gomaa were the leading contenders by far. Sadat clearly could not fill Nasser's shoes. In every position he'd held, Shamir wrote, "Sadat was little more than a courier of diplomatic mail, or a pillar in the meeting room." On the basis of the information available to MI at the time, Sadat was taken to be dull-witted, narrow-minded, "lacking in independent political thinking, a 'gray' diplomat with little color of his own." Beyond discussing his intellectual limitations, the report emphasized that according to various sources, Sadat was "thought an opportunist, lacking in scruples, a demagogue and a hypocrite; seen as a boor, talentless and incapable of making his own contribution to the conduct of policy." Shamir's assessment concluded that "Sadat is not a personality with the skills needed to run a country. He lacks the basic qualifications to hold the reins of government in any real way, or to be accepted in Egypt as Nasser's successor and a leader of the Arabs."[3] Similar assessments were formulated by other intelligence agencies around the world, and some of them made their way to Israel as well.

Some have argued that Sadat's image as one of the least competent men in the Egyptian leadership was deliberately crafted. According to Anis Mansour, a veteran Egyptian journalist and a friend of Sadat's, Nasser's successor was in fact exceptionally clever and ambitious, much more so than was assumed. According to Mansour, Sadat understood that drawing too much attention to himself would risk creating the impression that he was trying to compete with Nasser and undermine his leadership. So he always kept a low profile, appearing as unthreatening as possible, the entire aim of which was to survive. If Mansour is right, Sadat's strategy proved itself amply, because it was precisely that unthreatening image that earned him the vice presidency in 1969, a largely ceremonial post that only became truly important when Nasser suddenly died the following year.

Regardless of whether Sadat's weak image was deliberate, one can understand why men like Sabri, Gomaa, Sami Sharaf, and former vice president Hussein el-Shafei were initially willing to go along with a Sadat presidency. Such an arrangement offered two advantages. First, it would send a signal of continuity and constitutionality of the regime. And second, his political weakness would mean that he could pose little threat to their own status; they would still be able to depose him when the time was right. He was not an especially popular figure in Egypt and had no independent power base. A common saying in Cairo at the time was that God had given Egypt two catastrophes: taking Nasser away and putting Sadat in his place. During a May Day celebration of 1971 held at a steel factory in the city of Helwan, Sadat gave the keynote address. Thousands of people chanted "Sadat! Sadat!"—while waving posters bearing Nasser's picture.

Sadat's political weakness was also a function of the specific governmental structure that had come together under Nasser. It was the result of having a charismatic and powerful leader who knew how to speak directly to the masses but who still needed mechanisms of authority, oversight, and motivation for the Egyptian people. What emerged was a layer of second-tier leaders, about fifteen in all, who were close to Nasser and became known as the "centers of power" (*markaz al-kawi*). Each of them was responsible for an area of operation—diplomacy, defense, infrastructure, party politics. And each built his power not so much on his connection to Nasser or his personal skills but on his ability to build and maintain a long train of loyal followers, known as a *sheelah*, or "comet tail."

As a result, these leaders often put a far greater emphasis on keeping their followers happy than on faithfully discharging their duties. And so, when Field Marshal Abdel Hakim Amer fell from grace in the wake of the Six-Day War, some people said that he had invested more in maintaining his military *sheelah* than in preparing for war. Similarly, the true loyalty of the vast networks of intelligence operatives run by Interior Minister Shaarawy Gomaa and presidential secretary Sami Sharaf was less to the security of the country and more to the two men in charge. Because Nasser's personal leadership was so dominant throughout Egyptian life, his support among the population unrivaled, there was no fear of competition between his status and that of the individual power brokers with their comet tails. When Sadat came to power, however, this was no longer the case. His continued rule would depend entirely on his ability to work with, or manipulate, the centers of power.

This was no easy task. In addition to building comet tails, the power brokers also developed their connections with each other. In some cases, such as between Sami Sharaf and the minister of war, Mohamed Fawzi, the connection was based on blood ties. In others, alliances were built on common worldviews or political convenience. The result was a fairly well-oiled leadership machine that had worked alongside Nasser and held most of the power in the country. The most notable of these included Ali Sabri, chairman of the Arab Socialist Union, who continued to hold power even after Nasser dismissed him as vice president and appointed Sadat in his place; and Interior Minister Shaarawy Gomaa. Many people, including in IDF Military Intelligence, saw these two as the natural successors to Nasser and expected that Sadat would swiftly be replaced as president by one of them. The centers of power, however, had someone else in mind. They may have planned on Sadat being quickly replaced, but in the long run, it was Sami Sharaf, Ashraf Marwan's boss, who would end up leading the country. Or so they believed.

Anwar Sadat never built himself a power center or comet tail. Not only did it go against his leadership style, which relied heavily on a small number of loyal aides, but the posts he filled were also mostly ceremonial, making it hard to build a following when he had so little to give his followers. Thus in the first few months of his presidency, he cooperated with the centers of power, even though he knew what they planned to do to him. At the same time, however, he took popular steps like releasing political prisoners and improving the overall standard of living in Egypt.

These steps improved Sadat's position and gave him, within a few months, confidence in his ability to stand his ground in the face of the centers of power. In their view, Sadat was no Nasser, but at best a primus inter pares—and a temporary one at that. Sadat, however, began making decisions on his own, and tensions with the leadership rose. This was especially the case concerning efforts to get the Sinai back from Israel. Believing that Egypt had no way of retaking it by force, in February 1971 Sadat proposed an interim settlement in which the IDF would pull back from the Suez Canal just enough to allow Egypt to reopen it to maritime traffic. The proposal angered Ali Sabri, who believed that the only solution to the Israeli occupation was war; Sabri pinned his hopes on the Soviets to help Egypt overcome its military inferiority. Many of the leaders either supported his position or at least voiced their concern about Sadat's acting on his own.[4]

The tension between Sadat and the centers of power reached its climax in the second week of May 1971. In the drama that unfolded, Ashraf Marwan played a central role. In Sadat's telling, Marwan was the one who handed him the winning card, enabling him to vanquish his opponents once and for all.

ONE OF SADAT'S weaknesses was the fact that his adversaries, especially Sami Sharaf and Shaarawy Gomaa, controlled the intelligence agencies; they had tapped his phone lines and infiltrated his closest circles. Knowing this, Sadat looked for ways to circumvent the normal means of communication—a task made especially difficult by his lack of a comet tail of his own. He was forced to rely on his own family. When he wanted to verify a warning he had received from Mohamed Hassanein Heikal, editor of *Al-Ahram* and one of Nasser's closest friends, about a plot to assassinate him, he sent his thirteen-year-old daughter Noha to Heikal's apartment with a request that he meet Sadat in the president's home. Similarly, on May 13, when he sensed that the moment of truth in the power struggle was drawing near, he sent his older daughter Lubna in her private car to Alexandria, where she met the mayor of the city, Mamdouh Salem. Salem was a former officer in the Interrogation Corps, a police unit charged with, among other things, protecting the person of the nation's leaders. Lubna's message was brief and clear: "The president wishes to see you immediately. Tell no one." Salem rushed to Cairo. Sadat asked him whether he was willing to assume the position of minister of the interior. Salem accepted the offer and was quietly installed to replace Shaarawy Gomaa.

IMMEDIATELY UPON BEING sworn in, Salem took the commander of internal security forces in Alexandria and appointed him to be Egypt's new chief of interrogations. Sadat gave Salem a list of all the people he identified as conspirators against the president. They were all to be arrested.

Even before Salem was sworn in, while Sadat sat in his office waiting for him to arrive from Alexandria, the president decided to test the loyalty of Gen. El-Leithy Nassif, commander of the Presidential Guard, who had been personally appointed by Nasser and whose job it was to keep Sadat safe. The general and his guard, however, were under the command of Sami Sharaf, and Nassif owed his direct allegiance to the presidential secretary. But the day before, in what in retrospect was a major blunder on Sharaf's part, he had given Nassif the unusual directive that in all circumstances, he must remember to honor the chain of command as part of his professional duty. The result was that when Sadat now asked Nassif about his personal loyalty to the president and his willingness and ability to imprison government officials conspiring against him, Nassif understood what was happening and swore his total loyalty to the president. Sadat made him swear not to tell anyone of their conversation. Nassif swore, and kept his oath.

Himself a seasoned conspirator, Sadat now felt that everything was in place to make his move. The timing was decided, in no small measure, by Ashraf Marwan, who was still working under Sami Sharaf in the President's Palace.

Though all sources agree that Marwan played a central role in helping Sadat overcome his opponents and establish his rule over Egypt in May 1971, there are disagreements as to what, exactly, he did. Sadat's memoirs, *In Search of Identity*, which are strewn with basic factual errors, say that Marwan came to him at 10:57 p.m. on May 13, bringing the letters of resignation of the chairman of the popular council, the war minister, the presidential secretary, and members of the Supreme Executive Council. The purpose of their collective resignation, Sadat believed, was to create a constitutional crisis that would force the president himself to resign. Instead, Sadat wrote, "I accepted their resignations."[5]

Sadat's wife, Jehan, who also wrote a memoir, *A Woman of Egypt*, in which she claimed for herself an important role in guiding her husband in general and upending the conspiracy in particular, gives a more dramatic and detailed account. In her telling, she and the president were watching the ten o'clock news in their home when they heard a knock on the door. It was Ashraf Marwan, who, in addition to his family connection to Nasser and his role in the President's Office, was also a personal friend. He handed them the letters of resignation and added, uncomfortably, that a public announcement would be made in just a few minutes, during the news broadcast they were watching. Sadat shook his head in disbelief. Then, indeed, the anchorman reported on the mass resignations. Marwan continued standing there uncomfortably, and when Jehan asked him why he hadn't given them more notice, he answered that Sami Sharaf hadn't let him leave the office. Jehan understood from this that Marwan, whose loyalty to Sadat she had never doubted, had genuinely been unable to get around Sharaf's orders—before adding that "I no longer knew what to believe." Perhaps she said this because, according to one of the conspirators, Marwan was given the order to deliver the letters at 8:00 p.m.[6] At this moment, according to Jehan, Marwan's role ended and El-Leithy Nassif's role began. Sadat ordered Nassif to jail everyone on the list immediately.

Sadat and his wife both describe Marwan as having mostly played the role of messenger. From their accounts it is unclear whether he came to them on Sharaf's orders, in order to create the impression of bureaucratic propriety in delivering the mass resignations aimed at destroying the regime; or at Marwan's own initiative, as an ally to Sadat in the President's Office who brought them the letters, albeit belatedly, which they were not supposed to know about until after the announcement. Other sources, however, describe Marwan not only as having decided on his own to deliver the letters but having risked his life to get his hands on incriminating evidence against Sadat's opponents and then bring it to the president—handing Sadat the tools he needed to destroy his enemies.

Nasser, apparently, kept two secret safes in his house. In the larger one he held cash that was used to pay for top-secret projects. In the smaller one he kept ultrasensitive documents about the intelligence and security agencies. After Nasser's death, his widow, Tahia, gave the keys to the safes to Sami Sharaf. On May 13, Sharaf sent his personal secretary, Muhammad Said, to take the documents from the smaller safe to a different hiding place. According to two accounts, Marwan heard about it and tracked Said down. He saw him leaving Nasser's house with the documents in hand and then starting to drive off. Marwan pulled up, took out his gun, and started shooting. Said stopped the car, and Marwan took the documents and brought them to Sadat.[7] They included founding documents of the Socialist Union Party, which was the central base of power of the conspirators, personal papers of Sami

Sharaf and other opposition leaders, and bank account information where, presumably, they kept their bribe money. According to
one account, certain documents also showed that Sami Sharaf and
Ashraf Marwan had been bad-mouthing Sadat—and Marwan took
the time to destroy them before bringing the rest to the president.[8]
A different account contradicts this, however, saying that Marwan
brought Sadat everything that Said had taken.

In yet another version of the events, the CIA played a central
role in preventing the coup, discovering the conspiracy through
their wiretapping of some of the conspirators, and also via Vladimir Sakharov, an officer in the local KGB office who was secretly working for the Americans. The deputy director of the CIA's
Cairo station, Thomas Twetten, who would later become the agency's director of operations, passed the incriminating evidence to
Marwan, who gave it to Sadat that evening.[9] A similar account
has the Mossad passing information to James Angleton, head of
counterintelligence in the CIA and key Israel liaison, about an intended coup that included Sadat's assassination at the hands of pro-
Soviet elements in Egypt. The information was passed to Twetten
in Cairo, who gave it to Marwan, who warned Sadat.[10]

As against all these accounts, there is also Sami Sharaf's own
description of the events. He claims that on the evening of May
13, he gave Marwan the order to take the letters of resignation to
Sadat. Nasser's son-in-law refused and offered his own resignation
instead. Sharaf refused the resignation and insisted that he remain
in his post until someone more loyal could be found to replace
him. When Marwan, having no choice, agreed to do the job, Sharaf
told Said to give Marwan three leather suitcases full of documents
relating to people connected to Nasser, not including government
ministers, members of the Supreme Executive Council, or members of the president's family.[11]

What everyone seems to agree on is that immediately after the arrests of Egypt's key power brokers the next day, Sadat rewarded Marwan for his faithful service.

THOUGH IT IS hard to tell what exactly Ashraf Marwan did to prevent the coup of May 1971, his role clearly went far beyond just delivering the letters of resignation. Marwan also, it seems, gave Sadat incriminating evidence against the conspirators. Neither Sadat nor his wife mentions it in their memoirs, but reliable Egyptian sources say that in the years that followed, Sadat would say that Marwan had "lit his path" regarding the events of May 1971.[12] Given this, combined with Marwan's immediate and dramatic promotion, his role must have been substantive and decisive.

Even the story about Marwan robbing Said at gunpoint, as farfetched as it sounds, seems more likely than Sami Sharaf's claim that he was the one who told Said to give Marwan the documents. One may accuse Sami Sharaf of many things, but he was no naïf. To suggest that he deliberately gave Sadat the documents that led to his own arrest just hours later seems implausible.

So if it is safe to assume that Marwan gave Sadat, on the night of May 13, the evidence he needed to prove the conspirators' guilt, it seems pretty likely that he first removed anything that might have tainted him in the president's eyes. We know that Marwan did not hold Sadat in the highest regard;[13] if evidence of this appeared in the documents, he would have done everything he could to make sure the president never saw it. This also dovetails with Jehan Sadat's account that Marwan appeared uncomfortable during the visit, apologizing that he had come so late. After all, if he was bringing the president smoking-gun evidence of the wrongdoing of others, material he had risked his life to acquire, why would he feel ill at ease for being late? It seems reasonable, then, that Marwan took the time to go through all of the documents and remove anything that might get him in trouble—and this was the real reason for his delay.

THE CONFLUENCE OF INTEREST that brought Sadat and Marwan together is a central pivot around which the Angel's whole story
turns, and it warrants a closer look. How did Sadat, who seems
to deliberately downplay Marwan's role in the whole conspiracy,
come to rely on him so heavily and appoint him, despite his lack
of experience and connections to the military-intelligence establishment, to so sensitive and important a position as the director
general of the President's Office instead of Sami Sharaf? Questions
run the other way as well: What led Nasser's son-in-law to jump
on Sadat's horse, which, according to most observers at the time,
was a long shot at best, risking his status with the most powerful
men in Egypt?

As to the first question, two considerations made Ashraf Marwan
especially attractive to Sadat. The more important one was the
aura he carried as a member of the nation's founding family. The
centers of power presented themselves as Nasser's true heirs, and
Sadat needed to build up his own legitimacy through association
with Nasser's family. Marwan was the only member of Nasser's
family available to help. Tahia, Nasser's widow, had cut herself out
of public life during her husband's lifetime, and all the more so
after his death. Nasser's three sons were still too young; Khaled,
the oldest of them, was just twenty-three and despised Sadat. Just a
month before the attempted coup, Sadat placed a call to the Nassers' home, asking that they let him use their bulletproof Mercedes
limousine, which had cost the state $36,000. Since the president's
death, the car had sat untouched in the family's garage. The family
refused, however, saying it belonged to them and not the government. Sadat insisted. In the thick of the argument, Khaled went to
the garage, poured gasoline on the car, and torched it.[14]

While he may have expressed it in an unusually impulsive
manner, Khaled's animosity to Sadat was shared by much of Nas-

ser's family. His oldest daughter, Hoda, and her husband were the only family members who could be considered natural heirs, but they were deeply ensconced in the centers of power. Sadat, therefore, had little choice but to turn to Ashraf Marwan if he was to benefit from the family's imprimatur at all. Nasser himself might not have approved. But the Egyptian people didn't need to know that.

The second consideration was the fact that Marwan worked in the President's Office, which had paradoxically become the nerve center of the conspiracy. Sadat desperately needed someone there who could tell him what was really going on in the one institution most clearly identified with serving his interests. Marwan, who felt little loyalty to the Nasserites who filled the office, fit the bill perfectly.

No less important for Sadat, however, was the fact that Nasser's son-in-law was available. He was not beholden to any "comet tail" or "center of power," not even that of his boss, Sami Sharaf. This made him immensely valuable to a president trying to find his footing when almost all the players were committed to preexisting alliances. Marwan's situation was different. He was both Mona Nasser's husband and a close friend of Anwar and Jehan Sadat. This friendship, of course, was not without interest. In her memoir, Jehan describes Marwan as a man whose character and ambitions resembled those of her husband more than did anyone else's in the Nasser family. She took advantage of her friendship with Souad al-Sabah, the wife of the Kuwaiti sheikh who helped Marwan in London, to deepen the connection between Marwan and Sadat.[15]

The question of why Marwan chose to ally himself with Sadat is a trickier one—especially given Sadat's ostensibly weak hand in the struggle for succession. Even more problematic, perhaps, was the fact that in the Nasser family, support for Sadat was taken as a repudiation of the family itself, with everything that might entail.

From Marwan's perspective, helping Sadat could easily have ended his political career and ruined his public stature as a member of the family. His decision to take that risk tells us a great deal about both his calculus and his character.

First off, there was the question of alternatives. True, it would have been safer to support Sami Sharaf and the other leaders. But that was not especially appealing. Marwan felt shamed by his lowly position in the President's Office and had no reason to believe things would improve if Sharaf were to become president. Sharaf knew exactly what Nasser had thought of Mona's marriage to Marwan—and that Marwan had married her out of ambition rather than love. What's more, Sharaf and the others probably had plenty of incriminating evidence of his taste for the good life that clashed so sharply with Nasser's puritanism, evidence that could easily be used against him. In the best possible scenario, he would be one of many people struggling up the comet tail. This was not what he had planned for himself.

By comparison, the idea of becoming a part of Sadat's entourage looked a lot more promising. Sadat had no comet tail but rather a small number of loyal people on whom he relied. For Marwan, working directly with the leader was much better than joining one *sheelah* or another. The way to achieve this was by swearing loyalty to Sadat. The most important thing Marwan could offer the president was the link to Nasser's family, which could lend Nasserite legitimacy, inauthentic as it might have been, to his independently pursued policies.

Beyond this there was also a financial angle. Marwan well knew that as opposed to Nasser, who demanded that his family members refrain from graft or other gain, Anwar and Jehan Sadat saw things differently. Nasser's Spartan lifestyle was alien to them. Before Sadat had replaced Nasser, they married their oldest daughter off to Osman Ahmed Osman, one of the richest men in Egypt, who

made much of his money as one of the main contractors building the Aswan Dam. Another daughter later married Sayed Marei,
scion to one of the wealthiest families in Egypt. Nor were the
Sadats sticklers when it came to their own finances. According to
the rumors around Cairo at the time, shortly before Sadat became
president, his wife fell in love with a house in Cairo. The owners
had no interest in selling, however. In early July 1970, Nasser traveled to Moscow; Sadat, as vice president, took the helm and immediately slapped an order of forfeiture on the house and everything
inside it. When Nasser came back to Egypt a few days later, the
owner petitioned him about the confiscation of his property. After
a brief inquiry, Nasser canceled the order and gave the man back
his home. According to one account, Nasser was so angry that he
decided to fire Sadat, but he didn't get around to it before his death
in September.

Regardless of whether the story is true or just an example of
the rumors about the Sadats' attitude toward corruption, what is
clear is that the new leader's intimate circle was far more open
to this kind of behavior than Nasser had been. Marwan, whose
greatest crisis with his father-in-law happened because he took
money from Souad al-Sabah, could be certain that under Sadat's
aegis such a crisis would never have occurred. Marwan, finally,
needed a plausible explanation for his newfound wealth since he
started working for the Mossad. Personal corruption was the perfect excuse.

But beyond all these considerations, there was also a psychological element at play. Again, Marwan had a deep-seated urge for
stimulus and risk. By tying his fate to Sadat, he got his "fix" of
risky behavior—certainly much more so than if he had joined the
comet tail of Sami Sharaf. But there was another psychological
factor as well, what we might call the "alliance of losers." Marwan
felt rejected by Nasser, and Sharaf and the other power brokers

had treated him accordingly. But they held Sadat in contempt as well, and Marwan may have felt a sense of common cause with the beleaguered president. Not that Marwan himself thought all that highly of Sadat, as he told his Israeli handlers more than once. But he may well have also identified with him. In so complex a soul as Ashraf Marwan's, a soul driven by powerful urges mixed with cool calculations, this sense of common fate may have played a crucial role in the choice he made at that pivotal moment.

Finally, we should remember that Ashraf Marwan lacked any sense of true political loyalty or, for that matter, moral standard. The only people to whom he was consistently loyal, it seems, were his wife, Mona, who stood by him in the face of her father, and his two sons. After all, for a man willing to sell his homeland's secrets to its most vicious enemy, giving Sadat the evidence that put Sami Sharaf and his coconspirators in jail was really no big deal.

WHEN ANWAR SADAT picked Ashraf Marwan to replace Sharaf as presidential secretary, the Mossad's most important spy ever suddenly became much more valuable. He was now in charge of the nerve center of the most powerful regime in the Arab world. Marwan, of course, was no Sami Sharaf: The position alone did not automatically confer anything like the power Sharaf had wielded. As "Secretary of State for Presidential Affairs," Sharaf had turned the President's Office into a terrifyingly effective intelligence agency, as well as a clearinghouse for every piece of intelligence relevant to the security of the state and Nasser's regime. But it had taken years for Sharaf to grow into that role. Beginning in 1954, when Marwan was about ten years old, Sharaf began weaving his web, gaining influence and experience gathering information. His network extended into every dark hole in Egypt, and there was very little that Sami Sharaf didn't know or couldn't find out. It was a custom-built, handcrafted masterpiece, and he did his best to ensure that it was staffed entirely of people of unflinching personal loyalty to himself. That was his comet tail.

None of that was passed on to Ashraf Marwan when he took Sharaf's post.

Moreover, Marwan entered the position almost entirely lacking relevant experience. True, he had worked under Sharaf for two years. But since his boss had never trusted him, he had learned little about the office's inner workings and had rarely been given sensitive assignments. Neither did Marwan have any especially useful connections with the other "centers of power" such as Interior Minister Shaarawy Gomaa or the military chiefs. Once in office, he tried to take command of Sharaf's intelligence network, but to little effect. Very quickly it became clear that Sharaf's people weren't giving their loyalty to someone as young and untested as he was. Moreover, as opposed to Nasser, who turned the President's Office into the fulcrum of his entire regime, Sadat worked differently. He preferred not to get overly involved in day-to-day affairs but rather to put most of his focus on the grand, strategic decisions— on war and peace—and to let other people run the country, people he felt he could trust. Marwan's youth, inexperience, and political weakness, alongside his personal habits and especially his extreme ambitiousness that brought him into conflict with other leading figures—all these made it impossible for Sadat to place the full portfolio of Sharaf's responsibilities in Marwan's hands.

So, while Marwan continued to hold the title of presidential secretary for some time, in practice his role was dramatically re-duced, and he became a kind of "liaison for special affairs," above all acting as the president's personal emissary to key leaders in the Arab world. Marwan's youth and family ties made him perfect for maintaining contact, for example, with the new Libyan regime led by Col. Muammar Gaddafi, which had overthrown King Idris in a military coup in September 1969. Gaddafi, who was an enormous fan of Nasser, was just two years older than Marwan. Abdessalam Jalloud, who was Gaddafi's second in command, was Marwan's age.

Sadat's choice proved wise. Jalloud and Marwan worked together closely, most importantly on a deal that enabled Egypt to get around the weapons embargo France had imposed in 1967 as part of efforts to keep arms from reaching conflict states. In return, Marwan helped Jalloud work around prohibitions that the United States and Great Britain had put on selling weapons and replacement parts for civilian aircraft to Libya. But the relationship went beyond the work itself. Soon rumors spread in Cairo about illegal dealings the two had been cooking up together, as well as wild parties they attended in London, Rome, and Cairo.

In addition to the Libyan brief, Sadat also asked Marwan to work on relations with Saudi Arabia, which underwrote a large part of Egypt's state budget. Marwan's contact in the Saudi royal family was King Faisal's brother-in-law Kamal Adham, who had founded the Saudi intelligence services in the mid-1960s and continued to direct them. Oddly enough, those agencies had been created mainly to stop the spread of Nasserite Pan-Arabism in the Arabian Peninsula. But after Egypt pulled its forces out of Yemen, relations between the Saudi royals and Nasser had markedly improved. Here, too, Sadat's choice proved wise. Beyond the professional relations between Adham and Marwan, the two also became close friends, a relationship that included no small amount of personal economic gain for both of them. Shortly after being given the Saudi brief, reports started appearing in the Egyptian press about various kinds of corruption that Marwan was allegedly involved in, and on at least one occasion the name of Kamal Adham was raised. We will return to both Marwan's corruption during this period in general, and the case involving Adham in particular. It is important to note, however, that Marwan's reputation for corruption made it hard for anyone to notice the money he was getting for his treason.

But even without having the full responsibilities that Sharaf had, Marwan's value to the Mossad nonetheless skyrocketed after May 1971. His closeness to Sadat, previously based on personal connections alone, now became official. Marwan could legitimately ask anyone for any piece of information he wanted. From now on, there was no limit to the intelligence Israel could get out of Egypt.

Chapter 5

THE DREAM OF EVERY SPY AGENCY
ON EARTH

Even before the Corrective Revolution of May 1971, Ashraf Marwan had impressed his handlers more than any other agent in Israeli history. In his first meeting with Dubi in December 1970, he delivered top-notch documentary intelligence, and in subsequent meetings he continued providing remarkably accurate information about everything happening in the Egyptian leadership. The addition of Lt. Col. Meir Meir to the meetings in London helped sharpen Marwan's effectiveness, focusing his efforts on attaining whatever Israel considered the most important information. In his first meeting with Marwan in April 1971, Meir asked Marwan for the Egyptian plans for crossing the Suez Canal. In their next meeting, Marwan carried with him the actual written army orders for the crossing, which gave every detail about how the Egyptians would attack. The orders described which forces would be building the bridges, where they would be positioned, who would cross first and who later on, and many additional operational details. A copy of the orders lay in the safe of every division commander stationed anywhere near the canal. According to Marwan, exercises had been conducted based on these plans since before the War of

Attrition had ended in August 1970, but they had continued with far greater urgency since then. These orders, we now know, were exceptionally accurate, with the first phase being carried out to the letter on the day of Yom Kippur, October 6, 1973.

The second document Marwan gave Meir was the order of battle for the entire Egyptian army. It comprised the military structure, lists of commanders, division numbers and their chiefs, the weaponry at their disposal, detailed listings of warplanes and their locations for every squadron of the air force, and a vast collection of details about every operational unit in the Egyptian military. Until then IDF Military Intelligence had pieced together a fairly accurate map of the Egyptian army, based on a variety of human and technical sources. But this added a level of depth and detail that went far beyond anything they had known. It was unprecedented in its quality, and also helped establish the level of certainty of what they already knew. And because of the high degree with which it corroborated the information already in their hands, it dramatically increased their confidence that Marwan was no double agent. For anyone who still wondered, this should have removed all doubts.[1]

The dramatic developments in Marwan's life and status, and especially his appointment to the post previously held by Sami Sharaf, created an exceptionally rare situation in the history of espionage: The direct assistant to the leader of a country preparing to launch an attack on its enemy was a secret agent on behalf of that enemy. At around the time when Marwan started working for the Mossad, the East German spymaster Markus Wolf succeeded in planting an agent, Günter Guillaume, in the position of personal assistant to West German chancellor Willy Brandt. As with Marwan, Guillaume's handlers never imagined that he would reach so high a position; their aim was just to have someone in the upper ranks of the ruling party. Guillaume worked closely with Brandt for four years, passing strategic top-secret information to East Germany and, by extension, to Moscow. He was caught in 1974, and Brandt was forced to resign.[2] Unlike Egypt in 1970, however, West Germany did not have immediate plans to attack East Germany; the information that Guillaume passed along was political and diplomatic, not military. Marwan, on the other hand, handed the Mossad Egypt's most closely guarded military secrets concerning concrete plans to attack—the top items on the Israeli intelligence community's wish list.

Today, the documents that Marwan gave Israel take up four very large binders in the Mossad archives. They include not only the documents and their Hebrew translations, but also the transcripts of his own orally given impressions, known as "source assessments." They cover a range of topics. Some are relatively minor, like planned government appointments, Sadat's take on his country's economic challenges, the restructuring of the police and internal security forces, and other domestic issues. All these allowed the very small number of Israeli intelligence officers who read them to have an unmediated sense of life in the upper echelons of Egyptian society.[3]

The most important material, however, was military. A large part of it included stenograms—notes of conversations that, unlike formal minutes, were written during rather than after the conversations—dealing with the most critical subjects in the most important bodies in the country. They included, for example, discussions of the Supreme Council of the Armed Forces, the army's General Staff meetings, conversations between top generals and their Soviet counterparts, meetings with officials from other Arab states, including summit meetings, and Sadat's meetings with foreign leaders in his trips abroad. Sadat's management style caused him to skip meetings covering subjects he was not too interested in, even if the forum was extremely sensitive, such as the military's General Staff meetings. He would often send Marwan in his place. In such cases, stenograms were just the icing on the cake. In his conversations with Dubi and Meir, Marwan left no doubt that he had attended the meetings himself. "The room was noisy," the source assessments tell us. "Sadat seemed annoyed the whole time." And so on.

The information Marwan provided about discussions with the Soviets—a subject of top interest to Israel because of the Egyptians' belief that they needed Soviet weaponry in order to attack—was exceptionally thorough, including not just stenograms and minutes of conversations between Sadat and Soviet leaders, but also a detailed account of lower-level meetings between ministers of defense, army chiefs of staff, and intelligence chiefs. Taken together, these reports opened a wide window through which Israel's top political and intelligence leaders could see not only what Egypt was thinking vis-à-vis war with Israel, but also what the Kremlin was thinking—namely, that the Egyptians were not ready to take on the IDF.

Probably the best example of just how thoroughly Marwan helped Israeli intelligence penetrate Egyptian-Soviet relations has to do with Sadat's talks with Soviet leaders in Moscow in October 1971. The purpose of the visit was to convince the Kremlin to supply "deterrent" weaponry, the mere threat of which would prevent Israel from launching deep-bombing raids at sensitive Egyptian targets. In an earlier round of talks with Soviet premier Leonid Brezhnev in March 1971, Sadat asked for a shipment of Kelt missiles—air-to-surface rockets launched from Tupolev Tu-16 bombers. This time around, he was asking for Scud missiles, surface-to-surface rockets with a range of about 170 miles—enough to reach most major targets in Israel.

Military Intelligence and the Mossad had received only partial information about the two visits, including the fact that an arms deal had been inked in the current October talks. Since these were taking place just as Sadat's "year of decision" about war with Israel was coming to an end, the Israelis were especially eager to find out what had been discussed and what the deal included. Soon after Sadat left Moscow, Marwan met with Meir and Dubi in London. Meir peppered Marwan, who had not accompanied Sadat, with questions, prepared mostly by IAF intelligence. How had Egypt presented their war plans? What were the details of the agreement—which weapons systems, and when would they be delivered? Marwan answered as best he could, but there was much he didn't know. At the end of the meeting, Meir asked him whether he could produce an account of the conversation between Sadat and Brezhnev, and emphasized the high importance of such a document. Marwan said he would get the document.[4]

If on previous occasions the time that passed between meetings was weeks or months, this time Marwan got back to his handlers within days, giving them the actual minutes of the meeting. The Soviets, it turned out, promised to give Egypt the Kelt missiles, without demanding (as they had back in March) that Egypt get Moscow's permission before using them against Israel. But the Soviets still refused to commit to a delivery date—or to selling Egypt the Scuds they so eagerly wanted.

Beyond this highly valuable concrete information regarding weapons procurement, the Israelis also got a direct look at Egypt's preparations for war, the Soviets' impressions of them, and the dynamic of relations between the two states. Standing in front of a large map of the Sinai that had been hung in the conference room at the Kremlin, Egyptian war minister Mohammed Ahmed Sadek described Egypt's plans for crossing the Suez Canal and sending its tanks into the Sinai, toward the Mitla and Gidi Passes in an effort to cut across the peninsula. At this point, Brezhnev stood up and asked to see the two passes on the map. Sadat hurried over and pointed them out. The minutes revealed the Soviets' doubts about

Egypt's ability to carry out the plan. More than once during the meeting, they told Sadat and his men that the Egyptian army was not prepared to take on the IDF on land or in the air, and that the plan being shown on the map therefore had no chance of succeeding. "You have T-34s," one of the Soviet experts said. "With these you would fight against the Jews?" The T-34 was a thirty-year-old tank that had been the core of the Soviet armor during World War II but was useless against the IDF's modern weaponry. In truth, the Soviets had sold Egypt the next-generation tanks, and for years Egyptian armor had been based on T-54s and T-55s. But they refused to sell Egypt the newest T-62s, which had been built to fight against American M60s, the IDF's mainstay. The comment, the Israelis understood, was not meant literally, but to express the Soviet expert's low opinion of Egyptian armored capabilities—and, by extension, the Kremlin's desire to discourage Egypt from launching another disastrous military campaign against Israel.[5]

The details Marwan gave Israel about Sadat's talks in Moscow became a central component of the intelligence assessment that IDF chief of staff Lt. Gen. Chaim Bar-Lev sent to a very small forum that included Prime Minister Golda Meir, Defense Minister Moshe Dayan, Deputy Prime Minister Yigal Allon, and Minister Without Portfolio Yisrael Galili. On November 21, 1971, Bar-Lev reported that the Soviets had agreed to sell Egypt a squadron of twelve Tupolev Tu-16 bombers capable of launching Kelt air-to-surface missiles with a half-ton payload at a range of up to 125 miles. Bar-Lev said that Egypt now hosted some 9,500 Soviet advisers, technicians, and trainers, and more than 10,000 Red Army troops deployed in an antiaircraft division including SAM sites, as well as fighter squadrons manned by Soviet pilots. He also had information about intensive military activities taking place along the Suez Canal, including exercises for crossing the canal and earthworks for the crossing. Much of the intelligence, we may assume,

came not only from Marwan but from MI's own sources, including surveillance, reconnaissance flyovers, wiretaps, and more. The
Mossad, too, had sources besides Marwan. But he was probably
the source of one additional, especially worrisome piece of intelligence: Sadat, it was learned, had entered the army's underground
war room known as Center 10, a move that showed the seriousness
of his intentions. A similar picture emerged from a speech Sadat
gave to officers and soldiers stationed at the canal, in which he
declared that since he saw no chance of getting the Sinai back
through diplomacy, the only way forward was war.[6]

Marwan's data proved decisive in Israeli attempts to decipher
Egyptian intentions as Sadat's "year of decision" drew to a close.
The Soviets, who knew more about Egypt's military capabilities
than anyone else, may have thought that Egypt couldn't win a
war and wouldn't try; for Israel, however, a number of indicators
combined to raise a red flag. To figure out what Egypt had in store,
MI-Research held a series of intensive meetings that focused on
the apparent contradiction between Sadat's hostile public declara-
tions, combined with Egypt's preparations for crossing the canal,
on the one hand, and the prevailing belief in Military Intelligence,
on the other, that Egyptian commanders were so thoroughly aware
of their inferiority on land and in the air that the likelihood of
their launching an attack must be low. Eventually, Meir Meir, who
headed up MI's Egypt branch, concluded that without further indicators that the Egyptians had completed their preparations for war,
there was no need to sound an alarm. Some analysts have claimed
that this sober assessment was what earned Meir his promotion to
full colonel.[7] But even if his sobriety at the time proved wise—the
Yom Kippur War was still another two years off—Egypt's procure-
ments from the Soviet Union were cause for serious concern. The
defense minister, in a meeting of the cabinet in November 1971,
said that even if Egypt would still take a beating in any war with

Israel, it would now have the ability to do some damage as well. He was especially worried about the Kelt missiles. If such a missile "were to fall in the area of Tel Aviv, Ramat Gan, or Bat Yam," he warned, "there will be an avalanche, because these areas have high-rise buildings."[8]

THE MATERIALS MARWAN gave the Mossad also had an impact on relations between Israel and the United States. Sometimes the Mossad would send reports to the CIA based on Marwan's intelligence, after it was carefully edited in a way that made it impossible to identify the source—a process known as paraphrasing. Moreover, the most sensitive items were handed directly by Mossad director general Zvi Zamir to CIA director Richard Helms, to ensure that on the American side, too, the number of eyes that saw the documents was kept to a minimum.

The minutes of the October meeting between Sadat and Brezhnev, however, were too important to leave in Israeli hands alone or to pass along to the CIA as a paraphrase. Prime Minister Golda Meir decided that Israel had to present it to the White House in its original form, giving the Americans a rare glimpse into the USSR's relations with one of its most important third-world client states. The document also offered a firsthand account of the Kremlin's attitude toward the Middle East, and would enable the Americans to draw conclusions about a number of other aspects of Soviet foreign policy. Fearing the exposure of his source, Zamir was reluctant. But he accepted Golda Meir's decision and summoned the head of the Mossad station in Washington, Efraim Halevy, who was in Israel mourning the loss of his mother, to take care of the handoff. Zamir then joined Golda Meir on her trip to Washington. Sitting with President Nixon and National Security Adviser Henry Kissinger, the prime minister handed each of them a copy of the minutes. Meanwhile, Zamir met with CIA chief Helms in a nearby room to get his thoughts on the document. The CIA, Helms affirmed, vouched for its authenticity and congratulated the Mossad on its success in developing so valuable an intelligence source. In the intimate relations between the two agency heads, there were clear rules of conduct. Helms didn't ask anything about the source's identity, and Zamir gave him nothing to go on.

Golda Meir wasn't much of a note writer. But at the end of the visit to Washington, she wrote a few words to Zamir on a photograph of her taken with Nixon, expressing her admiration and gratitude for Zamir's work. Orally she added that not only were Nixon and Kissinger deeply impressed by the Israeli achievement and by Israel's willingness to share the document in its raw form, but the president was now ready to sell Israel additional F-4 Phantoms.

Not long afterward, Marwan passed along additional top-secret information about Soviet-Egyptian relations, and Golda Meir wanted to give that to the White House as well. This time, Zamir was more adamantly opposed, convinced that now the CIA would certainly figure out who the source was. The prime minister insisted, and a stalemate ensued. In a top-level meeting that included military secretary Brig. Gen. Israel Lior and Minister Without Portfolio Yisrael Galili, Zamir informed Meir that if she forced his hand, he would carry out her orders, but he would continue to insist that it was endangering the safety of the source. Meir, no less stubborn, told him to get on a plane and deliver it himself. Zamir said that Efraim Halevy could deliver it just as easily as he could. Meir insisted that Zamir not just carry out her orders but accept her position *in principle* regarding the decision to hand the material over. Zamir refused, and Golda Meir got up and stormed out of the room. Unimpressed by her passive-aggressive tactics, Zamir stood his ground.

In the end, the prime minister capitulated, and the Americans never laid eyes on the document.[9]

BEGINNING IN LATE 1968, when the Egyptians had finished rebuilding most of their military after their defeat in the Six-Day War, the question of whether and when they would attack had been the foremost concern of the Israeli intelligence community. Military Intelligence had done an impressive job answering that question early on. That fall, it had estimated that Nasser was going to attack in March 1969. It would be a static conflict, at least at first. On this basis, IDF chief of staff Bar-Lev gave the order to complete its preparations for war along the Suez Canal front by March 1. The Bar-Lev Line, a string of earthworks and fortifications along the canal, was completed on time, including the logistical infrastructure to support it during a prolonged conflict with Egypt. When the War of Attrition began on March 8, 1969, Israel was ready. That war ended on August 7, 1970, without any diplomatic or military gains on Egypt's part.

Egypt's failure, however, immediately raised two questions. Would they now look for a diplomatic or a military way to get the Sinai back? And if their plan was war, when would they feel ready to attack?

Marwan's promotion into Sadat's inner circle after the Corrective Revolution of May 1971 enabled him to pass on to the Israelis, the following July, the actual thoughts of Egypt's president regarding the first question. According to an MI memorandum disseminated that month,

> According to a high-ranking source in Egypt, there is no longer hope for a diplomatic agreement, and according to all indications Israel has no intention of withdrawing from the territories it conquered. A "diplomatic agreement," in

their view, would require Israel's commitment to Egypt that it return all territories taken in 1967, not just Sinai [i.e., also the West Bank and Golan Heights to Jordan and Syria, respectively]. The Egyptians came to the belief that the Americans had been leading them on, when the truth was they had neither the will nor the way to press Israel to withdraw. Egypt concluded that in light of the situation, there was no way to convince the Egyptian army and the Egyptian people that there was still hope for a diplomatic agreement, and there would therefore be no choice but to employ military force.[10]

At around the same time, Israel's ambassador to the United States, Yitzhak Rabin, was asked to prepare a personal, for-your-eyes-only message that he would deliver to Nixon and Kissinger. This, too, was based on information passed along by Marwan concerning the Egyptian perspective, and was to include four specific points:

1. Egypt is prepared for a full peace agreement with Israel on the basis of the Rogers Plan [which proposed returning the Sinai in exchange for peace];

2. The United States has repeated to the Egyptians its commitment to the Rogers Plan;

3. If the United States refuses to put pressure on Israel, Egypt will have no choice but to go to war;

4. The emphasis of the Sadat regime in its political and military struggle is not on the fate of the Palestinians, but on reclaiming Egyptian territory.[11]

It is unclear what convinced Golda Meir that she ought to send a message to Washington depicting Egypt as peacemaker and Israel and the United States as belligerents. Most likely, she was trying to show the Americans how Israel was working in line with the administration's hard-edged Middle East strategy—a central part of which was refusing any peace deal that would give Sadat back the Sinai without his switching over to the American side in the Cold War. And since Israeli decision makers had little faith in Egypt's peaceful intentions anyway, and were thus uninterested in giving up control over the eastern third of the Sinai under any conditions, the confluence of American and Israeli interests wound up torpedoing any Egyptian effort to move forward with a peace treaty in exchange for a full return of the Sinai—the same terms that, seven years and many lives later, became the basis of the Camp David Accords. Rabin, however, never delivered the message, for fear that it would result in increased US pressure on Israel.

Regardless of how these moves may be judged in hindsight, the fact remains that because of Ashraf Marwan, Israeli decision makers developed a very accurate picture of Egypt's intentions regarding war and peace. The Egyptians knew that they couldn't retake Sinai by force, and the Israelis knew they knew it. Among the analysts of IDF Military Intelligence, the belief emerged that if Egypt were to start a war, it would not be with the aim of recapturing the Sinai, which was unrealistic, but only "to force the powers to intervene and impose a solution."[12]

Having successfully answered the first question, MI got to work on the second: Under what circumstances would Egypt see itself ready to attack, even for more limited aims? Their efforts here would constitute a major step in developing what became known as the *kontzeptzia*—or Concept—which became the overarching paradigm that guided Israeli intelligence and decision making for most of the period between 1970 and the October 1973 Yom Kippur War. According to the Concept, Egypt would never attack without first solving the problem of its military inferiority. Here, too, Marwan's intelligence made a decisive contribution.[13]

The number one problem facing Egypt was Israel's dramatic air superiority. With the loss of the Sinai Peninsula, an Egyptian surprise attack on IAF air bases similar to the one that the IAF used to destroy the entire Egyptian air force on June 5, 1967, had become nearly impossible, for two reasons. First, the much greater distance Egyptian fighters would now have to fly, combined with improved Israeli radar coverage, made it extremely unlikely that Egypt could surprise the IAF the way Israel had done to Egypt. And second, the Soviets had yet to produce a fighter plane that could penetrate Israel's air defenses. As opposed to Western countries that were producing advanced aircraft like the US-made F-4 Phantom and A-4 Skyhawk (which Israel had) or the French Mirage 5 (which had been developed specifically for the IAF), Soviet manufacturers had focused their efforts on short-range interceptors and strategic long-range bombers meant to carry nuclear payloads. The Kremlin simply didn't have the kind of planes Egypt needed. The commander of Egypt's air force, Gen. Ali Mustafa Baghdady, expressed his frustration in a meeting of the Supreme Council in early 1972: "What I need is a deterrent aircraft. A fighter-bomber, about Mach two, with a good payload and range, that lets us go deep into enemy territory."[14] At the time there was only one plane that met Baghdady's demands: the F-4 Phantom. So long as Egypt was a Soviet client, the problem of Israel's air superiority had no solution.

But without neutralizing Israel's air superiority, any Egyptian effort to advance into Sinai would run into a wall. Egypt's main military achievement since the War of Attrition had been the deployment of massive antiaircraft batteries along the western bank of the Suez Canal, with Soviet help and in flagrant violation of the cease-fire agreement. These would provide an effective air umbrella for Egyptian troops and tanks crossing the Suez Canal. These SAM batteries, however, were fixed in place, creating a situation in which any Egyptian forces that remained under the antiaircraft umbrella—extending about six miles to the east of the canal—

were safe from IAF attack; but the moment they tried to advance beyond that range, hell would rain down upon them. Under such circumstances, retaking the Sinai was impossible. And since in every attack plan the Egyptians produced through the end of 1972, the main objective was retaking a significant portion of the Sinai, Israeli air superiority continued to be the decisive consideration in determining the likelihood of war. Both to Israel and to Egypt, in other words, it was clear that unless something significant changed, Egypt could not attack.

Marwan made two decisive contributions to Israel's understanding of the conditions under which the Egyptians would launch an attack, and of how close the Egyptians thought they were to fulfilling them. His oral reports and the documents he provided confirmed Israel's assessment that the air superiority issue was decisive. In conversations he had with Meir Meir when Marwan was still working for Sami Sharaf, only one solution was offered: After crossing the canal under cover of antiaircraft guns, the Egyptians would try to physically move their stationary antiaircraft sites eastward, gradually allowing the tanks to penetrate the peninsula, always under the umbrella, toward the Mitla and Gidi Passes. But from everything known at the time about Egypt's war plans, it was clear that they had put far too much emphasis on designing and training for a ground assault and not nearly enough on the Achilles' heel of IAF attacks. In 1970 the Egyptians did not yet have mobile SA-6 antiaircraft batteries, just stationary SA-2s and SA-3s. The SA-3s were manned by Soviet troops, and it was unclear that the Kremlin would approve their use if Egypt decided to launch an aggressive attack on a close ally of the United States. But even without this caveat, moving a SAM site across the canal was an extremely complex operation, and the small number they could successfully relocate would not have been enough to counter Israel's massive air power—power that had been significantly augmented since the late 1960s, with the arrival of large numbers of F-4s and A-4s from the United States. So even if the Egyptians had plans for crossing, and were conducting exercises according to those plans, everybody knew they were impracticable.[15]

But if the Egyptians knew they couldn't launch a successful campaign with the weapons they had, what did they think they needed to make it possible? After Nasser's death, and especially after May 1971, the Egyptians began looking at the problem of Israeli air power more realistically. Under the direction of the new minister of war, Mohammed Ahmed Sadek, a number of scenarios were worked out, and it became clear that the idea of gradually moving SAM batteries eastward wasn't going to work. Neither could Egypt tolerate a resumption of the deep-bombing raids. The only real solution to both of these problems was well known: convincing the Soviets to sell them better weapons, including long-range bombers that could carry serious payloads to Israeli air bases, and air-to-surface and surface-to-surface missiles that could reach Israeli population centers, in order to deter Israel from launching deep-bombing raids on the Egyptian home front.

From the details Marwan gave Israel about Sadat's talks in Moscow in March and October 1971, it became clear that Egypt was most interested in weapons that could threaten Israel's home front, in order to deter Israeli attacks on Egypt's own home front. As recalled, by October 1971 the Soviets agreed to sell Egypt a squadron of Tu-16 bombers carrying Kelt missiles but still refused to sell them Scud surface-to-surface systems. Around September 1972, Marwan gave the Israelis a copy of a letter by Sadat to Nikolai Podgorny, president of the Supreme Soviet, in which Sadat complained about the Soviets' continued unwillingness to give Egypt "weapons of retaliation that will deter the enemy from attacking Egyptian targets in the depth of our territory." Sadat added that "it was and remains clear that if we do not have retaliatory weapons of this kind, we will be without any military options whatsoever."[16] The information that Marwan passed on later described in detail the next stages of the process, including the arrival of the Kelt missiles to Egypt in late 1972 and their becoming operational in 1973. Marwan was also the first source who told Israel about the Soviets' change of heart regarding the Scud missiles in late May 1973, and their delivery—along with Soviet personnel to man them—in August 1973.

The matter of the long-range fighter-bombers was a tougher nut to crack, mainly because the Soviets didn't have any. The Egyptians pinned their hopes on the MiG-23, but by 1971 the plane had not yet entered mass production. An interceptor version of the MiG-23 became operational in the Soviet air force in June 1972, and a ground-attack version for export to third-world countries went into production in 1973. The earliest possible date for their becoming operational in the Egyptian air force was 1974—and as far as Sadat was concerned, waiting that long was not an option, especially since there was no guarantee that the planes would really be ready by then. The Egyptian war planners determined a minimum need of five attack squadrons (between sixty and seventy-five warplanes) for effectively attacking Israeli air bases.

Some time after Sadat came to power, Marwan reported on a meeting with his top generals, who presented the president with their need for a warplane comparable to the Israeli F-4 Phantoms as a condition for going to war. From later reports, Israeli MI and IAF intelligence could follow precisely the evolution of the Egyptian views regarding the precise aerial forces required to neutralize Israeli air superiority. At a certain point, these assessments included the five fighter-bomber squadrons as the minimal condition for Egyptian action—precisely what the Egyptian war planners, we now know, were in fact saying.

More important is the fact that beginning in late 1972, the

assessments suddenly stop referring to the need for long-range fighter-bombers as a condition for going to war. Specifically, Marwan informed Dubi on June 3, 1973, about four months before war started, that the Egyptian generals ceased regarding the supply of such aircraft as a necessary condition for launching war. Instead, they now counted on their massive air defense layout west of the canal, the split of the IAF efforts between the northern and the southern fronts, and the achievement of surprise as the main means to overcome their air inferiority.

Although the Israelis were aware of the shift, they failed to grasp what it meant. MI-Research and IAF intelligence continued, all the way until the Yom Kippur War in October 1973, to believe that the Egyptians would not attack without the fighter-bombers. And so, for example, on September 24, 1973, less than two weeks before the war, Military Intelligence chief Eli Zeira asserted that the purchase of fighter-bombers robust enough to attack targets in Israel continued to constitute, from the Egyptian perspective, a necessary condition for going to war—and that at least until 1975 this condition could not be met.[17] This mistake would haunt Israeli intelligence analysts who, having developed their *kontzeptzia* largely on the basis of information Marwan had given them, refused to revise their thinking even when Marwan began painting a very different picture.

THE NEAR IMPOSSIBILITY of procuring effective warplanes from the Soviet Union began to sink in with the Egyptians, forcing them to look for an alternative. MiG-17s, Sukhoi Su-7s, and even Sukhoi-17s, which arrived in small numbers about a year before the war, couldn't do the job. The only country other than the United States producing even vaguely relevant airplanes was France. Ironically, the French plane designed for ground assault was a variant of the Mirage 5J, tailored to specifications provided by the Israelis and intended for the IAF. But the French embargo on the conflict states halted the delivery of fifty such planes to Israel, and France was now looking for buyers for these as well as other models like the Mirage 5D, which had a low-altitude attack radius of 425 miles and a payload of two 1,900-pound bombs. These numbers didn't compare well with Israel's F-4s, but they were still better than anything the Soviets could offer.

But getting the Mirages was not so simple. The French embargo, after all, applied to Egypt no less than to Israel. And so, in November 1969, just months after a coup in Libya brought Muammar Gaddafi to power, negotiations began between Libya and France to purchase Mirages, ostensibly for the Libyan air force but in fact for Egypt. In January 1970, Libya and France signed an agreement to purchase 110 planes, half of which were 5Ds headed for Egypt. Delivery to Libya began in 1971, around the time that Sadat gave Marwan the Libyan brief. Naturally, all the information related to the deal, delivery via Libya, and integration of the planes into the Egyptian air force in July 1971—every detail was fully known to Israel. During the Yom Kippur War, Egypt's 69th Squadron would deploy forty-two Mirage 5s of different types out of its Tanta base. The number of Egyptian pilots trained to operate them was smaller—about twenty-five. These planes undertook the most important of Egypt's aerial missions in the first days of the war. Thanks to Marwan, Israeli intelligence knew everything there was to know about the squadron, who was commanding it, the names of its pilots, and the locations of its secret hangars.

The arrival of these aircraft did not change the persistent conception held by MI chief Zeira and his key staff. The 3,800-pound payload of each Mirage was less than a quarter of the 18,000-pound bomb payload of the hundred Phantoms that were in the service of the Israeli Air Force when the war began. Even if used to strike Israel's well-protected air bases, they could cause no serious damage to the sheltered aircraft. Moreover, from the information that Marwan delivered it was clear that the Egyptians thought so, too. While they viewed the Mirage 5s as their best attack aircraft, they did not regard them as an effective means to neutralize Israel's air superiority.

SINCE THE YOM KIPPUR WAR, a great deal of information has been released, mostly in the form of official memoirs and documentary research, about the long chain of events that led up to the war: the Egyptian perspective about what they needed in order to attack, the weaponry they received that made it possible, and the decisions surrounding the date of attack. From all of this it emerges, without a shadow of doubt, that the intelligence that Ashraf Marwan gave the Israelis proved consistently accurate, reflecting precisely what was happening in Egypt.

In examining the sources of Israel's massive intelligence failure in the days preceding the Yom Kippur War, one thing is clear: It resulted not from a lack of accurate information, but from the refusal of Military Intelligence to abandon the *kontzeptzia* even after it had clearly, irrefutably, been obviated by events. Thanks to Marwan, the Israelis understood precisely how the Egyptians saw both the necessity of war and the conditions necessary to launch it, through October 1972. But then, at around that time, Sadat changed his mind, deciding he would go to war without waiting for the weapons he would need to win. Ashraf Marwan, as we will see, reported this faithfully to Israel. MI, however, failed to adjust its assessments accordingly. This, and only this, led to Israel's failure to be ready when war struck.

MARWAN'S CONTRIBUTION TO Israeli intelligence, however, was not limited to the creation, and eventual dissolution, of the *kontzeptzia*. Marwan's intelligence also proved incredibly accurate in everything surrounding Egypt's specific attack plans. Here, too, MI benefited from a wealth of sources; Marwan's information, however, both raised the level of confidence in Israel's assessments and added rich, crucial details.

Since 1968, when the Egyptian military began its Tahrir exercises simulating the recapture of the Sinai Peninsula, Egyptian moves had been followed closely by MI, especially through the vast surveillance apparatus of Unit 848, its Signal Intelligence (Sigint) unit.

The report issued by MI-Research after one exercise in early 1969 concluded, "In its exercise, Egypt addressed the conquest of the western Sinai and the creation of a defensive line to the east of the [Mitla and Gidi] passes within four to five days, at a strength of five infantry divisions, one to two mechanized divisions, and two armored divisions."[18] In the summer of 1971, Marwan gave Col. Meir Meir the details of a plan called Granite, which gave MI a more detailed and reliable picture of how the war would look from the Egyptian side. Another plan that Marwan gave them in early 1972, similar to the earlier plans, allowed MI-Research to issue a special forty-page intelligence survey on April 16, which also included maps detailing the Egyptian assault. The first phase of the war, which was supposed to take no more than twenty-four hours, was built on five infantry divisions crossing the canal at five different points, securing the crossing points and their immediate areas, and then moving two armored divisions, the 4th and the 21st, across to the eastern bank and capturing land up to the IDF fortifications. This could be done either in daylight or at night. Because of the IAF's limited capabilities at night, MI's best guess was that the Egyptians would attempt it under cover of darkness. To isolate the canal zone from the rest of Sinai, the Egyptians would airdrop, via helicopters, between seven and ten commando battalions at the eastern openings of the Mitla and Gidi Passes. A marine brigade, comprising one tank and two infantry battalions, would

land at Rumani Beach, and another brigade-size infantry force
was to rendezvous with it by the eastern reef passage, with the aim
of blocking the northern Sinai road to Israeli reinforcements. The
Egyptian plan also included amphibious crossings at Lake Timsah
and the Great Bitter Lake, along the line of the canal. All of these
were to take place on the first day of battle.

On the second day, the armored divisions would advance to a
depth of about eight miles into Sinai; on the third day they would
take the passes, effectively conquering that portion of the Sinai
along a parallel up until their eastern entrance. In the fourth and
final phase, the Egyptian armies would complete their conquest of
Sinai up to the Israeli border.[19]

THE EXCEPTIONAL PRECISION of the documents that Marwan delivered, combined with the impressive breadth of Egyptian activity
that it covered, made him into what Mossad director Zvi Zamir
called "the greatest source we have ever had."[20] Marwan, he said,
"was a first-class source, because he could cover a whole area that
was very hard to get to, and the level of reliability of what he said
was high. There were others who gave us information here and
there, which confirmed or complemented things that he said. But
he knew it inside out. He could describe what things had been
like in the past, how things developed. From this perspective he
was unique."[21]

Other people who knew about Marwan's contribution confirm
Zamir's impressions. Brig. Gen. (res.) Amos Gilboa, who headed up
MI-Research during the 1980s, carefully went over the materials
Marwan had provided and concluded that there had never been
a spy in Israel's history who had made Egypt transparent the way
he did.[22] Brig. Gen. (res.) Aharon Levran, who was deputy commander of MI-Research before the Yom Kippur War, concluded
that the material Marwan had given Israel was "high-quality in-

formation of the sort that intelligence agencies wish for all their lives, and only get to see once in many generations."[23] He called Marwan "the kind of source that lands on the intelligence community's doorstep once in a generation. Worth his weight in gold."[24]

Intelligence officials were not alone in applauding Marwan. Years after the war, Moshe Dayan had the following to say:

> The Concept was not the invention of some mad scientist at MI, or the MI chief or the defense minister. It came together for us on the basis of very concrete intelligence information that we thought was the best that could possibly be achieved. . . . I can say with absolute confidence that any intelligence agency in the world, any defense minister or army chief of staff, who received this material and knew how it was attained, would have come to the same conclusion.[25]

From all the people who came into contact with the materials that Marwan provided, there were only two who—after the fact—called into question his commitment to helping Israel. One was the head of MI-Research Branch 6 (Egypt) who replaced Meir Meir beginning in the summer of 1972, Col. Yonah Bandman. In his view, one serious problem with Marwan was the fact that he kept warning that Sadat was about to launch a war, and then it didn't happen. Bandman's take was that Marwan had been crying wolf, and that it was therefore reasonable to ignore his warnings leading up to the Yom Kippur War. Moreover, Marwan failed to give good answers to the questions Bandman had given Dubi to ask, questions that tried to get to the bottom of Sadat's behavior patterns. Instead, the answers he kept getting were technical, dealing with issues connected to Egypt's war plans. And though he never went as far as calling Marwan a double agent, Bandman clearly believed, in hindsight, that the information he passed along was unreliable and that "for someone in his place in the hierarchy, there were certain things he should have known" that Marwan did not tell the Israelis.[26]

The other person who seriously doubted Marwan was Maj. Gen. Eli Zeira, chief of Military Intelligence during the war. Zeira became far more extreme in his views than Bandman, arguing that Marwan was a double agent who served as the central pillar in Egyptian attempts to divert Israel's attention before the war. In order to support this claim, Zeira distinguishes between the materials Marwan delivered and his oral assessments:

> Some of his "information" was spectacular, including verified data that was the dream of any intelligence agency in the world. . . . The "information" provided was, for the most part, copies of documents and minutes of meetings at the highest levels. As opposed to this, the warnings regarding the anticipated timing of the war usually came in the form of reporting, partly in writing and partly orally, but all of them came *without supporting documentation.* By October 1973, all of them had been revealed to be *inaccurate.*[27] [emphasis in the original]

Although he never says it explicitly in his book, Zeira presents an array of arguments to show that Marwan was the point man in an elaborate con game that Sadat was playing on Israel leading up to the war. In Zeira's view, Marwan gave false alarms of war in late 1972 and April 1973 in order to lull the Israelis into dropping their guard—and then deliberately failed to raise the alarm in the months that preceded October 1973. When he finally did give a warning, it was vague and so late in the game that, in the Egyptians' view, it was already too late for the IDF to mobilize.[28] In a televised interview promoting a revised edition of his book, Zeira hesitated to put things in a cut-and-dried manner. True, he said, he had no proof. But he nonetheless believed that Ashraf Marwan duped Israel "at the behest of Sadat, and I think they worked it out together."[29]

In considering Zeira's far-reaching claim, two points must be made. First, other than Zeira and to some extent Bandman, everybody who knew about Marwan and saw the material he provided over many years has completely rejected the double-agent hypothesis. Brig. Gen. Arieh Shalev, who served directly under Zeira as commander of MI-Research, for example, conducted a series of investigations and concluded unequivocally that Ashraf Marwan was no double agent—even if he never fully sold his soul to the Jewish state.[30] Aharon Levran, a self-described admirer of Eli Zeira, still believes that Marwan was an authentic spy and takes issue with Zeira on that subject.[31] Other, more junior officers from MI at the time, such as the chief of the political desk at MI-Research Branch 6 (Egypt), Albert Sudai; the chief of the same division's military desk, Yaakov Rosenfeld; and his predecessor at the military desk, who saw a great deal of Marwan's intelligence, Zusia Kaniazer—all of them are convinced that Marwan was a true agent, as are all of the Mossad officials who saw the material.

The second point has to do with how wide the double agent theory has spread both in Israel and around the world. But if it has become something of an urban legend, it is because almost everything published about Marwan until now was heavily influenced by conversations conducted with Eli Zeira. Zeira was, simply, the only Israeli in the know who was willing to speak with anyone on the subject—because until Marwan's death in 2007, no one who knew the truth dared talk about it for fear of risking his life. As a result, the great majority of what was said in public was said either by people directly influenced by Zeira, or senior Egyptian officials, members of Marwan's and Nasser's family, and others who had far too much to lose by saying that Marwan was anything but a loyal citizen of Egypt.

ANY ANALYSIS OF one of the most fascinating agents in the history of modern espionage would be incomplete without discussion of the methods used in his handling. Over the years, outlandish claims have been made about the amounts he was paid, with some putting the figure at up to $200,000 per meeting, or about $1 million in today's dollars.[32] The Mossad was willing to go very far to satisfy Marwan—but the actual numbers were far smaller.

Marwan would meet with Dubi whenever he traveled to Europe, sometimes as part of an official delegation, sometimes on business or even vacation. Every trip included one or more meetings over a few days. After the first few encounters, when payment was not even discussed, he began receiving $10,000 per set of meetings, but only when he asked for it. Later he asked to double the fee. Naturally, some in the Mossad were alarmed by the unprecedented outlays for a single agent. But after he threatened to cut off contact, they met his demands. In rare cases he received even more. Payments were made directly by Dubi to Marwan in cash, in used bills of smallish denominations in a small Samsonite case. At the end of each meeting, Marwan would take the case with him without opening it.

Yet even if the amounts were smaller than legends told, they were still big enough to cause a major deficit in the Mossad's European Operations budget. Covering it required express authorization from the Finance Ministry. Golda Meir did, at one point, hint to Finance Minister Pinchas Sapir that the Mossad had secured a top-level source with direct access to Sadat, but she wasn't more specific than that. The deficit kept growing, and at a certain point Sapir sent one of his bureaucrats to demand an explanation from the Mossad's chief of European Operations, Shmuel Goren.

Goren needed several bottles of French wine, and more than one gourmet dinner, to secure the Finance Ministry's approval for the expenditures—without even giving him the explanation he had wanted.

Another nagging question for the Mossad was that of the handler. Again, from the very beginning, top officers had insisted that such a source must be directed by a top-notch, veteran intelligence gatherer. But Zamir kept Dubi on despite his having joined the Mossad only three years earlier. The decision was spot-on: Dubi successfully managed the relationship in a way that minimized trouble and maximized Marwan's effectiveness. The core of Dubi's approach was his insistence on always giving Marwan the impression that Dubi's first loyalty was to the Angel rather than the Mossad. "Alex," he would come to believe, was somehow different from the rest of the agency. He could effectively represent Marwan's interests, taking his side in disagreements with the hierarchy on questions like the level of payment, who knew his identity or joined the meetings, and even who should be his handler.

Handling Marwan was no simple task. For starters, he didn't take the basic steps needed to ensure his security. Despite being given alternative phone numbers, for the first few months he kept calling up the Israeli embassy in London to set up meetings. To get him to stop, Dubi set up an offsite phone line manned by a go-between known as a "dead letter box." Marwan was told to call that number, rather than the embassy, whenever he needed to get a message to Dubi. The go-between was a London woman in her fifties who rarely left home. Whenever Marwan called, she immediately contacted Dubi. At just around this time, the first answering machines had been introduced, and Dubi installed one in the apartment so that Marwan could call at any time of night.

Yet Marwan continued to take needless risks. At least once he arrived at a meeting in an Egyptian embassy car, with an Egyptian

embassy driver. Another time, Dubi and Meir Meir met Marwan
in his apartment in London's Mayfair district. The entire time
they were talking in the living room, a local prostitute was waiting
for Marwan in the bedroom. She could have heard every word.
Marwan didn't care.

He took risks in the documents he brought, as well. Many of
them were originals—not even photocopies. When Dubi asked
why he wasn't worried about getting caught with the documents,
he just smiled and said, "They won't search me." In some cases he
gave them to Dubi. In others, when they were especially sensitive,
Dubi would photograph them with a handheld camera and give
them back. Only in extreme cases, when the documents were too
sensitive to bring along, would he write down the key points and
then dictate them to Dubi.

Marwan's recklessness went further. A few months after Marwan
started working with the Mossad, Dubi once noticed the butt of a
handgun popping out from behind his jacket. When he asked him
about it, Marwan drew the loaded Smith & Wesson .38 and offered
it to Dubi as a gift. Dubi was aghast. He explained to Marwan that
what might be acceptable in Cairo was entirely unacceptable in
the British capital, where even mafia bosses refrained from carrying
firearms. Marwan was unmoved. His diplomatic passport, he said,
meant that the local authorities couldn't touch him. He offered
the gun again. It was a beautiful weapon, with the hammer hidden
inside the stock so you could shoot it from inside your pants or
jacket pocket without worrying that the fabric would get caught
in the mechanism. Dubi was tempted but turned down the offer.
The next meeting, Marwan brought another gun, this time as a
clear and premeditated gift. Dubi had little choice. He took the
gun and thanked his Angel.

The one area where Marwan was pointedly risk-averse was in
anything having to do with wireless communication. Given his easy

access to the most important Egyptian secrets, the Mossad wanted to position him as an "alarm agent" who could give a real-time warning if the Egyptians were about to attack. They sent an expert to London to give Marwan a crash course in using a wireless device. He sent Marwan off with the device, means to hide it, and a list of frequencies. Marwan, however, wasn't very good with gadgets. Somebody in the Mossad defined him as having "two left hands." At his next meeting with his handlers, Marwan told them that it was just too dangerous and that he had tossed it into the Nile. In all his years working for the Mossad, the greatest spy in Israel's history never once passed information via wireless communication.

And yet, despite the relatively smooth relationship that developed, the question of the handler kept coming up. Dubi, it was claimed, had "defected" to Marwan's side, a problem of overidentification common to inexperienced handlers. There were other questions as well, like what would happen if Dubi were unavailable to meet when Marwan needed to—say in the event of illness, vacation, or professional transfer. Indeed, intelligence agencies usually try to prevent a situation where a single handler becomes too closely connected with an agent over an extended period of time, so they change handlers from time to time or add a second handler. But Marwan adamantly refused any effort to replace Dubi or bring in someone else, and every time the subject came up he threatened to quit. Zamir found himself at a dead end, with only one, somewhat unusual, way to move forward. He would directly involve himself in handling the Angel. To this, even Ashraf Marwan could not object.

Beyond just solving the problem of Marwan's exclusive connection with Dubi, Zamir also wanted to boost the Angel's motivation. From the outset it was clear that his psychological needs— particularly the need to compensate for the insult he had received at the hands of Nasser and his men—played an important role in his decision to work for the Mossad. So it was only natural that if he were allowed to meet on a regular basis with a former general in the legendary Israeli army, who now headed the most storied intelligence agency on earth, this would serve to pump up Marwan's ego and to motivate him to work hard for Israel. And indeed, from the moment Dubi brought it up, Marwan was happy to go along.

The first meeting between Israel's top spymaster, "the General," as Marwan used to call him, and Israel's greatest spy was a success. From Marwan's perspective, the very fact of the meeting reflected an upgrade in his status, an expression of his importance in the Israelis' eyes. Zamir enjoyed it as well. Beyond the operational challenge that this sort of secret meeting entailed, one he had never personally experienced during his military career, it turned out that Marwan was charismatic and interesting, with a wonderful sense of humor—a true conversationalist. Small wonder, then, that their relationship developed very quickly; the two met, with Dubi in tow, whenever the opportunity arose. Sometimes, due to operational requirements, they would even stay at the same hotel and meet on successive days.[33]

Zamir did not get into specifics about the information Marwan had delivered. Instead they spoke broadly, about global affairs, with Zamir asking just a few questions and letting Marwan do the talking. For Zamir, hearing what Marwan had to say on these issues was less important than giving him the feeling that the chief of the Mossad was hanging on his every word. When it came to Egypt's war strategy, Marwan's insights were more important. Since their first meeting, he described the gap between Sadat, who wanted to initiate hostilities as soon as possible in order to generate a political process to get back the Sinai, and his generals, who clung to what Marwan termed as "the Nasser plan," which aimed at the occupation of the whole of the Sinai by military means alone. Since the generals knew that their plan was not feasible without receiving additional weapon systems from the Soviets, they refused to go to war. At the same time, Sadat was looking for generals who would accept his strategic vision and would be ready to launch a war with limited territorial goals.[34]

The Mossad helped Marwan in other ways as well. His quick climb up the Egyptian hierarchy and his careless behavior drew attention, much of it negative. The Mossad tried to help him deflect the accusations, apparently with no small measure of success. Sometimes a little gesture went a long way. For example, when Marwan went through marital troubles, Zamir ordered his people to buy a diamond ring in Tel Aviv and pass it to Marwan, who then gave it to his wife. Thus the flowering of renewed affection between Nasser's daughter and her husband was subsidized by the Israeli taxpayer.

Yet despite Zamir's participation in meetings with Dubi and Marwan, there were still officials in the Mossad who thought it would be better to involve a more experienced officer to replace Dubi. Zamir was convinced that Dubi was doing an excellent job, but the pressure finally had its effect. In advance of one of their London meetings in 1971, it was agreed that the designated replacement, a man with significant experience in the Egypt branch at MI-Research, would wait outside the room until Zamir had explained to Marwan the reasons for the change of handler. Yet as soon as Zamir began raising the issue, Marwan immediately and forcefully refused. Zamir asked the intended handler to join them, and the latter began telling Marwan about himself and his experience, in Arabic. Marwan wouldn't even look at him. After the man left, Marwan took Zamir and Dubi to task for bringing "that Iraqi" to the meeting. Zamir explained that the man was Jewish, an Israeli intelligence officer, an expert. Marwan was unimpressed. "In the Arab world," he explained, "there is a hierarchy. The Egyptians are on top. Then come the Syrians, the Jordanians, the Saudis, and on it goes." Marwan blinked, and then continued. "The Iraqis are at the bottom. Egyptians step on them when they walk," he concluded, illustrating these last words with a gesture of walking.

Zamir needed no further convincing. The question of replacing Dubi would not come up again as long as he remained the Mossad chief.

MARWAN'S STELLAR SUCCESS posed an unprecedented professional dilemma for the Mossad. On the one hand, Zamir was aware that responsibility for the Israeli government's overall intelligence assessment was not in the hands of his agency, but of IDF Military Intelligence. For this reason, MI-Research was supposed to be the address for everything Marwan provided. There it would be analyzed, processed, and integrated with all the other information that reached Israel, and then packaged for use by Israel's top military and diplomatic decision makers. On the other hand, because of the sensitivity of the source and the fear that Marwan's identity might be compromised if more than a handful of people knew he existed, his materials could be given to MI only in bits and pieces. But that, in turn, would run the serious risk that when his materials were integrated with all the other data, the unique quality of his intelligence would be drowned out, and it wouldn't enjoy anything like the weight it deserved in helping the Israeli leadership understand what was happening in Egypt.

As noted already, in order to overcome these problems Marwan's reports were sent in their entirety, and in their raw form, directly only to the prime minister, the defense minister, the IDF chief of staff, and the chief of IDF Military Intelligence. A fifth person in the loop, secretly, was Minister Without Portfolio Yisrael Galili, who was Golda Meir's personal confidant. Zamir himself distributed the reports; in his absence, his trusted chief of staff would do it. For integration into MI's overall assessments, MI distribution officers would take that information and divide it into categories like Soviet-Egyptian relations, the Egyptian army, the Egyptian air force, and so on, passing it to the different branches of MI-Research and changing the code names to hide the fact that so much information was coming from a single source.

The most avid consumer of Khotel reports was certainly Moshe Dayan, who often summoned Zamir to his office for clarifications or more information. But Golda Meir was not far behind, picking them apart intensely with Galili and discussing them with Zamir in their weekly consultations in her home in Ramat Aviv. Even in these closed forums, but especially in telephone conversations, reference to Marwan was always made using an improvised code name. Dayan, for example, would often refer to the "last information I received." During the first days of the war, this caution was somewhat dropped; according to the minutes of the top government meetings, both Bar-Lev and Meir spoke frankly about "Zvika's friend," referring to Zamir's nickname, "Zvika." This, too, was an improvisation that emerged from the war's heady first days, when on the one hand the need to try to understand Sadat's motives and plans was at its peak, and on the other, the circle involved in the discussions and decisions often included people out of the loop about Marwan.

And indeed, the fact that Khotel reports were given only to the four key decision makers placed a strict limit on the discussions that could be held about them and on the variety of opinions that could be voiced in interpreting them. This fact was especially worrying to MI chief Aharon Yariv. From his professional standpoint, understanding intelligence required that it first be digested, combined, and prioritized within a broader picture of all the different sources and evidence that was constantly flowing into the hands of the analysts in MI-Research; by giving decision makers the raw material from one source, it could paint a very inaccurate picture of what was really happening in Egypt. Yariv talked to Zamir about the problem and suggested that Zamir keep sending them out in their present form, but to the prime minister alone, who was anyway the Mossad chief's direct superior. Zamir respected Yariv's opinion and the next report did not go to Dayan or the chief of staff. After Meir received it, however, she called Dayan to ask him what he thought about "what Zvika sent." A few minutes later an outraged Dayan called Zamir, demanding to know why he hadn't received his copy. Zamir tried to explain that Yariv had thought it wiser to stop sending them to him for fear that they might skew the defense minister's intelligence analysis. Dayan cut him off. Using the Hebrew acronym for Military Intelligence, "Aman,"* he simply said, "Aman, schmaman. Send it to me." With this, the attempt to limit distribution of Marwan's raw intelligence material, for all its professional merits, met a swift end.[35]

---

* *Aman* is an abbreviation of *agaf modi'in*, or the intelligence branch of the IDF.

Chapter 6

SADAT'S EMISSARY FOR SPECIAL AFFAIRS

Anwar Sadat's decision to appoint Marwan as his personal liaison for a very specific, crucial assignment—namely, handling relations with Libya and Saudi Arabia—fit well with Sadat's overall approach to managing the country's affairs. While he had at his disposal all the traditional tools of rule, such as the army, foreign ministry, and intelligence agencies, he rarely relied on them in crafting his policies. He had little patience for rambling policy papers or long meetings aimed at striking a compromise among competing ministries plying contradictory policies. His most important decisions usually followed a period of seclusion. He would cut himself off from advisers and reports, sit alone, and find the answer. The result was that instead of taking measured steps and walking a fine line, Sadat preferred bold, often risky moves. This was his methodology when he offered an agreement for a partial Israeli withdrawal from the Suez Canal in February 1971; when he had his opponents arrested rather than trying to cut a deal with them three months later; when he went to war in October 1973 against a clearly superior enemy; or when, in November 1977, he went to Jerusalem and addressed the Knesset without first reaching clear understandings with Israel or the United States about the peace negotiations that were about to begin. Every one of these decisions could have ended his political career. Sadat, however, was blessed not only with excellent political intuitions, but—at least until 1981—no small amount of luck as well.

Sadat's tendency to cut through bureaucracy rather than work with it made his use of exceptionally loyal assistants crucial for his ability to function. In this sense, Ashraf Marwan fit Sadat like a glove. He was part of no hierarchy and had no other loyalties. Sadat believed that Marwan would remain true to him personally, not just as head of state, but also because Sadat was the man who had elevated him. Marwan brought with him his boundless ambition, cleverness, networking skills, charm, and above all the incandescent glow that came with being a member of the Nasser family.

From Marwan's perspective, it was his ambition, youth, and lack of a power base in the Egyptian establishment, alongside his lust for money and love of intrigue, that turned his life into an ongoing drama. In the decade between his rise in 1971 and his political downfall and departure from Egypt in 1981, he held a number of senior positions, made many personal enemies, engulfed himself in scandals, faced public accusations—usually to no effect—of various forms of corruption, enmeshed himself with the most intimate aspects of the Sadat family, and amassed a sizable fortune that, according to critics, reached £400 million in 1981.

WHAT REALLY ENABLED Marwan to forge fruitful ties between the Egyptian president, on the one hand, and the Saudi royals and Libyan revolutionaries, on the other, were his relationships with two people in particular: Kamal Adham and Abdessalam Jalloud.

Kamal Adham was born in 1929, the son of an Albanian father and a Turkish mother, scion of one branch of Saudi royals. Adham's family moved to Saudi Arabia when he was just a year old. His half sister, Iffat, became the beloved wife of Crown Prince Faisal. In 1961, Faisal, who was already the regime's strongman, appointed Kamal to negotiate with a Japanese consortium called the Arab Oil Company on the rights to produce oil in the neutral zone between Saudi Arabia and Kuwait. In return Adham, who had won Faisal's confidence, received 2 percent of the sales of any oil the company produced. The Saudi oil minister at the time, Abdullah al-Tariki, correctly estimated that the value of that appointment was in the billions of dollars, and he informed Faisal of his opposition to it. In response, the prince fired Al-Tariki. Adham was soon a billionaire and became known in Middle Eastern business circles as "Mr. Two Percent."

In 1964, following the death of King Saud and the ascent of Faisal, Adham was officially appointed adviser to the new king. Among his other duties, Adham created the Mukhabarat al a-amah, the kingdom's central intelligence agency, and led it for many years. The decision to create it arose from the need to find an effective solution to the problem of Nasserite infiltration into the Arabian Peninsula, which had worsened because of the Yemenite civil war, in which Egypt had taken the opposite side from the Saudis. An additional responsibility of the agency was to raise the profile of Saudi Arabia around the world, especially in the United States. This would be achieved mainly through bribery.

According to the Saudi way of doing things, stopping Nasserite agitation in Saudi Arabia meant, among other things, building positive relationships with members of Nasser's inner circle. For Adham that meant befriending Jehan Sadat, wife of the man who at the time was chairman of the Egyptian National Assembly. According to journalist Bob Woodward, in 1970 Sadat received a regular stipend from the Saudis, with the implication that the various business projects conducted between Jehan and Kamal were little more than cover for the bribes. Given Kamal's close ties with the

CIA, the Americans clearly were aware of the relationship; whether they were also behind some of the bribes remains unclear.

The connection between Adham and Jehan Sadat became especially important after Nasser's death. Saudi-Egyptian relations had substantially improved after the Six-Day War and Egypt's withdrawal from Yemen, and the Saudis had begun giving Egypt significant economic aid as compensation for the loss of income from the Suez Canal, Sinai oil fields, and tourism. Once Anwar Sadat took power, those relations strengthened even more. Faisal picked Kamal Adham to be his personal liaison to the new Egyptian president. Adham secretly visited Cairo with the aim of sounding out Sadat on new understandings between the two countries. He expressed the Saudis' concern about Soviet influence on the region and emphasized that the Soviet presence in Egypt was forcing the Americans to support Israel much more than they wanted to. Sadat answered that he needed the Soviet units on Egyptian soil so long as there was the risk of war. But he stressed that if the Americans were to pressure Israel to find a solution to the Sinai problem, even just a partial accord, he would gladly send the Soviets home. These words made their way to Washington, where they were leaked to the press by Senator Henry "Scoop" Jackson, one of the Senate's leading opponents of the Soviet Union. The leak embarrassed the Kremlin and did little to improve ties between Moscow and Sadat. But the dialogue that had begun between Sadat and Adham became the central channel of communication between the United States and Egypt, which had severed diplomatic ties during the Six-Day War. Through this channel, Adham relayed messages between the two sides, including assurances from National Security Adviser Henry Kissinger that if Egypt were to end its strategic alliance with the Soviets and send the advisers home, the United States would help it get the Sinai back.[1]

The tight connection between Adham and Sadat bore fruit in

the darker aspects of Egyptian–American relations, as well. According to Mohamed Hassanein Heikal, when Sadat came to power the intelligence agencies told him about a secret operation called Dr. Birdie (*doktor asfour*). In this operation, which according to Heikal was known to no more than ten people in Egypt and was carried out during 1967 or early 1968, listening devices were planted in the American interests section in Cairo, which had been housed in the Spanish embassy after relations were cut. The operation had been approved by Nasser himself, and he had received regular surveillance reports. Soon after taking power, Sadat told Adham about the devices. Heikal, who learned of the conversation from Sadat himself, and who had influence on the program, was shocked that the new president would tell a known CIA informant about so incredibly sensitive an operation. Whatever Sadat's motives were, the result of his conversation with Heikal was swift: The operation was stopped and the devices turned off.[2]

Ashraf Marwan and Kamal Adham had been close even before Sadat picked Marwan to handle relations with Saudi Arabia. The introduction had been made by mutual friends, including Jehan Sadat, as well as Sheikh Abdullah al-Sabah and his wife, Souad. According to one source, it was Adham who had pressured Sadat into picking Marwan to replace Sami Sharaf in May 1971. Sadat quickly found himself having to strictly limit Marwan's role. Practically, however, by leaving him in charge of relations with the Saudis in general and King Faisal in particular, he had turned Marwan's relationship with Adham into the central channel of communication between the two states, circumventing the traditional channels of diplomats and embassies. Whatever advantage this may have given their states' respective leaders, Marwan and Adham learned very quickly how to turn it to their own personal advantage as well.

In the Saudi political and business culture of the time, the concept of a conflict of interests had yet to be introduced. On the contrary, taking advantage of your position to build your estate was an accepted, even admired, norm. And it was a norm that suited Marwan's personality well. Kamal Adham, who proved his aptitude with his famous 2 percent, but also through other deals involving oil, aircraft (mostly through deals with Boeing), and weapons, was a perfect business partner for the shady deals Marwan started making soon after he ascended to power in Sadat's government.

Their first joint venture was in real estate. Marwan purchased, in the name of his wife, Mona, a twenty-three-acre plot of land in the Kardassa region, near the pyramids at Giza. He paid 150,000 Egyptian pounds ($60,000). Later he took advantage of his status as adviser to the president in order to raise the value of the land and sold it at a large profit. A few months later, Marwan used that money to buy another, larger piece of land, again in Mona's name. Again he sold it for a huge gain. This time around, the buyer was Kamal Adham.

When Marwan's rivals learned of the deal, they made sure to bring it to public light. A journalist named Jalal al-Din al-Hamamsi accused Marwan of a range of corrupt activities. How was it, Hamamsi asked, that a public servant's family, no matter how senior, got its hands on that kind of money? How did the land appreciate so dramatically in so short a time? Amid the public outcry, Sadat had no choice but to have his attorney general launch an investigation of the first real estate deal. Marwan answered that he got the money from selling the cars his wife had received as a gift from one of the other Arab governments because she was Nasser's daughter, and that she was the one who had sold the land. The excuse was accepted—in part because of the public's abiding loyalty to Nasser's family—and the case was closed. Calls for an investigation of the second deal went nowhere. Years later, Marwan admitted he had lied about the source of the money but denied taking advantage of his position. "I borrowed money from a friend and we bought the

land together," he said. "We were lucky, and the value multiplied
five times in two years."[3] Another time when he was asked how he
began to make his money, he said that it was from a real estate deal
in Abu Dhabi. What made it succeed, he claimed, were not any
special gifts of his own but dumb luck.[4]

It may be fair to assume that the "friend" who lent Marwan the
money to make the first purchase was Kamal Adham. Whether because he wanted to buy political influence in Sadat's regime, or out
of sincere friendship, he did everything he could to make Marwan
wealthy—including buying the land at a high price in the second
deal. There is another possibility, however: that the financing for
the first purchase came not from Adham but from the Mossad. In
that case, Adham merely made it possible for Marwan to parlay it
into something much bigger.

Marwan's close relations with Kamal Adham offered him not
only financial opportunities but also a key to new social circles.
The most important of these included graduates of Victoria College in Alexandria, the most elite secular institution of higher
learning in the Arab world. Since its founding in 1902, Victoria
counted many alumni who went on to power and leadership.
As with the elite schools in other countries, students maintained
friendships for years, even decades, after graduating. Adham, too,
was an alumnus, and his circle included King Hussein of Jordan;
Hussein's prime minister, Zaid al-Rifai; and the brothers Adnan
and Essam Khashoggi, sons of the Saudi king's personal physician,
who became global tycoons. He introduced Marwan to his friends,
and the young Egyptian took full advantage of the connections
for business (as with Adnan Khashoggi) or political advancement
(as with Mansour Hassan, the Egyptian information minister who
was one of the strongest people in the President's Office as well
as a friend of Jehan Sadat). At other times, it was the Victorians
who leveraged their connection with Marwan to advance their

projects with the president. In September 1978, for example, King Hussein met with Marwan in London, asking him to pass along a secret message to Sadat saying that he wanted to join the peace conference about to be held at Camp David together with Israeli prime minister Menachem Begin and US president Jimmy Carter. Despite Hussein's efforts, which included a phone call to Sadat at Marwan's encouragement, Sadat refused the king's request.[5]

AND THEN THERE WERE the Libyans. The Libyan issue was especially complex because of the volatility, messianism, and rash behavior of the country's young leader, Col. Muammar Gaddafi, who led a military coup in September 1969. Gaddafi was an avowed Nasserite who wanted to put his country on a path to social and economic progress, while at the same time emphasizing its Islamic, anti-imperialist, and pan-Arab qualities. As part of this worldview, he repeatedly tried to bring about the unification of Libya and Egypt—a permanent headache for Sadat. Sadat, however, saw good relations with Libya as an important goal, both because of the latter's newfound wealth resulting from renegotiated oil deals with the major companies and because it was the major conduit through which the Egyptian air force could purchase fighter planes with enough range to attack Israeli air bases.

Whereas with the Saudis, Marwan's contact was a billionaire, a spymaster, and a confidant of the king, with the Libyans his point man was no less exotic: Maj. Abdessalam Jalloud, Gaddafi's right hand, the prime minister of Libya beginning in 1972. Born at some point in the early 1940s (the year has been cited by various sources as 1940, 1941, 1943, and 1944) into the tiny, impoverished al-Magharba tribe, Jalloud shared with Gaddafi his low socioeconomic origins. Yet unlike other members of his tribe of his age, he acquired a high school education and even set his sights on a career as a doctor. He first met Gaddafi in prison after both were arrested during a 1959 demonstration, and he decided to change the course of his life toward the military, enrolling in the officers' academy. During his military years, Jalloud immersed himself in the revolutionary literature that was popular at the time—mostly based on the experience of the Egyptian and Cuban revolutions. And yet, as opposed to Gaddafi, who grew up in a kind of pristine, puritanical tribal ethos, Jalloud had a tribal experience that was more open. This combination of his relative openness with his tendency toward revolutionary Arab nationalism rather than Gaddafi's ascetic fundamentalism made Jalloud far more ready to enjoy the "good life" than his boss was.[6]

Even amid the kaleidoscope of colorful characters who populated the young Libyan leadership under Gaddafi, Jalloud stood out. One of his most memorable qualities was a tendency to show eccentric disrespect for representatives of foreign powers. On the morning the king was deposed, for example, the embassies of the United States, the Soviet Union, the United Kingdom, and France sent emissaries to get briefed on the events of the previous night and to learn what they could about the new regime. Each one waited outside his embassy as a military jeep drove around picking them up, the four of them ending up squeezed into the backseat. Dressed in fatigues next to the driver was a man who introduced himself as "Sergeant Mohammad." They were driven to the headquarters of radio and television, where Sergeant Mohammad, along with other commanders, briefed them about the situation. The "sergeant," of course, was none other than Jalloud, the commander of the forces that had taken over all the key government offices in Tripoli the night before.

Abdessalam Jalloud was also the central figure in the negotiations that opened between the new regime and representatives of the foreign oil companies over the percentage that the new government would take on all exports. These had not changed for nearly ten years, and Jalloud now demanded a dramatic increase. During the negotiations, Jalloud would summon the companies' representatives to meetings late at night, hand them his demands or proposals in writing, and send them back to their hotels. Soon after, he would call them at the hotel and demand immediate answers—sometimes threatening that if his demands were not met, the company would be nationalized. Once, Jalloud sauntered into the conference room, wielding an automatic rifle, railing about how Western powers had to sell arms to Libya. In the end, the oil companies acceded to Libya's demands.[7]

To his credit, Jalloud never discriminated between the global powers, on the one hand—whom he despised for what he considered the pillaging of his native soil—and those who were supposed to be Libya's closest friends and allies, on the other. In March 1973, he came to Egypt for talks about military cooperation between the two countries. Participants included the Egyptian minister of war, Gen. Ahmad Ismail Ali, as well as Ashraf Marwan. During the talks, an argument flared between the young Libyan and the Egyptian minister, a career military man in his late fifties, over the range of a certain ground-to-ground missile. Ismail claimed it was twenty-five miles; Jalloud said it was only two and a half miles. To resolve the dispute, an authoritative reference manual was produced that listed the missile's specifications. Jalloud was right. But he could not restrain himself, and told Ismail that something as small as a decimal point could have big implications, and it would be better if officers were better at reporting the little details so that the political leadership could make better decisions. The minister was furious at the implicit accusation, coming from the mouth of someone who, less than four years earlier, was still a junior officer. "I fought in three wars," he retorted, "when you were still a little boy." Jalloud responded that those wars were all failures, and that the failures resulted from false details that military officers gave their leaders. He then stalked out of the room, causing a crisis in the talks.

Marwan ran after him, hoping to calm him, but Jalloud barged into Sadat's office demanding that his honor be respected. As he was explaining himself to Sadat, the war minister stormed in as well, pointed to Jalloud, and yelled, "This unschooled boy humiliated me before my officers!" When Jalloud tried to respond, Ismail threatened, "If this child doesn't shut his mouth, I will smack him with my boots!" The war minister then walked out, slamming the door. He returned to his house and refused to go back to work for three days. Jalloud, no less furious, went back to Libya, causing a rupture in the talks. Marwan, who needed all his diplomatic finesse to bring the talks back on track, followed Jalloud to Tripoli and returned with an answer from Gaddafi to Sadat: The Libyans demanded that Ismail be fired. Sadat was unwilling to hear of it; preparations for war with Israel were well under way. In the end Ismail remained in his position, but Egypt accepted Jalloud's demand that a different diplomatic channel be created to work around the minister of war. Jalloud was still not satisfied. He told his Libyan lawyer to file a suit against Ismail and did not withdraw it even after the Yom Kippur War. Ismail never again visited Libya; he died in late 1974.[8]

As opposed to Kamal Adham, who was significantly older than Marwan, Jalloud was Marwan's age. This fact, combined with Marwan's impressive family connections and his ability to charm the bark off a tree, quickly moved their relationship from formalities to friendship. Jalloud would often steal out of Tripoli, which under Gaddafi had become a bastion of Islamic asceticism, and head for places where the good life awaited. Often that meant Cairo, where he and other Libyan officers spent nights drinking and doing the town with Marwan. Sometimes Jalloud and Marwan would meet up in Rome or London. During one of these getaways in London, Marwan actually called up his Mossad handler, demanding that the Israelis arrange for prostitutes—in plural—for his high-ranking Libyan friend. Dubi had little experience with this particular aspect of London nightlife, and he turned for help to his friends at the Mossad's London station. They, in turn, found a reputable escort service to fulfill Jalloud's needs. The tab for Jalloud's debauchery was picked up by the Israeli taxpayer.

Marwan's opponents, of course, did everything they could to make these adventures a matter of public record. Once, during a party in a private home in an upscale Cairo neighborhood, somebody locked Marwan, Jalloud, and their revolutionary Libyan friends into the apartment. When they began shouting to get out, the pranksters called the police to complain about the shouting, and officers arrived at the scene. Sadat received a report on the incident but chose to let it slide. Even if it made Marwan look bad in Cairo, Egypt could not do without his services.

The friendship between Marwan and Jalloud became the pivot of Egyptian-Libyan relations, bearing fruit in the most important joint initiative of the time: the purchase of Mirage warplanes from France.[9] The deal, which included the procurement of 110 Mirage 5s, was valued at over $200 million. To make it happen, Marwan traveled often, not just to Tripoli but also to France, even though the Libyans were supposedly fronting the operation. Sadat himself said on more than one occasion that Ashraf Marwan personally overcame many obstacles that the French government, as well as the manufacturer Marcel Dassault, put in the deal's way during the trying days leading up to the October 1973 war.[10] As usual, Marwan's achievements weren't purely in the service of his country: Some Egyptian sources reported that he took a hefty fee as well.[11] According to the *Al-Shaab* newspaper, his take was $10 million.[12] Whether or not Marwan profited, it *is* clear that the Israelis quickly learned everything there was to know about the deal.

MARWAN'S TALENT FOR keeping the volatile Libyans under control, alongside his stable relations with the Saudis, made him a fixture in Sadat's world. He also took great advantage of the relationships he developed with some of those closest to Sadat, first among them his wife, Jehan, to secure Sadat's continuing political support. Ashraf Marwan understood that his affinity for dubious dealings and tendency to make harsh enemies at home made the president's support for him all the more crucial.

From the outset, many in Sadat's office bristled at Marwan's meteoric rise. The support he gave Sadat during the May 1971 Corrective Revolution, and the imprisonment of many of Nasser's closest friends that resulted, made him a traitor in the eyes of many ranking Egyptians—especially Nasser's family, including his widow, Tahia, his daughter Hoda and her husband, and Nasser's sons. Marwan often turned their hostility to his advantage, complaining to Sadat about the heavy price he and Mona had paid for supporting him, and using it to bolster his position and to cover for his corruption.[13]

Another source of antagonism, however, was jealousy of what Marwan represented: a handsome and eloquent upstart, propelled, without any prior experience or discernible achievement, to the top echelons of Egyptian life. His closeness with the president, who backed him unblinkingly, and with the president's wife, who was far more involved in affairs of state than was her predecessor, only added to the ill will directed against Marwan, fueling rumors of his misbehavior. Marwan himself once explained the animosity against him this way: "Seventy percent of Egyptians hated me. For 10 percent of them, it was because of my connection to Gamal Abdel Nasser; for 60 percent it was my age. According to the law, no one under the age of 35 could be appointed a government minister . . . and I had oversight authority over all the ministers when I was still in my twenties. It was unthinkable."[14] Even if he overstated his status and understated his responsibility for the ill will, there was plenty of truth in his words.

At the end of the day, however, it was Marwan's behavior that contributed more than anything else to the relentless attacks against him. For he was indeed corrupt. One example concerned a 1971 procurement of Mercedes automobiles for the President's Office. When investigators from Egypt's General Intelligence Service (Mukhabarat) went over the details of the agreement and documents from the importer, they discovered check stubs made out to Ashraf Marwan totaling $1 million. The chief of intelligence, Gen. Ahmad Ismail Ali, brought the findings to Sadat's attention, but the president ordered the case closed. Intelligence officers involved were exceptionally frustrated, and one of them passed the details to a journalist, who went to Sadat exhorting him to reopen the case. Sadat finally agreed, and Marwan was interrogated, as was Marwan's father. Marwan tried to pin it on another employee in the office, to no avail. But because the investigation failed to produce clear evidence incriminating Marwan, no steps were taken against him.[15]

The fact that Ashraf Marwan was questioned along with his father was not a big surprise. After a long military career, the elder Marwan entered the business world, and during the 1970s he became known as "Mr. Fifty Percent" because of the large commissions he charged. Jalal al-Din al-Hamamsi, the same journalist who uncovered Marwan's real estate deals with Kamal Adham, investigated Marwan's father as well. The Egyptian minister of trade, Zakaria Tawfik, confirmed that Abu al-Wafa Marwan was suspected of bribe taking, adding that he was under considerable pressure to retire. Further inquiries revealed that both Marwan and his father were under heavy suspicion; according to a number of different sources, it was Marwan who, taking full advantage of his position, brokered the bribes for his father. In this instance, too, the case against him was dropped on orders from the top—despite considerable evidence.[16]

Nor were Marwan's scandals limited to financial dealings. A big one concerned his rivalry with Ahmad al-Masiri, an officer of the Republican Guard who also served in the President's Office. Here, too, the details are sketchy, and many interested parties have offered contradictory versions. But what they all seem to agree on is that Al-Masiri, young and talented and promising, ambitious and broad-minded, was Marwan's biggest rival in the President's Office; and that Marwan was worried that Al-Masiri would replace him. The more Al-Masiri won Sadat's confidence, the more his power grew. Like Marwan, Al-Masiri knew how to maneuver around the president's family—especially Sadat's oldest daughter, Lubna, who was in her early twenties. Whether out of genuine interest or cold ambition, Al-Masiri asked Lubna to marry him. Marwan, who knew full well the implications of joining the presidential family by marriage, saw the proposal as a direct threat to his status and became obsessed with scuttling the marriage. Sadat's byzantine management style made his goal achievable.

In what followed, Marwan teamed up with two immensely powerful people: Jehan Sadat, who was less than thrilled about her daughter marrying a public servant, even one as promising as Al-Masiri; and Fawzi Abdel Hafez, Sadat's private secretary, friend, and confidant. According to one version of the events, Jehan actually invited Marwan into the conspiracy. Clearly both of them wanted Al-Masiri as far away from Lubna as possible. Jehan sent him a letter, declaring that her daughter did not love him and that he should stop courting her. Fearing that this was not enough, Jehan, Marwan, and Hafez put pressure on Sadat to have Al-Masiri transferred out of the President's Office in order to minimize the opportunities for the two to meet. Sadat agreed to send the young man on a diplomatic mission to Yemen. His mission was successful but limited, and with his return, there also returned the threat of his marrying Lubna—and the pressure on Sadat to put a stop to it.

Direct pressure was applied to Al-Masiri as well, in the form of a long train of visitors telling him that he had no chance of winning Lubna's hand. There were additional efforts made to lower Sadat's impression of Al-Masiri, as well. He received reports from intelligence, for example, that the young man's behavior was less than exemplary. These, too, had their effect.

In the end, Sadat decided he had no choice but to transfer the smitten fellow to the Foreign Ministry, where he embarked on a diplomatic career. The romantic liaison was over. Not so long after, Lubna married someone else—a wealthy businessman from an aristocratic Egyptian family—and her mother was satisfied.[17]

Marwan's victory, however, came with a less gratifying epilogue. In the mid-1970s, after a mountain of complaints about Marwan had piled up on Sadat's desk, the president finally decided to investigate them. To lead the inquiry, he appointed none other than Ahmad al-Masiri. Al-Masiri went to London and conducted a secret investigation. He uncovered documentary evidence pointing to financial irregularities on the part of Nasser's son-in-law. He brought back with him, among other things, documents showing that in 1972 Marwan purchased two million shares of a large London company at a price of £2 per share. This time Marwan had no way of explaining where he had gotten the £4 million, and when Sadat saw the proof, he could no longer turn a blind eye. Al-Masiri's investigation started a process that would end with Marwan's being banished from Sadat's inner circle, and ultimately leaving Egypt entirely.[18]

ALL THAT, HOWEVER, was still a long way off. In the early 1970s, Marwan was busy building three different careers, and excelling remarkably in all three. In his official, publicly known career, he was confidant and emissary for the president of Egypt, with a focus on Saudi and Libyan relations. He carried out dozens of international missions, met with Arab leaders in Cairo, and flew to Arab capitals to deliver messages from the president. In June and July 1973, the Arabic press published accounts of his official visit to Riyadh, where he met with Saudi king Faisal; the following month they reported on his meeting with the emir of Kuwait, Sheikh Sabah al-Salim al-Sabah, to whom he delivered a message from Sadat. Other meetings were kept secret. The best-known of these, after the fact, took place in Saudi Arabia in August 1973, when Marwan accompanied Sadat on a secret summit meeting with King Faisal, in which the Egyptian president informed the Saudi king of his intent to launch a war in the near future.[19] Marwan also was involved in efforts to acquire weaponry from Arab states in the days before the war. This included not only making sure the Mirages arrived via Libya, but also trying to steward another deal to acquire thirty-two more Mirages via Saudi Arabia, along with British-made Sea King helicopters. This deal, which fell through in the end, was negotiated between Marwan and Faisal, without consulting Egypt's minister of war, army chief of staff, or air force commander.[20]

In his second career, Marwan took advantage of the contacts he made to build his personal fortune. Even if the rumors that swirled of his corruption were exaggerated, he definitely became wealthy quickly. His £4 million stock purchase on the London exchange— far beyond anything the Mossad ever paid him—took place in 1972. Whether through his real estate deals or through other shady moves, it is clear that within three years of returning to Cairo with his tail between his legs after taking money from the Al-Sabahs to cover his debts, Ashraf Marwan was wealthy enough to live the high life in London, or anywhere else, without borrowing a penny. His dream of riches had come true.

His third career was as a spy. Here, the main question involves his motivation. His two biggest reasons for turning to Israel in

1970—his need for cash and his resentment toward Nasser—were no longer relevant. He was now rich and famous and carried immense power and status. So why would he keep selling his nation's secrets?

As far as we know, the Mossad never tried to force his hand. Prior to the war, Marwan never asked to stop helping the Israelis. Part of the reason was probably inertia: His work for the Mossad may have now seemed less dangerous, and more lucrative, than he had once expected. This work also, it seems, satisfied his deep need for risk and stimulus—the gambler inside him—that let him feel not only the thrill of danger but also the power of personally moving history and the sense that, unlike everyone around him, he was really on the stronger, more clever side in the Arab-Israeli conflict.

This would dovetail well with additional rumors that during this period Marwan began working for other intelligence agencies as well, including the CIA, MI6, and Italian intelligence. If such connections existed at all prior to the Yom Kippur War, they were on a low flame. The fact is that these countries' intelligence about Egypt during the time was far weaker than what Marwan had given Israel. The CIA, for example, passed on to Israel the most detailed information they had from their best sources—including sensitive sources like King Hussein of Jordan. If Marwan had given the CIA anything really important prior to the war, the Americans would have passed it on to Israel. But they didn't, probably because they didn't have it. Howard Blum, who investigated the connection between Marwan and the CIA using sources at the agency, concluded that although Marwan did indeed work for the Americans, it happened much later, mostly during the 1980s.[21] The same may have been true with the British and the Italians. One unidentified Italian source claimed that Marwan gave them "a warning of the war a few hours before he met the Mossad officials in London."[22]

This seems unlikely, however, because—as we will see—Marwan was very busy in London that day.

So despite the rumors, there is little reason to believe that Marwan worked for any foreign intelligence agency other than Israel's prior to the war. But it is also hard to accept that he managed to keep his treachery a complete secret. British intelligence, for example, probably knew about it, since they knew that Dubi worked for the Mossad—which should have been enough for a competent intelligence agency to draw the right conclusions. Indeed, one MI5 officer met with a Mossad official at the time, and after bringing up Marwan's name, he added, "But of course you know him well." Yet in the absence of any evidence that he actually worked for anyone else, it should be assumed that he did not; and even if he did, he certainly saw the Israelis as his principal client, to whom he gave the very best intelligence. In the months that followed, until the outbreak of war, his contribution to Israeli security would reveal itself, time and again, to be indispensable.

Chapter 7

EGYPT GIRDS FOR WAR

In July 1972, after failing repeatedly to secure "weapons of deterrence" from the Soviets, Sadat suddenly announced that the Red Army troops that had been stationed in Egypt since early 1970 were going home. The Soviets had sent them, along with advanced SAM sites and squadrons of Soviet fighters and aircraft, to help Egypt neutralize Israel's air superiority. But they had undermined Egypt's autonomy in crucial decisions about its security. For as long as Soviet units defended Egyptian skies, the Kremlin had veto power over any Egyptian decision of war—a fact that Sadat knew too well. And so, as the prospects of getting the Sinai back through diplomatic means faded, the shackles on Egypt's war options grew more and more painful.

The man who probably took greatest advantage of Sadat's predicament was Henry Kissinger. In his indirect contacts with Egypt—mostly through Saudi channels overseen by Kamal Adham—Kissinger made it clear that the United States did not believe Egypt had a realistic war option, and that as long as the Soviets were on Egyptian soil, the White House would not exert pressure on Israel. As far as Kissinger was concerned, the only war that mattered was the Cold War, and he dangled the Sinai as bait to get the Egyptians to switch to the American side.

And indeed, Egypt had no realistic war option. Without the Scuds that the Soviets refused to supply and the long-range fighter-bombers that the Soviets didn't have, Egypt was completely vulnerable to Israeli aerial attacks, on both the battlefield and home front. And while the Soviet antiaircraft division may have helped, it didn't make it possible for Egypt to launch an attack on its own, since the Soviets would probably veto anything that would risk their own troops engaging with the IDF. So Sadat sent them packing—keeping the missile batteries and planes for Egypt, of course. Despite the crisis in Soviet-Egyptian relations the Kremlin, being now less obliged to participate in Egypt's defense and more concerned about an Egyptian-American rapprochement, eased its arms sales policy. Beginning in late 1972, new weapon systems such as the T-62 tank, SA-6 batteries, and modern water-crossing equipment started flowing to Egypt.

Sadat called Kissinger's bluff—and the Americans failed to deliver. In the ensuing months, nothing new came from the American side, and Sadat realized that the White House had no intention of getting Egypt back the Sinai in exchange for a peace agreement with Israel. He had reached a dead end.

On October 24, 1972, Sadat summoned the Supreme Council of the Armed Forces for a special meeting in his residence in Giza. He informed the chiefs of the military that in light of the futility of efforts to convince the Americans to move diplomacy forward, he had decided to launch a war, "using whatever means are at our disposal." The implications were clear. If until then, the Egyptian war paradigm (and, by extension, the Israeli intelligence *kontzeptzia*) had held that Egypt could not launch a war without getting "weapons of deterrence," that barrier had now ceased to exist. Egypt would find the way to go to war without these means. Sadat emphasized how crucial the time factor had now become, ordering his military to prepare for the attack as soon as the beginning of 1973—two months hence.

Many of the participants in the meeting voiced forceful objections. Some spoke of the home front's vulnerability to Israeli
bombing raids. Others, especially the commanders charged with
crossing the Suez Canal, complained about the operational difficulties involved in fending off Israel's superior armor and the
enormous earth embankments Israel had positioned along the
canal to prevent an Egyptian crossing. The army's chief of staff,
Saad el-Shazly, and his chief of operations, Mohamed Abdel Ghani
el-Gamasy, urged the president to petition other Arab states for help
in the war effort. And the minister of war, General Mohammed
Ahmed Sadek, said that the goal of the war should be conquering
the entire Sinai Peninsula, and that the Egyptian military was very
far from being able to do that.

Sadat was not moved. He repeated that he saw no alternative to
war, that an assault must be launched in the coming months, and
that the goal would not be the conquest of all of Sinai but rather
shattering the status quo and triggering a diplomatic effort that
would end in restoring all Egyptian territory. Two days later, he
made his resolve as clear as could be: He fired the minister of war,
the minister's deputy, and the commander of the navy, replacing
them with men less hesitant about war.

In the months that followed, Egypt's military leaders translated
Sadat's directives into operational plans. The objective of the war
was to challenge Israel's belief that occupying the Sinai would, in
itself, provide security for the country, by (a) undermining Israel's
economy through a prolonged conflict that would require an extended mobilization of reserves, (b) isolating Israel diplomatically,
and (c) changing the balance of power in the region by convincing
the Americans to put pressure on Israel to give up the lands it took
in 1967, especially the Sinai. Egypt's new war concept meant new
territorial objectives as well. Until the summer of 1971, when Sadat
appointed Shazly to take over the military just months after the

Corrective Revolution in May of that year, the goal had been to conquer the whole Sinai using a plan known as Granite II; when Shazly took over, more limited plans were developed, known as Operation 41, which sought to conquer land up to the Mitla and Gidi Passes that cut through the mountains of western Sinai—about twenty-five to forty miles east of the Suez Canal. But these plans still needed "weapons of deterrence" to combat Israel's air power. With Sadat's new directive to prepare for war by the start of 1973, it was decided to limit the war aims to what seemed reasonable to believe the Egyptian army was capable of achieving even without the long-range missiles and aircraft.

These new plans were ready by January 1973, as ordered. The new plan, known as Operation High Minarets, aimed both to solve the problem of Egyptian military vulnerability to IAF attacks and to fulfill Sadat's demand for something that would shake up the region and force progress on the diplomatic front. The focus of the plan was the crossing of the Suez Canal—using the very same plan that Marwan had given Israel back in 1971, with five infantry divisions crossing at five points. But as opposed to earlier plans, which saw the crossing as the first phase meant to enable the armored divisions to launch themselves toward the Mitla and Gidi Passes, with Operation High Minarets the crossing of the canal and capture of its eastern bank would be the final goal of the whole war. In this way, Egyptian troops could avoid having to move eastward beyond the antiaircraft umbrella, which extended no more than six miles east of the canal.

Operation High Minarets was kept top secret—and not just from the Israelis. It was crucial to keep the Syrians from knowing just how limited Egypt's actual territorial aims were. For Sadat, the cornerstone of his military strategy was forcing the Israelis to fight on two fronts simultaneously, dividing both their manpower and their attention. For this, however, he would need the Syrians to attack from the north on the Golan Heights. And because the conquest of the Golan could allow the Syrians to cross the Jordan River and invade northern Israel, while the Suez Canal was very far from the Israeli border, Sadat understood that if Syria were to attack, Israel's principal occupation would be fighting off the onslaught in the north—making it much more likely that Egypt would successfully capture and hold the east bank of the Suez Canal. Yet in order to secure the agreement of Syrian president Hafez al-Assad, the Syrians had to believe that Egypt planned on putting everything they had behind a full invasion of the Sinai, not just keeping their troops under the antiaircraft umbrella in the canal zone. If Assad were to find out about Operation High Minarets, the whole plan would be scrapped.

In order to keep Assad in the dark while securing his cooperation in the planned joint attack, Egypt developed a second military plan, completed in April 1973, known as Granite II Improved. In this version, which was shared with the Syrians and formed the basis of all of their discussions with Egypt about the war, the infantry would cross the canal in the first phase, and then the armored divisions would cross into Sinai and head for the passes.[1]

Granite II Improved also included some serious improvements for crossing the canal. To deal with the problem of the embankments, water cannons would blast away enough to make room for amphibious vehicles landing on the eastern bank. To minimize loss of Egyptian forces and maximize the territory secured on the eastern bank, Egypt would encircle and cut off IDF fortifications rather than try to overrun them. And to prevent or delay IDF reservists from reaching the front, commandos would be dropped by helicopters at key locations in Sinai, cutting off approach roads. On the first day of combat, Egypt would send its five infantry divisions to establish five beachheads on the eastern bank. On the second day, they would expand the beachheads, and on the third day they would link them up, creating a strip of conquered territory along the canal and extending up to seven and a half miles deep into Sinai. Once this was complete, two armored divisions, the 4th and the 21st, would cross the canal and launch an eastward attack heading for the Mitla and Gidi Passes.

That was Granite II Improved, the official plan shared with the Syrians. The plan that Shazly actually intended to implement, however, was Operation High Minarets—identical to Granite II Improved, just without the final step of bringing the armored divisions across the canal or attacking deeper into Sinai. It was so secret that even the division commanders were unaware of it.[2]

Meanwhile, Egypt began its exercises to train for the attack. While in the past, exercises focused mostly on training the tank divisions for combat in Sinai, now they focused on the crossing itself—especially preparing the assault boats that would ferry 32,000 soldiers across the canal in the first phase, and building bridges to carry over the heavy equipment in the second. They also practiced bursting through the earth embankments on the Israeli side. As for the tanks, many of them were now attached to infantry divisions to help out in the first phase, rather than practicing their fictitious plan to invade Sinai.

By the spring of 1973, Egypt was ready. It was the first time since 1967 that the Egyptians had workable, operative plans for attacking Israel without waiting for "weapons of deterrence." Now they just needed to set a date.

ASHRAF MARWAN, WHO played so decisive a role in developing Israel's *kontzeptzia* regarding the minimal conditions Egypt thought were necessary to launch a war, was also the key source of information about Egypt's change of heart, which should have convinced the Israelis that the paradigm was no longer relevant. What happened instead was that a number of top figures in Israeli Military Intelligence remained so deeply committed to the *kontzeptzia* that they just dismissed Marwan's new reports as false or irrelevant. Their inflexibility continued all the way to the morning of October 6, 1973—and was the single biggest reason that things went so deeply wrong from Israel's perspective.

Marwan did not participate in the fateful meeting a year before the war, on October 24, 1972, when Sadat announced his new vision. But one of his assistants did and took notes. Just over a week later, Marwan met with Zamir and Dubi in London, and handed them documents that testified clearly to Sadat's decision to go to war soon. It explicitly described the expulsion of the Soviets in July 1972 as a first step toward maximizing Egypt's freedom to maneuver. The document did not say outright that Sadat would no longer wait for the weapons he had once believed he needed in order to attack. But whatever it was missing in print was made up for by Marwan's oral account of the October 24 meeting and its implications. He told the Israelis that Sadat had come to the conclusion that the diplomatic option had reached a dead end, and the only way to start it again was through military action; and that he had fired his minister of war because the latter had refused orders to prepare the attack. Marwan also explained that Sadat had fired other generals who had doubted the Egyptian army's readiness— all in the effort to ensure broad agreement that would enable the most efficient path to launching an attack. Marwan also provided a timetable: Preparations for the defense of the Egyptian home front were to be completed by the end of November 1972; during December, the army would complete its preparations for a low-level "static" war. The crossing of the canal would not take place before the end of 1972. Finally, he told the Israelis that Syria was in on the plan. Already at this stage, Israeli intelligence had all the information it needed to conclude that the *kontzeptzia* was a dead letter.

Three weeks later, Marwan met them again. What became clear

this time was just how great the gap was between Sadat's determination to attack and Egypt's actual readiness for war. The Soviets continued to refuse to supply the Scuds and long-range fighter-bombers; the Sukhoi Su-17 fighters they gave Egypt couldn't stand up to Israel's Phantoms. Yet as Marwan kept pointing out, Sadat was far from dissuaded. The president would order the attack—and the army would not refuse him.

How did Marwan account for Sadat's determination to fight a war he was bound to lose? Sadat, he answered, was willing to pay a very heavy price in order to get something moving on the diplomatic front.

The unavoidable conclusion from all of this is that any claim to the effect that Israeli intelligence had no idea that the *kontzeptzia* had become outdated, that they had no idea the Egyptians had changed their minds about the conditions needed to launch an attack, and that Marwan had somehow tricked the Israelis into sticking to the old way of thinking in order to maximize the effectiveness of the surprise attack a year later—such a claim is completely unfounded. Neither was Marwan the only source Israel had about Sadat's change of heart or the decision to prepare for war—far from it.

Nor was this understanding limited to the Mossad. On November 26, 1972, one month after Sadat fired many of his top military figures who disagreed with his new approach, and just days after the second meeting with Marwan in London, Moshe Dayan reported to the government that "there are reports . . . which we must relate to with utmost seriousness, of an emerging trend in Egypt to restart the hostilities . . . including escalation, if possible by the end of the calendar year." According to the reports, Dayan said, the Egyptian move would be taken together with Syria, with the aim of "creating an 'Eastern front' together with Jordan."[3]

The warnings coming in from Egypt caused the Israeli prime

minister to convene her "kitchen cabinet," the government's top decision-making body. On December 1, 1972, she met with Dayan, Yigal Allon, and Yisrael Galili, as well as the IDF chief of staff, David Elazar, who had replaced Chaim Bar-Lev; the new chief of Military Intelligence, Eli Zeira; and Zvi Zamir from the Mossad. The sole agenda item was Egypt's immediate war intentions. On the basis of information MI had received about the October 24 meeting, Zeira declared that "Sadat has given the order to finish preparations by the end of December, [but] he hasn't given a date of attack." He estimated that the chance of an attack was therefore "not high," and the likelihood that Egypt would actually try to cross the Suez Canal "close to zero." At the core of Zeira's error stood a misunderstanding of Sadat's expulsion of the Soviet troops just a few months earlier: Instead of seeing it as a preparation for war, he took it as a dramatic set-back to Egypt's defensive capability, which therefore made Sadat *less* likely to attack rather than more so.

The Mossad chief's assessment was more cautious and took more seriously the latest information from the Angel. "In light of what we know, we need to go on the assumption that there could be an exchange of fire," Zamir told them. "When I say 'fire,' it doesn't necessarily mean restarting hostilities along the whole canal, but rather harassment here and there." The IDF chief of staff, for his part, was skeptical about the possibility of war in the near term, but he expressed a healthy caution when he added: "We can't look at ourselves as free from the need to be prepared . . . we can't say there is 'no chance' of fire and we can sleep easy."[4]

In fact, the only person at the meeting who took Marwan's warnings very seriously was Moshe Dayan. "We need to assume that Egypt will launch an attack at the canal in early 1973," he declared, adding that "Egypt and Syria are in collusion." Dayan then insisted that Israel send Egypt a message via the Americans, or pos-

sibly the Soviets, warning against even a limited Egyptian assault—
and affirming that Israel "has no inclination to enter another war of
attrition, and if they start a fight, we will hit back hard." Given the
possibility that Jordan would join the fight, Dayan also suggested
that a similar message be sent to King Hussein.[5]

Despite Zeira's assessment that the chances of an Egyptian attack
on the canal were "close to zero," Golda Meir and Moshe Dayan
decided to alert the Americans. That same day, Yitzhak Rabin, Israel's envoy in Washington, sent a message to Kissinger reporting
that they had received word that Egypt was planning an offensive
by the end of December; a similar message went to the CIA from
the Mossad. It was unclear, the communiqués added, whether the
Egyptians were planning a full-scale war to take back the Sinai, or
something more limited such as shelling the canal area or commando raids without trying to take the eastern bank.[6] The Americans answered that they, too, had received information confirming
that Egypt had indeed changed its mind about launching a war.
The CIA, however, shared Zeira's assessment that Sadat was fully
aware of his military inferiority and that therefore the likelihood
of a new war was not high.

The outlook shared by Dayan, Elazar, and Zamir at the meeting
had its merits. On the one hand, it took into account the new
warnings about a change of heart in Egypt. On the other hand, it
took seriously the fact that Egypt's military disadvantage had not
changed, that Sadat knew it, and that many top-ranking Egyptian
officials opposed it for that very reason. War, in other words, was
taken to be unlikely but possible, and Israel had to prepare accordingly. Dayan, who took the most aggressive stance at the meeting,
reiterated a few days later that although an Egyptian attack was not
likely in the coming weeks, "it could certainly happen before the
spring."[7]

The gap between the positions of the MI chief, who believed

the likelihood of an Egyptian crossing of the canal was "close to zero," and the IDF chief of staff, who believed that the likelihood was low but not low enough to ignore, reflected a difference in their basic approaches. When Zeira took up his post, he was already committed to the *kontzeptzia*. Elazar's view was more nuanced. He had seen the original materials, supplied by Marwan, on which the *kontzeptzia* had been based. But from the day he replaced Bar-Lev as chief of staff on January 1, 1972, he viewed war as quite possible in the coming two years. So he was much more open than Zeira to changing his assessment based on new information that came in.

This difference of opinion had dramatic results. In the summer of 1972, before Sadat had decided on war, MI estimated that the Egyptians would not come to the conclusion that they had the necessary armaments to go to war before April 1973. At the same time, MI allowed for the possibility that, because of the pressure to show progress on the diplomatic front, Sadat would find it necessary to take military steps without first acquiring the equipment. Ironically, only after information started flowing from reliable sources suggesting that the time pressures were indeed becoming more critical for Sadat, MI's assessment of the possibility of war in the short term started going down rather than up. On January 20, 1973, some six weeks after the meeting of Golda Meir's kitchen cabinet, MI-Research issued its semiannual intelligence assessment, in which it declared that the possibility of war was "farther away than at any time in the past."[8] This was based mostly on the belief that the dismissal of the Soviet air defense division in July 1972 had significantly weakened Egypt—even though Marwan had said otherwise. Indeed, it is hard to ignore the fact that everything Marwan had given Israel with regard to Sadat's decision for war in October 1972 appears to have left no impression whatsoever on Military Intelligence's assessment.

Elazar, on the other hand, was much more impressed by the

Angel's latest warnings. He had taken up his post about a year and a half after the end of the War of Attrition and against a backdrop of relative calm on all fronts. As a result, he was under intense pressure to cut the IDF budget. The government was trying to push through a new social agenda, diverting resources to absorbing tens of thousands of new immigrants who had begun arriving from the Soviet Union, and addressing the social inequities that had sparked demonstrations by the Sephardic "Black Panthers," named after the American movement. Quiet borders and a general sense that there was no war in the offing, combined with the belief that Israel's superior military could swiftly repel any attack—all these made it possible, Israel's leaders believed, to shift the Treasury's priorities. Cuts had already begun in 1970 and were threatening to deepen.

Elazar, however, saw an Egyptian attack during his tenure as a real possibility, and he argued that these cutbacks were the gravest threat to Israel's future. The worst of them was a plan to reduce mandatory service by three months, which would dramatically reduce the number of active-duty troops, who would be crucial for holding off an Arab assault until reserves could be deployed. Elazar fought the plan tooth and nail, making use of Marwan's warnings to that end.[9] In effect, Ashraf Marwan's warnings prevented a situation in which the IDF would have been even less prepared than it was when war came the following October.

IN EARLY 1973, Israel received further reports about Egypt. One batch added details to the October 24 meeting, telling of disagreements that arose because most of the participants were convinced that the Egyptian military was far from ready for war, and because of Sadat's decision to fire War Minister Sadek and others because of their "defeatist" attitude. This report also correctly reported the order of the new war minister, Ismail, to prepare a plan for crossing the canal using infantry divisions followed later by tanks (Granite II Improved), and on the new wave of Egyptian military exercises preparing for the crossing.

A second group of reports came from Ashraf Marwan. On January 17, he reported that Sadat had ordered the army to prepare for attack without waiting for new weapons. At the same time, the same intelligence batch suggested that Egypt was not planning on crossing in a general way but preferred to launch open-ended static hostilities involving commando and air force raids in Sinai, as well as an air attack on Israel proper. According to what Marwan himself said, the Egyptian initiative would begin in May 1973 and would be carried out in coordination with Syria.

These reports, too, should have strengthened the belief that Sadat had changed his mind about attacking Israel. Yet, again, they fell on deaf ears at MI-Research. In a survey written in response to Marwan's report of January 17, the commander of MI-Research Branch 6 (Egypt) Lt. Col. Yonah Bandman wrote that it did not "testify to a decision that Sadat had made to open fire in the coming months; all the more so did the decision not reflect any operational plan whatsoever." In Bandman's view, Marwan's reports reflected little more than Egyptian fantasizing, in an attempt to create an atmosphere of crisis in order to spur on the diplomatic effort; the military exercises, too, had been falsely interpreted as hostile purely because of the sense of crisis in the regime, which itself was engineered to put pressure on Israel.[10] Bandman's reflexive rejection of any report that contradicted Israel's now-outdated *kontzeptzia* found expression in other ways as well. Unlike his predecessor Meir Meir, Bandman did not meet Marwan once during his entire tenure in the position. And when the opportunity to meet with Dubi presented itself, either in London or in Israel, he never once took it.

EGYPTIAN WAR PREPARATIONS continued apace during the first months of 1973. In addition to writing up plans and holding exercises, Egypt now began receiving a stream of arms from the Soviets as well. They included SA-3 and SA-6 surface-to-air batteries, SA-7 Strela personal antiaircraft missiles, Sukhoi Su-17 fighter planes, T-62 tanks, Sagger personal antitank missiles, additional artillery, and bridging equipment. At the same time, Egypt started getting Western aircraft that improved, if not dramatically, its attack capabilities deep in Israeli territory. These included British-made Hawker Hunters from Iraq, relatively old planes that gave Egypt little more than a boost in morale. They also started receiving the new Mirages that Libya had bought from France. During March and April, Egypt received eighteen of these, mostly IIIEs, which had a long enough range to attack Israeli air bases.[11] It was still not enough to neutralize Israel's overall air superiority, but the combination of these planes with the scaling back of Egypt's war aims gave a better response than ever before to the vulnerability of Egyptian ground forces to attack from the air.

At the same time, war preparations were ramping up. Sadat held a series of meetings with the leadership of his Socialist Union Party as well as the cabinet, in which he made clear that in light of the diplomatic stalemate, there was no choice but to go to war, with the aim of "shattering the cease-fire." As the spring approached, for the first time since the end of the War of Attrition, the Egyptians believed they were ready to take on the IDF.

IN EARLY APRIL 1973, the chief of Egyptian military operations, General Mohamed Abdel Ghani el-Gamasy, presented a number of possible dates of attack based on optimal conditions—such as when the currents in the canal would be slowest and tides would be ideal, the amount of moonlight, and which dates would be the most difficult for the IDF to organize a swift and effective response. The earliest of these was in mid-May. On April 5, Sadat met with his cabinet and explained the logic behind his decision to go to war. The cabinet approved the decision unanimously. Several days later, the preparations were made public. Radio Cairo began broadcasting war slogans. The government began meeting in Center 10, the underground war room, and issued a call for volunteers to join the "people's resistance" if the IDF were to occupy territory west of the canal.

All of these preparations ran aground, however, as soon as the Syrians were brought into the picture. On April 23, President Hafez al-Assad came to Egypt for a secret two-day meeting with Sadat in Burj al-Arab on the Mediterranean coast. The Egyptians presented the Granite II Improved plan, which included the armored assault to capture the Mitla and Gidi Passes. The crossing of the Suez Canal was presented as a first stage toward the conquest of all of Sinai. For their part, the Syrians presented their plans for conquering the Golan Heights. But even though the two sides agreed to coordinate their attack, Assad was unwilling to pull the trigger: Neither Egypt nor Syria, he believed, was ready for war. The central problem, Assad said, was Syria's lack of surface-to-air batteries to protect its ground forces from aerial attack. The two presidents agreed to delay the entire operation until the late summer. A few days later, Assad flew to Moscow, where he signed a huge arms deal; within a few weeks, new weapons began flowing to Damascus.

THESE DEVELOPMENTS WERE not lost on the Israeli intelligence community. As early as March, reports started coming in about Egypt's heightened war preparations. They all confirmed what Marwan had said in January—that the target date for war was in May and that Egypt was coordinating with Syria.[12] Once the war plans had concretized and specific dates were discussed, the intelligence flow became more intense.

Ashraf Marwan was far from alone in supplying information to Israel, but he was the most important source. On April 11, he gave

EGYPT GIRDS FOR WAR

Dubi a detailed account of Egypt's intentions to launch an attack in the middle of May. The opening assault would include a thirty-eight-minute-long artillery barrage to soften Israel's frontline defenses. Simultaneously, 178 warplanes would attack both military and civilian sites (mainly oil fields) in the Sinai, and another 40 Mirages would attack targets in Israel proper. After that initial assault, five infantry divisions stationed along the canal would begin crossing at five different points. The Egyptians would use the cover of darkness, making it difficult for the Israeli Air Force to respond effectively while Egypt began laying the bridges across the canal and moving the bulk of its infantry to the eastern bank. The infantry would have hundreds of Sagger antitank missiles to help them handle the Israeli armor. At the same time, the Egyptian navy would deploy sea mines and two destroyers to block the Bab-el-Mandeb Strait, where the Red Sea meets the Indian Ocean, to prevent trade from reaching Israel. Before the attack, Egypt would taper off its pumping from the Morgan oil field west of the Gulf of Suez, and eventually stop it completely, out of fear that Israel would attack the field and set it on fire.

Six months later, on October 6, 1973, Egypt would indeed attack. After thirty-eight minutes of shelling, five infantry divisions would cross the canal at the known points using the darkness to lay the bridges and send over the forces. The infantrymen would carry Sagger missiles and devastate the Israeli tanks—which would not be in position and whose teams would be taken completely by surprise. Egyptian warplanes in the first assault would number around two hundred, though they would not attack Israel proper, with the exception of a single attempt to shoot two Kelt missiles at Tel Aviv from a Tu-16 bomber. This change of plans probably resulted from the fact that they only had twenty-five Mirages operational rather than the planned forty, so they were diverted to the assault on Sinai.

In other words, almost every detail Marwan gave the Israelis on

April 11 ended up being carried out by the Egyptians on October 6.

In the meantime, however, additional information confirmed Marwan's estimate of a mid-May attack. Some sources specifically mentioned May 19, explaining the Egyptian considerations. But Marwan showed his remarkable quality as an intelligence source when he reported in early May (that is, a week after Sadat and Assad decided to push off the attack) that the date had been pushed off and was now closer to late May or early June. Three weeks later, he informed Dubi of further delays, of about a month. The Soviets, he reported, had put pressure mostly on Syria to hold off an attack that might create a sense of crisis in advance of the Nixon-Brezhnev summit scheduled for June 18 to 25 in the United States. Marwan added that there was some hope in Egypt that the summit would result in progress on the diplomatic front, making the war unnecessary.[13] Here, too, additional sources confirmed Marwan's information.

Marwan, moreover, was also one of Israel's main sources regarding Syria's war plans. At its center stood an assault by three infantry divisions that would advance, under cover of darkness, about six miles into the Golan Heights. At dawn the next morning, the Syrian 3rd Armored Division would push its way west to the 1967 border in order to occupy the entire territory that was lost in the Six-Day War. It later emerged, however, that Syria preferred to attack at first light rather than last, and after wrangling with the Egyptians, a last-minute compromise was reached putting the H-hour, or time of attack, at 2:00 p.m. The armored assault in October also ended up involving two divisions rather than one, because by October the Syrians had added another armored division, making it possible to use two in the assault. But other than these adjustments, the Syrian assault in October ended up being almost identical to the one Marwan described back in April.

The information that continued to come in about Egyptian and Syrian maneuvers confirmed the reports that Sadat had indeed planned to attack on May 19 but had shifted course after meeting Assad. The Egyptian army began amassing forces in the canal area in March, and in early April a reconnaissance flyover photograph showed the number of artillery pieces positioned at the front to be higher than ever. In late April, MI reported that the Third Army, which held the southern sector of the canal front, was preparing for a major exercise from May 20 to 24; at the same time or slightly beforehand, a combined-forces military exercise would be held under the navy's auspices. Exercises, of course, are often just a cover for a real attack, and MI estimated that during such an exercise, the Egyptians would raise their alert level, move forces toward the front, cancel officers' leave, and take other security precautions— the same steps that would be taken in the event of an actual war. In early May, MI reported on the call-up of reserves in every branch of the Egyptian military. At around the same time, Marwan reported on a massive movement of troops, including the 6th and 23rd Mechanized Divisions, toward the canal. But then, about a week after the decision was made to push off the war, the signs began to abate. During the second week of May, it was learned that the divisions that had been preparing to leave Cairo and head for the canal had stayed put, and along the canal itself there were no signs of the troop deployments that the Israelis were expecting based on the war plans Marwan had given them. Similar changes were seen on the Syrian front. Despite reports of intensive war preparations, the Syrian army, which regularly reinforced its front with the onset of spring, refrained this time, and even scaled back its deployments.

From all of this, it emerges that during the months of April and May, IDF Military Intelligence had all the data it needed in order to fully understand what was happening on the Arab side and why.

But despite this, MI consistently got its assessments wrong, rejecting out of hand the possibility that Syria and Egypt were getting ready for war. A special intelligence survey distributed on May 11 was supposed to assess the likelihood of war, but instead it simply ignored the multiple warnings and clung unblinkingly to the belief that Egypt would never attack without first procuring long-range fighter-bombers and Scud missiles. The report mentioned the arrival of the eighteen Mirages, calling it a "significant step" that could suggest a change in Egypt's approach, but then added that "it is doubtful that this addition would give the Egyptian leadership the wrong impression that Egypt can hold its own on the aerial front in a conflict with Israel."[14] Once again, the analysts in MI-Research, especially the head of Branch 6 (Egypt), Lt. Col. Bandman, who had been more than willing to embrace the *kontzeptzia* back when Marwan had first presented it to the Mossad, were now unwilling to recognize a large number of indicators, including those provided by Marwan himself, that strongly suggested that it was no longer viable. And when forced to address the warnings arriving from the best sources in Egypt, these officers chose any explanation that would let them continue believing in it. Exercises in Egypt were explained away as internal propaganda "whose aim was to lend credibility to the regime's declaration that their country was heading for a general conflict." The warnings themselves, which were described as a "wave of reports, some of which predict offensive Egyptian action and even named tentative dates," were dismissed as flowing "from the atmosphere of preparations for a 'general conflict'" that Egypt had undertaken. Years later, Bandman would explain that he never gave credence to the Mossad's sources, believing that they simply had mistaken preparations for an exercise as preparations for war.[15]

It is not clear, however, just how much of an impression all this left on the country's top decision makers. On April 18, in the wake of one of Marwan's warnings, Golda Meir convened her kitchen cabinet in her residence, at the request of the head of the Mossad, who had been concerned about the evidence that his agency had accumulated. The aim of the meeting was to assess the likelihood of war and how to prepare for it. For this reason, Zamir participated as well, even though formally his agency had no role in preparing overall intelligence assessments.

All the participants had been in on the Khotel reports. With the exception of MI chief Zeira, all of them assessed that Egypt was intent on war, possibly in the coming months. "I believe that they are going to war," said Defense Minister Dayan, setting the tone. It is clear that he no longer held fast to the *kontzeptzia* and was more focused on Sadat's political dilemma that might force him to attack before his army was ready. The IDF chief of staff, Elazar, said that "there is an inner logic that favors war . . . they could develop a [new] concept according to which war can get them out of their bind." Zamir emphasized that the conditions were ripening, in the Egyptians' own mind, for an attack. He said that the arrival of the Mirages was a major development and, apparently based on reports from Marwan, that the Egyptians believed more jets were on the way; at some point they would reach a critical mass that would allow them to attack IAF bases. And though Zamir, too, was still thinking within some version of the *kontzeptzia*, in the sense that he was still wondering what weapons the Egyptians thought they needed in order to attack, his version of it was far more flexible than that of his counterpart at MI. Zamir spoke of Egypt's improved SAMs, their new bridging equipment, new electronics, and improved home-front defenses as making war far more realistic from Sadat's standpoint—and quietly added his belief that war was on its way.

This contrasted dramatically with Eli Zeira's assessment. The MI chief rejected the possibility that Sadat would, under current conditions, launch a war. He dismissed the warnings and focused only on the actual preparations for conflict. And though he conceded

that "this time there are a few more signs of concrete preparations than there were in the presentation of November–December
1972," he quickly dismissed them, saying that any "logical analysis
of the situation will show that Egypt would be mistaken to go to
war." He was willing to accept the possibility of an Egyptian error,
and therefore clarified that MI would continue to search for additional indicators. "The truth is," he concluded, "we see more indicators that [Sadat] has no intention of acting than that he does plan
on going to war, but it is still too early to establish this." Given the
fact that these words were stated in the thick of Egypt's war preparations, when reports about the reinforcement of Egypt's battle
ranks at the canal front continued to stream in to MI, and at a time
when Israel's best intelligence sources were warning that Sadat intended to launch a war within a month, Zeira's statements at this
time seem increasingly far-fetched.

In the discussion that followed, the prime minister, as well as her
adviser, Galili, inclined toward the view that a combined Egyptian-
Syrian assault was a real possibility in the coming months; a consensus formed around this view.[16] The following day, Elazar ordered
the IDF to prepare itself for a sudden attack on two fronts. A month
later, Dayan held two meetings of the IDF general staff, and it was
concluded that from then on, the IDF would work under the assumption that over the summer, the Egyptians and Syrians (but not
the Jordanians) might launch a war. "Be ready for the summer,"
Dayan told the military brass. "It begins a month from now." This
was the beginning of what became known as the Blue-White
Alert, which included a rapid buildup of forces and preparations
for a war that was just months away.[17]

The Blue-White Alert was effective. Contrary to a popular myth
in Israel, it did not include a widespread call-up of reserves. It did,
however, include positioning on the northern and southern fronts
a total of 515 tanks—the full order of battle for Israel's standing

army, without reserves. True, for a couple of weeks surrounding Independence Day, two reserve tank brigades were called up to relieve those participating in the parade. Other than that, the large part of the Blue-White Alert's added budget of about $35 million was invested in building new military units, including one armored division and the headquarters of another division, bolstering the existing tank, artillery, and patrol battalions, relocating the emergency storage facilities closer to the front lines, developing the bridging system to enable the IDF to quickly cross the Suez Canal, and many other improvements. "Thanks to the Blue-White Alert," wrote the chief of IDF operations during the Yom Kippur War, Maj. Gen. Israel Tal, "the army that entered the war was much more powerful than the one planned for October 1973 in the regular work plans. This IDF was even more potent than what had been planned for 1974 and 1975."

The effects of April–May 1973 and the Blue-White Alert on the IDF's eventual readiness in October 1973 are not as clear as Tal puts it, for while the IDF's on-paper preparedness improved, the fact that war did not come in the spring and throughout the alert phase that officially ended on August 12 certainly lulled Israeli leaders and the IDF into a kind of complacency. The status of Eli Zeira, Yonah Bandman, Arieh Shalev, and other MI officers who had said all along that the Egyptians wouldn't attack, grew. The assessments of the IDF chief of staff and the defense minister, according to which war would erupt over the summer, were confounded. This had a real impact on Dayan, who over the months of June and July moved from believing that war was imminent to thinking it wouldn't happen in the decade to come, even without a peace agreement. This "crying wolf" effect was felt throughout the intelligence community as October approached. This may have canceled out any benefit from the upgrades in the IDF's physical readiness.

What is far more clear, however, is Ashraf Marwan's contribution to all these events. He was the main source of warnings of an imminent Egyptian attack in May, when Egypt in fact had planned on attacking, and was also the first one to tell Israel of its cancellation. He also provided Israel with the details of the Granite II Improved and the High Minarets attack plans, as well as Syria's attack plan. He gave Israel ongoing updates on the deployment of new Mirage fighters arriving from Libya, a process he personally oversaw. Beyond all of these, he also told Israel what they needed to look for in advance of an Egyptian attack. Some of these steps, such as specific deployments along the canal front and the states of alert in various parts of the military, had long been known to Israel. Others, however, such as positioning ships in the Bab-el-Mandeb Strait or shutting down the Morgan oil field, handed MI a string of clear, new indicators for when war would be launched. Had more attention been paid to those indicators in the days leading up to October 6, the Israelis would have known exactly when the attack was coming.

Marwan continued to supply crucial information even after it became clear that there would be no war in the spring. On May 20, he notified the Israelis of a new Egyptian surface-to-surface missile that carried a range of about 200 miles. It was the first sign of Soviet willingness to provide Egypt with the Scuds it had long asked for. Two weeks later, as recalled, he reported that the Egyptian leadership had stopped regarding the acquisition of long-range fighter-bombers as a necessary condition for launching war.

"THE MAIN REASON behind the failure to recognize that Egypt's war aims had changed," said Eli Zeira thirty-five years after the war, "was a failure of intelligence gathering. The intelligence gatherers did not provide any information about it. I can't remember a single report from any source about the shift. I can't remember a single report that even suggested that such a change in their war aims was possible."[18]

This was a smoke screen. Given the fact that Eli Zeira personally received Khotel reports detailing all the information Marwan provided, including the detailed war plans, he knew full well that the intelligence gatherers had seen it all and reported it all.

The real source of the Israeli failure, rather, was the inflexible commitment to the *kontzeptzia* on the part of Israel's professional intelligence assessors, above all Zeira himself, despite all the information they held in their hands, over the course of a full year, that pointed unequivocally to its irrelevance. So committed were they to the *kontzeptzia* that they continued believing in it up until the morning of October 6.

On that day, as hundreds of thousands of Israelis who made up the core of the nation's reserve army fasted and prayed in their hometown synagogues, the people on whom they relied to sound the alarm in case of war were caught with their pants about their ankles.

Chapter 8

FINAL PREPARATIONS AND AN INTERMEZZO IN ROME

The Blue-White Alert declared by the IDF on May 17 took effect just as the tide of indicators of impending war had crested. Marwan's report that the date of attack had been put off for at least two months created a sense, at least among some Israeli decision makers, that Israel may have jumped the gun when it started gearing up for a war that would never happen. The man who expressed this concern most clearly was Defense Minister Moshe Dayan. On May 21, he ordered the IDF to prepare for a war likely to begin "in the second half of this summer . . . at the initiative . . . of Egypt and Syria."[1] Two months later, however, in an interview for *Time* magazine, he asserted that "the next ten years . . . will see the borders frozen along the present line, but there will not be a major war."[2]

The defense minister's about-face was out of sync with what was really happening in Egypt and Syria. Although Sadat toned down the rhetoric in his speeches, and the overall atmosphere in Egypt was less belligerent, Egypt nonetheless kept arming, deploying new weapons, and conducting military exercises. A large weapons deal sealed in March 1973 and delivered over the summer brought in a squadron of MiG-21s, a brigade's worth of SA-6 surface-to-air missiles, armored personnel carriers (APCs), Sagger personal antitank missiles, and artillery pieces that included 180-mm cannons capable of blasting through the embankments of the Bar-Lev Line. And then there were the Scuds, which arrived from the USSR in July and were introduced in the summer exercises, beginning in August and continuing all the way up to the war. In addition, as Marwan told the Israelis, the Egyptian air force received its Mirages from France via Libya—and these, along with the Kelt missiles that would be carried on Tu-16 bombers, made an attack on the Israeli heartland a real possibility.

Egypt, meanwhile, accelerated its preparations for crossing the canal. The war's delay allowed Egypt to finish preparing the five task forces, each comprising 144 assault boats, to shuttle 32,000 Egyptian troops to the eastern bank, holding the beachheads until the bridges were completed. The five infantry divisions practiced pushing the boats into the water, climbing aboard, using oars or outboard motors to cross, and quickly positioning themselves on the Israeli side. Crews from tanks, armored personnel carriers, and amphibious assault vehicles drilled. The antiaircraft teams stationed at the canal were beefed up to give the ground forces the protection they would need from air attacks.

On Israel's northern front, war preparations entered an advanced phase as well, with the Syrian army taking an offensive posture even before Egypt did. The Syrian army, which with the onset of spring had shifted units from the front line on the Golan Heights back to the home front to train for the war, brought them back to the front lines again during the late summer. Israeli surveillance from Mount Hermon, reconnaissance sorties, and intercepted Syrian communiqués traced the troop movements, deployment of artillery batteries, high alert in the air force, and the movement of tanks associated with three infantry divisions that were meant to break through Israel's defenses on the Golan. MI experts had a hard time explaining Syria's moves, because normally the Syrians would pull back deployment at the front as summer waned and winter approached—for in winter it was more difficult to maintain troops, and a major military assault would be a lot harder to pull off. But now the Syrian army began a major buildup along the front exactly when they should have been scaling back.

Meanwhile, the Syrians began getting large shipments of advanced Soviet weaponry, especially SA-6 antiaircraft batteries. The way they deployed them should have raised Israeli concerns. Not only had they deployed the batteries very close together, in some cases—especially at the front line—more densely than anything the Egyptians had put at the Suez Canal; they had also deployed the batteries right along the border, spreading their umbrella over the whole Golan Heights. This came at the expense of effectively defending Damascus or other strategic targets in Syria. This unusual deployment was not lost on Israeli intelligence, but the opinion that emerged from MI-Research and IAF intelligence rejected out of hand the possibility that the Syrians would attack without the participation of Egypt, and that therefore the deployments must be defensive in nature.

With each passing day, the need grew for Egypt and Syria to coordinate the final details before the attack. The most important open question was the actual date of attack. On August 22 and 23, when the Syrian buildup was well under way, the military chiefs of the two countries met secretly to finalize the attack plans. The earlier planners had already zeroed in on a few different dates that provided optimal conditions. When the chiefs met now, at Egyptian naval headquarters in Alexandria, they narrowed it down further, to two date ranges: September 7–11 and October 5–10. They reported back to their leaders, and on September 12, during a visit by Assad to Cairo, it was agreed that the date of the assault, now called Operation Badr, would be October 6. Ten days later, they each officially informed their military chiefs of the date.

By this time, a significant part of the Syrian army was deployed along the Golan front, with more on the way. Now the Egyptian army started implementing its battle plans as well. The leaders still had to agree on the precise time of attack, or H-hour, but this would not be decided until about seventy-two hours before the attack.

THE ISRAELIS DID not know all the details of the collusion between Egypt and Syria. But thanks to Ashraf Marwan, the intelligence analysts at MI had at least a partial picture of what was happening in Egypt, and it indicated that the Egyptians were preparing an imminent attack. In the first half of the summer, a number of sources suggested that Egypt would attack in June or July. Wherever they got their information, it was not accurate. But some of them asserted that the war would be launched at the end of a planned military exercise—which is in fact what ended up happening in October. A source reported on June 12 that the war would be launched either in August or in September.

Also on June 12, Ashraf Marwan gave what was up till then his most accurate warning of the date of attack. He reported that President Sadat had already informed his Syrian counterpart that Egypt intended to launch a war in late September or early October. Of course, the fact that Marwan's report came three full months *before* Sadat and Assad picked October 6 as the attack date raises some questions about the reliability of the report. But since all along, Egypt had seen May, early September, and late September to early October as the three possible date ranges, many of Egypt's top people likely believed that the last of the three ranges was the most likely. Marwan apparently was passing along what he had heard from others.

During August, Marwan's diplomatic activities intensified. Sadat wanted to maximize international backing for the war, and he relied more on Marwan for this job than on the foreign minister. The most crucial meeting Sadat held was with King Faisal of Saudi Arabia, which was important not just because the Saudis were considered the senior player in the Arab world, or for the significant financial aid that the kingdom had given Egypt, but also because of plans that had started coming together at around that time which involved bringing together the twin powers of Saudi oil wealth and Egyptian military might to create a vise grip that would get the diplomatic process moving. But this would require Saudi support for the war. A few days after the Sadat-Faisal summit, the Saudis began putting together the operative aspects of the initiative, which resulted in the world's first oil crisis.

Naturally, the substance of the conversation between the two leaders was top secret. Even Ahmed Zaki Yamani, the Saudi oil minister and one of the king's closest confidants, learned nothing of what was discussed. All the dour and cautious king was ready to tell Yamani was that he was not to travel abroad for any extended period in the near future. The only person present at the meeting other than the two leaders was Ashraf Marwan, who accompanied Sadat on every trip to the Arabian Peninsula.

According to Marwan, Sadat explained to his host that the great war, the one everyone had been talking about but had yet to take place, would be launched "soon, very soon." In recalling the meeting years later, Marwan emphasized that Sadat had refused to invoke a specific date. "It wasn't because we were afraid that the Saudis would tell the Americans and that the Israelis would find out. No. There was simply no need to reveal anything further, other than that a war was in the works."[3]

Marwan met his Israeli handlers in early September, passing along everything he knew about the summit and about the late-August

Gamal Mubarak, son of Egyptian president Hosni Mubarak, reaches out to console Ashraf Marwan's widow, Mona Abdel Nasser—daughter of former Egyptian president Gamal Abdel Nasser—at Marwan's funeral in July 2007. *(AP Photo/Ben Curtis)*

Ashraf Marwan and Mona Nasser on their wedding day, July 1966. *(AFP Photo/STR)*

Egyptian president Gamal Abdel Nasser, with his youngest son to his left, meets his first grandson, Gamal Marwan, in April 1967. Nasser's wife, Tahia, holds the baby while Ashraf looks on.
(AP Photo)

Gamal Abdel Nasser with his wife, his two daughters, and their husbands. Ashraf Marwan stands next to Mona on the far right. *(Copyright © Maher Attar/Sygma/ Corbis)*

Zvi Zamir, director of the Mossad from 1968 to 1974, at his home near Tel Aviv in the early 1970s. *(Courtesy of Zvi Zamir)*

Lt. Col. Meir Meir receives the rank of colonel from the IDF chief of staff, Lt. Gen. David Elazar. Behind Meir is Military Intelligence chief, Maj. Gen. Aharon Yariv. Standing between them is Meir's wife, Gita. *(Courtesy of the Meir family)*

Israeli prime minister Golda Meir inscribed this December 1971 photograph of herself and American president Richard Nixon to Zvi Zamir. At the bottom she wrote: "To Zvika, in good friendship, Golda." *(Courtesy of Zvi Zamir)*

Maj. Gen. Eli Zeira, Israel's director of Military Intelligence during the 1973 Yom Kippur War, exposed Ashraf Marwan as an Israeli spy. *(Courtesy of the IDF Archive)*

Israeli defense minister Moshe Dayan, in the early 1970s. *(Courtesy of the IDF Archive)*

On September 7,
1973, President
Sadat signed a unity
declaration with Libya
as Col. Muammar
Gaddafi looks on.
Ashraf Marwan, in
charge of Egypt's
relations with Libya,
stands in the back row,
center. To his left is
Libyan prime minister
and personal friend,
Abdessalam Jalloud.
*(Keystone-France/
Gamma-Keystone via
Getty Images)*

Israeli prime minister
Golda Meir at a press
conference on the first
day of the 1973 Yom
Kippur War. *(Courtesy of
the IDF Archive)*

David Elazar, chief of staff of the Israel Defense Forces during the 1973 war. *(Courtesy of the IDF Archive)*

Ashraf Marwan in London toward the end of the 1990s. *(AFP Photo/STR)*

Ashraf Marwan fell from a fifth-floor balcony of Carlton House *(right)*. His body was found in the yellow rose garden. The group that was waiting for him watched his fall from a window in the Institute of Directors *(left)*. *(Courtesy of Heathcliff O'Malley)*

meetings between Syrian and Egyptian military officials in Alexandria. Sadat, he told them, continued to speak of war, but the date of attack would likely be later in 1973. At the same time, he emphasized that, as opposed to the past, this time Sadat was keeping his cards much closer to his chest.

Nonetheless, the real focus of the meetings between Marwan and the Mossad in early September 1973 was on something different: the prevention of what was very nearly the worst terror attack in Israeli history.

ON FEBRUARY 21, 1973, a day after IDF paratroopers overran a Palestinian terror base in the Lebanese city of Tripoli, a Libyan Boeing 727 airliner, Flight 414 from Benghazi to Cairo, entered the airspace over the Sinai. IAF jets scrambled to intercept the plane, making contact just after 2:00 p.m. The fighter pilots gave the universal signal ordering the jet liner to follow them. Their plan was to have the Libyan plane land at the air base in Rephidim, in the middle of the Sinai Desert.

At first it seemed that the Libyan pilot was following. But as they closed in on the air base, the plane suddenly veered west, back toward the Suez Canal. The fighter pilots reported its unusual behavior, and the fact that all the plane's window shades were shut, making it impossible to see into the aircraft. The airliner was now heading west for the Suez Canal area covered by the Egyptian SAM umbrella, which was off-limits to commercial traffic—yet despite this, the SAMs didn't open fire. The whole Sinai had been a no-fly zone for civilian aircraft since Israel had captured it in 1967. Add to this the fact that there had been explicit warnings about terrorists trying to blow up an airliner over Tel Aviv or another Israeli target, including the nuclear facility in Dimona, and the decision of IAF commander Maj. Gen. Moti Hod to request permission to shoot down the aircraft is not surprising. The IDF chief of staff, who had not slept the previous night because of the operation in Lebanon, was now awakened, and he promptly approved the request. A few minutes later, the smoking remains of the aircraft were strewn across the desert floor. One hundred five out of 112 passengers on board were killed. One of them was Salah Bousseir, the former foreign minister of Libya.

Later on, it would emerge that the airplane's communication system had failed. The pilot, who had strayed off course, at first thought the fighter jets were Egyptian, and the airfield was Cairo International Airport. When he realized his mistake, he panicked and decided to make a break for it. Worried about the terror warnings and finding themselves under intense time pressure, the Israelis made a tragic mistake.[4]

Israel was condemned around the world, but some of the most fateful consequences of the error were delayed. One was the adverse effect it would have on Marwan's ability to give proper warning in advance of the Yom Kippur War.

THE LIBYAN LEADER, Col. Muammar Gaddafi, could not ignore what he and his citizens viewed as an unprovoked Israeli attack on a defenseless Libyan civilian aircraft. His first phone call was to Sadat, to talk about retaliation. Gaddafi's proposals included attacking the Israeli port city of Haifa with Libyan bombers. Sadat, however, was concerned about ruining his surprise attack on Israel and urged restraint, though he could not say why. But Gaddafi was not a man to whom restraint came easily. He was frustrated, and his people wanted blood. The public outcry reached its peak during the funerals of the victims, when crowds swarmed the Egyptian consulate in Benghazi, enraged at Sadat's failure to protect the plane and his weak response to the crime.

Gaddafi decided to act without Egypt's cooperation. On April 17, he summoned the captain of an Egyptian submarine stationed in Libya, functioning as part of the Libyan navy according to a military pact Gaddafi had signed with Nasser. The Libyan leader ordered the captain to sail east into the Mediterranean and to torpedo the famed British cruise liner *Queen Elizabeth*, which was on its way to Ashdod carrying dignitaries to Israel for the country's twenty-fifth Independence Day celebrations. The captain asked for the order in writing, which Gaddafi supplied. After a full day undersea, the vessel surfaced and the captain radioed his commander in the Egyptian navy, reporting on his mission. The report quickly reached Sadat, who responded by ordering the captain immediately to head back to port in Alexandria. Soon after the *Queen Elizabeth* had left Israel and was back out at sea, Sadat informed Gaddafi that the commander had failed to locate the British ship.

Gaddafi didn't buy it. The downing of the plane, coupled with his inability to retaliate, had fostered in the dictator a deep sense of impotence and frustration—and he spiraled into a severe depression, even a personal crisis. He left the capital to find solitude in a tent in the desert. He told the members of the Revolutionary Council that he intended to resign. He then cut himself off from them completely. The council, however, rejected his resignation, and Gaddafi then traveled to Egypt and met with Sadat. During and after the visit, Libyan pressure on Egypt to unify their countries intensified; there was a mass march from Tripoli and other Libyan cities toward the Egyptian border. Egyptian pleas to stop the march were to no avail. In the end, the Egyptian army had to physically block about 40,000 Libyans trying to cross the border, with roadblocks and even freshly laid land mines.

In response, Gaddafi denounced Egypt and called for a popular revolution to root out the corruption and bureaucracy of Sadat's regime. Sadat, who wanted to focus on nothing other than preparing for war against Israel, capitulated. On August 29, 1973, after a lengthy negotiation, the two nations announced that on September 1—the anniversary of the Libyan revolution—they would sign documents to begin the process of unification.[5] This was enough to calm the choppy waters of Egyptian-Libyan relations for the time being. But it did little to sate Gaddafi's thirst for revenge.

In the often bizarre world of Middle Eastern politics, the Egyptian president's greatest fear was that a serious Libyan retaliation against Israel would trigger a new Israeli-Arab war, ruining any element of surprise Egypt may have had in its own plans to attack. In his contacts with Gaddafi, Sadat repeatedly emphasized that any Libyan action had to be fully coordinated with Egypt, both in planning and in carrying it out. Reluctantly, Gaddafi agreed.

The man Sadat appointed to handle the matter from the Egyptian end was his emissary for Libyan affairs, Ashraf Marwan.

In Muammar Gaddafi's moral worldview, the most fitting eye-for-an-eye response would be to shoot an Israeli airliner out of the sky. He said as much to Sadat in April when the latter visited Libya. When the Libyans and the Egyptians began plotting the revenge attack, around July, the first question was where and how such a plane could be downed. The planners quickly settled on Rome's main airport, Fiumicino International. As citizens of a former Italian colony, the Libyans knew Rome well. Fiumicino was notoriously lax on security, and the Italians were notoriously forgiving of Arab terror groups. On Marwan's orders, two senior Egyptian security officials traveled to Rome to learn the layout of the airport, the flight paths, and the best locations for attacking planes that were taking off or landing. They returned with blueprints and maps, and a plan was hatched for shooting down an El Al Boeing 747 passenger jet just after takeoff, using SA-7 Strela personal antiaircraft missiles that the Egyptians had just received from the Soviet Union. It was agreed that Egypt would take responsibility for delivering two missiles to Rome, where they would be picked up by Palestinians belonging to the Black September group—the same organization that had murdered eleven Israeli athletes at the Munich Olympics the summer before.

The first part of the operation went off without a hitch. On August 29, Amin al-Hindi, the leader of the Black September squad, arrived in Rome to prepare the attack with four other members of his group. A few days later, on Marwan's orders and without involving anyone from the Egyptian military, two missiles and their launchers were transferred from army stockpiles to Sadat's office. They were packed in diplomatic baggage under the name of Marwan's wife, Mona. She had planned on flying to London on an unrelated matter, but at her husband's request, she agreed to meet up with him in Rome. Mona was completely unaware of both the plan and the contents of the bags.

As expected, the Italian authorities didn't open them. Because they carried the name of Nasser's daughter, the bags were taken directly from the aircraft to a waiting pickup truck, which transported them to the Egyptian Art Academy in Rome.

Marwan arrived in the city the following day. He put the bags in his private car and drove to the Raphael Salato shoe store at 149 Via Veneto, in the main shopping district. Al-Hindi was waiting in the store. He recognized Marwan from a photograph he had been given. He approached Marwan and said the code word—several times.

From there, however, things went slightly awry. Marwan told Al-Hindi that he and his men would have to take the missiles out of his car, transfer them to their vehicle, and take them back to the apartment Al-Hindi had rented in Ostia, near the airport, from where the attack would be launched.

The trouble was, they didn't have a car. They hadn't been told they would need one.

The resourceful terrorists would not be deterred. They found a carpet dealer down the street, bought a few rugs, and rolled up the missiles and launchers into them. Then they carried them on their shoulders to the nearest subway station. They used public transportation to take the missiles to Ostia. Al-Hindi stayed in the apartment while the others headed for the Atlas Hotel, a downtown dive that doubled as a brothel.

None of it would matter. The Mossad was fully aware of the scheme from the early planning stages, thanks to Marwan. But unlike his other work for Israel, this time he wasn't really going against Egyptian interests. On the contrary, Sadat didn't want the plot to actually succeed, just a month before he was to launch his surprise attack. Shooting down an El Al plane would have triggered a massive regional crisis, and the discovery of SA-7 missile shrapnel among the wreckage would have implicated Egypt. Tensions would have risen dramatically, and Egypt would have lost the element of surprise. Such a scheme, in other words, could completely scuttle Sadat's plans for an attack on Israel.

Marwan knew Sadat's thinking. Sadat had learned to respect Marwan's stunning variety of talents, skills, and connections. He would know how to ensure the mission's failure, presumably by tipping off the Italians. But he never suspected that Marwan's contacts were Israeli.

In advance of the operation, Zvi Zamir arrived in Rome to update the local authorities on the plot and to oversee operations in the event that the Italians failed to stop it. In part, the Mossad chief was responding to the trauma of the previous summer, when German police had botched an attempt to rescue Israel's Olympic athletes. Zamir had stood by in the control tower at the Munich airport, helpless. After returning to Israel, deeply shaken, he realized that the Israelis could not rely solely on local forces to protect its citizens abroad.

Indeed, this time the Israelis did not count on the local security services alone. Upon learning about the planned terror operation, more than two weeks before it was to take place, a Mossad team headed by Mike Harari, a senior and veteran operations officer, arrived in Rome. The team thoroughly searched the area around Fiumicino Airport, looking for hideouts that could be used to launch the missiles. Even more important, they followed Marwan when he transferred the missiles to the Palestinian terrorists in Via Veneto and, then, followed the terrorists who took the missiles to their hideout. Harari wanted to raid the apartment, but Zamir, who had already arrived in Rome, decided instead to tip off his Italian counterpart, with whom he had an excellent working relationship. Zamir's only request was that the Italians give the Israelis one of the Strelas, with which the Israeli Air Force was unfamiliar at the time.

From Zamir's perspective, the greatest proof that Marwan wasn't working with the Italians was the surprise he now heard in the voice of his Italian counterpart when he told him he was in Rome to prevent a large-scale terror attack. This time, the locals did their job well. They organized quickly, and in the early-morning hours of September 6, a large force of police entered the apartment in Ostia and arrested Al-Hindi. The other men were picked up downtown at the Atlas Hotel. Al-Hindi later testified that he was surprised by the size of the force, at first thinking they were Mossad. In reality the Mossad team under Harari was ready to intervene in case the local forces faced problems, but there was no need for that.

The five terrorists were arrested. The missiles were confiscated, and the 747 carrying four hundred passengers that had been the intended target of the attack went on its way without the passengers knowing what had happened. Zamir and his men returned to Israel. Although the Black September plotters were later tried, the Italians feared reprisals, and the men were released and allowed to leave the country.

When Marwan learned of the arrest of Al-Hindi and his men,

he headed straight for the airport. Zamir did not tell the Italians who his source had been. Publicly, the question of how the Italians found out about the planned attack remained unresolved—though the following headline appeared in one of the papers: "Italian Sources: Arrest of 'Shoulder-Launched Missile Terrorists' Came After Hints from Israeli Intelligence."

After the dust settled, Marwan's Israeli employers gave him a sizable bonus for having, yet again, proved his dedication to Israel's security.[6]

THERE WAS A downside, however. Ashraf Marwan's involvement in both the planning and the disruption of the terror attack in Rome pulled him away from the center of decision making in Cairo and ended up affecting his ability to give a clear and timely warning of the war a month later. Whatever his distance from Sadat, he certainly knew that preparations for war had entered their final phase. And yet, between early September, when he told his handlers that Egypt intended to attack by year's end, and October 4—just two days before the attack—he gave the Israelis nothing.

Why? Three reasons may explain his silence. One is that Marwan was, for these crucial few weeks, largely out of the loop. He was taken by surprise when he learned on October 5 that the attack would be launched the following day. In his last update in September, he had told the Israelis that Sadat was disclosing less than ever before. Sadat did not let the Libyans or Saudis in on the secret of the attack's timing, so Marwan, whose job was to manage relations with those countries, had no reason to be in the know. Sadat likely took extra care with Marwan after the foiled Rome attack; Marwan was clearly well connected with foreign intelligence, and Sadat didn't want any leaks.

A second reason is that even the greatest spy in Israel's history, who handed over his own country's detailed war plans to the enemy, may have hesitated when it came to this particular secret regarding the date of attack. This may seem unlikely given everything we know about his personality. And yet, a number of intelligence officers who knew him insisted that this should not be ruled out.[7]

The third reason is that Marwan may have believed that no further warnings were necessary—that he had already given the Israelis everything they needed in order to come to the right conclusions. He had told them what signs to look for as the final preparations for war were made, signs that appeared in black and white in the war plans he had handed the Mossad, like the stoppage at the Morgan oil field, which could not be kept secret. So when Marwan finally did give the unambiguous warning of war on October 5, he thought he was telling the Israelis something they already knew.

These explanations are not contradictory and could all be true. They help us understand the final weeks and days leading up to the war, and especially the fact that for all their preparations and extensive espionage efforts, the Israelis were caught unprepared. It is important to emphasize that even without Marwan's warnings of October 4 and 5, during September Israel had accumulated plenty of crucial indicators that Egypt and Syria were about to attack. Under normal circumstances, Military Intelligence should have sounded the alarm no later than October 2—giving the IDF commanders more than enough time to call up reserves and fully deploy for war. But at that moment in history, Israel's Military Intelligence was under the command of a group of officers whose commitment to a specific intelligence paradigm—the *kontzeptzia*—was unwavering, almost religious, even though it had been obviated by events almost a year earlier. As a result, they overlooked a mass of critical data that had only one reasonable interpretation: that Egypt and Syria were headed for war.

OF ALL THE indicators, probably the most worrisome was the buildup of Syrian forces to the north. A reconnaissance flyover that showed the Syrian military in a full emergency deployment along the border, with redoubled artillery and the supporting armor of three infantry divisions advanced to their rear, troubled the IDF's northern commander. In a meeting of the IDF's top brass on September 24, Maj. Gen. Yitzhak Hofi expressed his concern about a Syrian surprise attack. Dayan did not see a full-scale Syrian assault in the offing but possibly something more limited, like an attack on an Israeli settlement on the Golan Heights, which could claim many casualties. A limited action, rather than full-scale war, became Dayan's biggest worry.

Even the warning King Hussein gave Golda Meir in their secret summit on September 25 did little to change Israeli assessments. Jordan had received a tip from a Syrian general who was secretly working for the Hashemite kingdom. Hussein told Meir that the Syrians were at battle stations and likely to attack along with Egypt. At the same time, the Mossad chief, together with Col. Aharon Levran, received details from the Jordanians about the Syrian deployments and plans, including the intent to mount a full-scale assault with Egypt. Neither of the meetings gave a date for the attack. The prime minister was deeply unsettled by the meeting with Hussein and demanded a response from Military Intelligence. The MI chief, Zeira, answered that the information Meir had received was unreliable. Though the king's intelligence included new information about the Syrian deployments—including the high state of alert, cancellation of leaves, the call-up of reserves, and the impounding of civilian vehicles—Zeira still insisted that Syria would never launch a war without Egypt, and Egypt had no such intention.

Nevertheless, the IDF chief of staff ordered the partial reinforcement of the Golan Heights. Two tank squadrons from the 7th

Armored Brigade and one artillery battery climbed the escarp-
ment to the Golan on September 26, the eve of Rosh Hashanah.

In the ensuing days, Israel received information about a heightened alert level in the Egyptian air force, as well as the movement
of armored units from Cairo toward the canal. On September 26,
a source that the prime minister had previously called "good"[8]
passed along a warning that Egypt intended to launch, very soon,
an attack that included crossing the canal. MI ignored it, asserting
that the Egyptians were moving their forces out of fear of an Israeli
preemptive strike. At the same time, the CIA passed along a report
that the Syrians were planning to attack, with the aim of recapturing the Golan Heights. This warning included an explicit plan
of attack. The officers at MI-Research, who knew that the CIA's
information was coming mainly from King Hussein, disseminated
a report that included both the warning and the key points of the
plan of attack but also their own opinion that the Syrian deployments were not offensive in nature. Nor did this opinion change
when MI received reports from its own sources in Unit 848 that
Syrian Sukhoi assault planes had been relocated to forward air
bases, or that the 47th Armored Brigade, which was charged with
the southern sector of the Golan front during a war, had left Homs
in the north and was making its way to the Israeli border in the
south. In early October, the Syrian army had completed its preparations and, in accordance with Soviet military doctrine, was now
in a position to attack without any further action.

On October 1, Egypt began a widely anticipated military exercise known as Tahrir 41. On the eve of the exercise, Israel received
yet another warning: Tahrir 41 would end with a real assault on the
Suez Canal. The aim would be to enter Sinai and grab territory up
to the Mitla and Gidi Passes. Other signs confirmed the warning.
In Military Intelligence, however, the warning was interpreted as
saying that the attack would take place the very next day—and

when that day passed without incident, the intelligence officers took it to be a false alarm. Their sanguinity about an Egyptian attack was also the reason for ignoring the signs of war on the Syrian front, which they insisted couldn't happen without Egypt. But still the indicators of real war, and not just an exercise, accumulated. The volume of wireless communications among the Egyptians, which in previous exercises had numbered in the thousands per day, was now far smaller; the amount of bridging and crossing equipment at the canal far exceeded anything in the past; an enormous munitions convoy was spotted making its way toward the Gulf of Suez with no reasonable explanation for it; and at the canal, dozens of ramps were built to ease rapid entry into the water—ramps that had never been seen in the previous Tahrir exercises.

In the face of all this, the head of the MI Research Division asserted, in an emergency meeting held in Golda Meir's office on October 3, that "Egypt believes it still cannot launch a war [and therefore] . . . the idea of a combined Egyptian–Syrian war doesn't strike me as reasonable." The mountain of intelligence that Marwan had been giving Israel for nearly a year still had not registered in his thinking.

It was only on Thursday, October 4, that Military Intelligence began to modify its approach. That afternoon—just forty-eight hours before the attack—Unit 848 began receiving clear indications of an emergency evacuation of all Soviet personnel, first in Syria and then in Egypt. While they were monitoring the air convoy shuttling Soviet advisers and their families back home, IDF surveillance units picked up on tense conversations taking place in Russian, in which the families of Soviet experts in Syria were ordered to pack their bags within twenty minutes and head for rendezvous points where they would be picked up and taken back to the Soviet Union. Further details about the evacuations streamed in throughout the night and into the next morning. At about the same time, the results of the latest flyovers, taken at midday over the Suez Canal, came in. "The Egyptian army," it was now reported, "is arrayed in an emergency deployment the likes of which we have never seen."

Although a definitive interpretation of the reconnaissance photos would take more time, and would only reach the decision makers on Friday morning, the tension began to rise sharply in the offices of Military Intelligence. The Soviet evacuations had taken the officers by surprise, and when combined with all the other indicators, the overall picture could not be easily interpreted as part of an exercise in the south and defensive preparations in the north alone. The top MI commanders, alongside the heads of MI-Research Branches 3 (Great Powers), 5 (Syria), and 6 (Egypt), spent the night at their desks, trying to integrate the raging river of information that now flowed. The commander of Unit 848, Brig. Gen. Yoel Ben-Porat, telephoned the MI chief and declared that war was coming. He had already put his unit on highest alert. Eli Zeira started to lose confidence in his belief that war was unlikely. Even he could not ignore the signs at this late hour.

At two thirty early Friday morning, the phone rang in the home of the Mossad chief. Zamir answered. His chief of staff, Freddy Eini, was on the line with an urgent message. The Angel had made contact. He was talking of war.

Chapter 9

SIGNING AT SUNDOWN ON SATURDAY

Ashraf Marwan left Egypt four days before the outbreak of war. He went to Libya, where he told Gaddafi about the intention to go to war soon, and then continued to France.[1] On Thursday, October 4, he was in Paris with an Egyptian delegation, making it difficult for him to operate freely, whether by telephone or to arrange a meeting with his Israeli handlers. Difficulties like these were not unusual for Marwan, however, who always found a way to overcome them. In the late afternoon on Thursday, he placed a call to the apartment of the woman in London who acted as the go-between between Marwan and his Mossad handler. He needed to speak with "Alex," he told her, and he would call again later on. The woman alerted Dubi, who quickly made his way to her apartment and then waited. Soon the phone rang again. It was the Angel.

Dubi could hear men speaking Arabic in the background. Marwan was clearly not alone and could not speak freely. And he was tense. He began by saying he couldn't talk for long. Dubi understood. Then the Angel got to the point: He wanted to talk about "lots of chemicals," and he needed to see the "General" urgently. Tomorrow he would be in London. They would meet.

Dubi thought he heard the message loud and clear. As part of the protocol that was set up to allow Marwan to give advance warning of an attack, they had chosen code words he would use to clarify the specific nature of the threat. Because Marwan had studied chemistry, they decided that warnings would incorporate elements of the periodic table, mixed with statements that seemed like normal conversation. The general term for war was "chemicals," but Marwan was also given more specific terms. If he wanted to tell them about a threat of immediate attack, he might have spoken of "potassium"; a less immediate warning might include mention of "iodine"; an air attack in the Sinai without crossing the Suez Canal could be called "sodium."

Some commentators have suggested that Dubi made a crucial mistake. He could have asked Marwan to name a specific element, rather than just "chemicals," as the basis for bringing the Mossad chief—the "manager"—to London. Instead, he chose not to press the point. Dubi, however, was unaware of the tense situation developing, from hour to hour, back in Israel. All he knew was what he learned from the press, and there were no public reports about a possible war. Dubi also did not have much of a choice. He knew that Marwan was pressed for time and that there were other people near him. He also believed that if Marwan had more precise information, he would have used a different code word. Since he didn't, Dubi concluded that the warning was not all that concrete. Finally, Dubi figured that in any event, Marwan would be more specific the next day when he met with Zvi Zamir.

Dubi, in any event, followed protocol. When he got off the phone with Marwan, he quickly called the Mossad's London bureau chief and then drafted a communiqué. Even though the immediate reason for sending a report was the warning he had just received from the Angel, the first paragraph dealt with other matters. Only farther down did Dubi write that the source wanted to

see the director of the Mossad urgently about the "chemicals," and
mentioned a time for the meeting in London.

The report was sent to Mossad headquarters in Tel Aviv, where
it arrived at around midnight Israel time. The officer on duty
promptly sent a copy to the office of Zamir and a second copy to
Military Intelligence.

The woman on duty at Zamir's office received the letter and
called his chief of staff, Freddy Eini, at home. Eini drove to headquarters to read it himself. According to his testimony before the
Agranat Commission—Israel's national commission of inquiry that
later investigated the events leading up to the Yom Kippur War—
Eini took it with utmost seriousness. It was "a warning of the start
of war. Nothing like this had ever happened." These last words, he
later recalled, referred not to the warning but to Marwan's request
to meet with the head of the Mossad. This was unusual because
Marwan had always been kept in the dark as to whether Zamir
would join their meetings, in order to keep the Egyptians, or any
other hostile actors, from setting a trap for him. Given these ex-
traordinary circumstances, Eini now felt he had to alert Zamir,
who was at home, about the communiqué.

It was now 2:30 a.m., Israel time, on Friday, October 5.

Their conversation included at least one misunderstanding. Eini
clearly thought he was calling Zamir to share a top intelligence
source's warning of war. Zamir, on the other hand, saw the call
as something more mundane. Eini did tell him that the Angel
wanted to meet him in London to discuss the "chemicals." But
because Marwan hadn't used the code word denoting an immediate attack, Zamir failed to interpret it as a concrete warning of
imminent war. He recalled that back in April, the same source had
used the code word for an imminent attack; that had been a false
alarm, and the Angel had quickly withdrawn the warning. This
time around, the other indicators of war were much more serious,

and as such, the less urgent implication of the word "chemicals" effectively lulled Zamir into concluding that war must be less imminent than he had feared.

Zamir believed that the purpose of Eini's call was to tell him about Marwan's request to meet the next evening in London. It was, therefore, up to Zamir to decide whether to go. But a decision to meet Marwan would mean a rapid change of plans in order to catch the morning flight, which was El Al's only flight to the United Kingdom on the eve of the Yom Kippur holiday. He had to tell Eini right away whether to make the arrangements. For days, the Mossad chief had been deeply worried by the stream of reports of war—and by Military Intelligence's insistence on downplaying them. Yes, he said, he would go to London. He told Eini to make the necessary arrangements for both the flight and the clandestine meeting, alerting local Mossad staff who would provide security and cover on the ground in London. With this, they ended their call.

Minutes later, Zamir's phone rang again. This time, it was the chief of Military Intelligence, Eli Zeira. This was the first time Zeira had ever called him after midnight, and this alone convinced Zamir that the situation must be serious. The MI chief updated him about the Soviet evacuations in Syria and asked Zamir if he'd heard anything new. Zamir, who had yet to internalize the urgency of Marwan's message about "chemicals," didn't mention the conversation he'd just concluded with Freddy Eini, and Zeira came away thinking that there was no news from the Mossad.

At about 3:00 a.m., Eini called again. He updated Zamir on the details of the morning flight. Zamir told him about the MI chief's call and the Soviet evacuations; Eini suggested that perhaps this dovetailed with Marwan's sudden desire to meet. Only then did Zamir realize that Eini, who had seen Dubi's communiqué, had understood Marwan to be delivering a warning of war. He told

Eini he would immediately call back Zeira to tell him about it, and instructed him to alert the prime minister's military secretary, Brig. Gen. Israel Lior, in the morning—both about the Angel's warning and about Zamir's plans to meet him in London.

Zamir called Zeira back. By now, three hours had passed since Dubi's communiqué had reached Mossad headquarters. According to the Agranat Commission report, Zamir now told the MI chief that "this is war. We don't have the exact date yet . . . but it is imminent."[2] According to Zamir's testimony, Zeira had agreed that yes, it was war.

The MI chief recalled the conversation differently, however. In his testimony before the commission, he said that Zamir had told him he'd be getting more information within twenty-four hours and that Zeira, in response, told the Mossad chief to pass it on to him in the fastest way possible if it was really about war. Contradicting Zamir's claim that the phone call was principally about an impending attack, Zeira claimed that he had not understood Dubi's message to be about war at all. "This," he told the commission, "I am now hearing for the first time." He later repeated the claim, saying that "a clear warning sign, as I now understand it? This I am now hearing for the first time."

The commission preferred the Mossad chief's testimony over Zeira's. Its members confronted Zeira with his own words as recorded in the minutes of his meeting with the prime minister on Friday morning, October 5. There it was clear that he understood Zamir to be waiting urgently for clarifications about the warning of war. When challenged, Zeira softened his position. "Zvika [Zamir] may have said something about it." Then he added: "I understood it, generally speaking, as a warning. Not something certain, not something imminent, not something clear. My sense is that such was the Mossad's understanding as well."[3]

Eini picked up Zamir on the morning of Friday, October 5,

from his house in the Tzahala neighborhood of Tel Aviv, and they made their way to the airport at Lod. On the way, they agreed that Zamir would update Eini by telephone right after the meeting that night. They also agreed on code words for Zamir to use while reporting. Zamir emphasized that the contents of Dubi's message must be passed to the prime minister. Eini had no need for the reminder: The rules were very clear, and Eini, who always followed them, understood their importance.

Zamir took off for London, and Eini drove to headquarters in Tel Aviv. He tried to reach Israel Lior, the prime minister's military secretary, at his office but was told that Lior was meeting with the prime minister and couldn't talk. Eini left a message to call him.

Prime Minister Golda Meir received the information in a meeting that took place in her personal office at IDF headquarters in Tel Aviv from 10:00 to 11:00 a.m. Other participants included Defense Minister Moshe Dayan, IDF chief of staff David Elazar, Zeira, and several of their closest aides. Zeira updated the prime minister about the Arab military preparations and the Soviet evacuations. He also mentioned the Mossad chief's trip to London, relaying the message from Marwan that "something's going to happen," and that Zamir went to check it out. At this point, the defense minister already knew about the warning. About an hour earlier, in a one-on-one meeting with Zeira, he had first learned that Zamir "last night received an alert from the Angel. He gave warning that something is going to happen, and asked Zvika [Zamir] to come immediately for a meeting. He'll see him tonight at 10 p.m."[4]

The matter-of-fact way that Zeira passed along what he heard from Zamir in their phone conversations the night before did little justice to the actual urgency of the warning. If Eini had called Lior immediately during the night (rather than the next morning), spoken to him directly (rather than leaving him a message), and told him in an unambiguous way what was in the communiqué

Dubi had sent several hours earlier, the prime minister likely would have heard and absorbed the information differently. Instead, what resulted was, in effect, a game of telephone: Marwan's warning was substantially diluted by the time it reached Golda Meir.

The ambiguous wording of Dubi's communiqué undoubtedly contributed to the misunderstanding surrounding Marwan's war alarm—namely, it was not understood as a war alarm during the crucial day that passed between Zamir's first hearing about it from Eini at 2:30 a.m. on Friday, and Zamir's own report after meeting Marwan in London the following night. If Marwan, who had given such accurate information all along, had known Thursday that the attack would be launched two days later, he almost certainly would have said so to Dubi, as clearly as possible and as soon as possible. Yet if Marwan was ambiguous during the Thursday-night phone call, it is probably because he only learned about the actual timing of the attack *after* he had spoken with Dubi—and purely by chance.

THE DELEGATION THAT had brought Marwan to Paris returned to Cairo on Friday morning. Marwan himself went to London. There he checked into a suite on the seventh floor of the Churchill, an upscale and relatively new redbrick hotel not far from Oxford Street. He lay on the couch that morning, reading.

There was a rap on the door. It was Mohamed Nusseir, a friend Marwan knew from Cairo. The forty-six-year-old Nusseir had been one of Egypt's first computer engineers. In 1967, at the request of Mohamed Hassanein Heikal, he joined the staff of the *Al-Ahram* newspaper, established the paper's data center and publishing house, and within five years turned it into one of the most impressive technological centers in the country. In 1972 he left the center and was now in a transitional phase; soon he would launch a career in computers and telecommunications that would make him one of the richest men in Egypt. He was married to the

daughter of Abdel Latif Boghdadi, a member of the Revolutionary
Leadership Council and vice president under Nasser. Through his
wife, he had met Mona, Nasser's daughter. Mona had introduced
him to Marwan.

Nusseir had a bizarre story to tell. That morning, he had spoken
to the director of the London office of EgyptAir, the national airline, who told Nusseir that he, as well as his counterpart in Paris,
had both received explicit, urgent orders from Cairo to reroute all
the carrier's planes in London and Paris to Tripoli, Libya. The order
came without explanation.

Neither Marwan nor Nusseir knew it, but the order sent to
London and Paris was the result of a decision made by the Egyptian aviation minister, who had, without consulting anyone, told
the CEO of EgyptAir to move all of his aircraft to friendly states.
The minister had just found out the date of the planned attack
and decided to take action to protect the planes. But when news
of the order reached the command center of the Egyptian military (Center 10), the defense minister and the army's chief of staff
were stunned. Fearing that the sudden change in EgyptAir's flight
schedules would tip their hand to the Israelis, they told the company's CEO to ignore the directive, and EgyptAir returned to its
ordinary flight schedule during the morning of Friday, October 5.[5]
The head of the airline's London office, who knew Nusseir, was
calling him to see if he knew any reason for the sudden order and
its reversal. Nusseir said he had no idea, but he thought he might
know someone who did: his friend Ashraf Marwan, the president's
confidant, whom Sadat had personally sent on many sensitive diplomatic missions, and who would be arriving in London that same
morning and staying at the Churchill.

According to an interview Nusseir later gave to an Egyptian TV
station, when Marwan heard the story he leapt up off the couch.
"There's going to be a war," he declared. "The war plans say that

we're worried about our planes getting damaged on the ground. Part of the plan is that we're supposed to reroute our planes to other countries." Marwan went into the bedroom, made a few phone calls, and soon came back out, saying that war would be launched the following day. He told Nusseir that he had to get back to Egypt immediately and asked him to go to their mutual friend, Kamal Adham, and tell him to lend Marwan one of his private planes so that he could fly back to Cairo. It was midday Friday when Nusseir called Adham, who was unable to help Marwan, since the plane he usually kept in London had just taken off. Nusseir left Marwan's suite and went back to his family. What was clear to him, he later recalled, was that "Marwan knew every detail of the war plans because he worked in the President's Office, but he didn't know exactly when it would happen . . . the proof of this was the great surprise he showed when he heard my story. It was clear that he didn't know when the war would begin."[6]

Most of the Israelis familiar with the war warning Marwan gave assumed that he was already fully aware when he left Egypt several days earlier that war would break on October 6. What emerges from Nusseir's account is that this assumption may have been simply false. In fact, Marwan learned that war will start on October 6 only on October 5 at midday, and only by accident.

In the entire debate about whether Marwan was actually a sophisticated double agent rather than the most important spy Israel ever had, no single question has been more decisive than Marwan's alleged "delay" in warning about the war. According to the double agent hypothesis, he knew all along that the attack would come on October 6; he gave the warning in order to maintain his credibility with the Israelis but withheld the information until it was too late for them to do anything useful with it. This, it emerges, is wrong on two counts: Marwan almost certainly didn't know about the timing until the day before the attack; and as we will see further on, he really did give the Israelis enough time to deploy the regular army for war, to start calling up their reserves, and to launch a preemptive strike. That they did not take these steps is due largely to their own confusion—and, in the case of MI chief Eli Zeira and those he influenced, their unwillingness to take Marwan's warning seriously.

There were several reasons for Israel's spectacular intelligence failure, which allowed the Egyptian and Syrian forces to catch the IDF unprepared when they attacked on the afternoon of Saturday, October 6. But Israel also benefited from a stroke of luck. If the Egyptian aviation minister hadn't given the order to change the national carrier's flight schedules and reroute the airliners to Libya; if Mohamed Nusseir hadn't heard about it from the chief of EgyptAir's London branch; if he hadn't known that Marwan was in the city and then tracked him down at the Churchill to see what he might know about it—the outcome of the entire war may have been quite different. Only through the confluence of all these events was it possible for Marwan to tell Zamir that night that war was not just on the way but would be at hand the next day. If his warning had remained without a precise date, it is hard to believe that Zamir's report that night would have started a process that would end in the call-up of Israeli reserves, as well as additional crucial decisions made in the final hours before the attack.

Egyptian efforts to keep the date of attack a secret were both comprehensive and remarkably effective, adhering strictly to the principle of "need to know." Foreign Minister Mohamed Hassan al-Zayat, for example, had no idea that war would break out on October 6 because he had been at the United Nations in New York and was out of the loop regarding military moves.[7] Sadat was careful, moreover, to keep the date a secret from other Arab leaders, including King Faisal of Saudi Arabia, with whom he was closest, as well as Muammar Gaddafi, who had been no small nuisance to him. If the leaders of Saudi Arabia and Libya didn't need to know, then neither did the man in the President's Office in charge of relations with those states. True, Marwan had excellent sources of his own who might have tipped him off. But even they may have been cut off or kept the information to themselves. Although more people in Sadat's office knew about it as the day of the attack drew closer, Marwan had left the country by October 3, when the number of people who knew was still relatively small. Only on October 3, for example, were the commanders of the infantry divisions at the front told that the attack would be launched three days later.

Other sources who reported to Israel in late 1972 and then again in the spring of 1973 that war was about to erupt, some even giving specific dates, gave no similar warning in the fall of 1973. The most likely reason is that Sadat did a much better job at keeping the secret this time around. Marwan's access was better than that of any other Israeli source in Egypt at the time, but even that was not enough to ensure that he'd know every secret. Moreover, he, too, had erred in the past, for example, when he reported in the middle of January 1973 regarding the supposedly upcoming hostilities the following May, that the Egyptians had no intention of crossing the Suez Canal; or when he reported in early September 1973 that the war would be pushed off to the end of the year.

It is thus far more likely that Marwan learned only on Friday, October 5, that war would break out the following day, and only as a result of the EgyptAir rescheduling. Israeli intelligence also picked up the unusual order given to the airline, but none of the intelligence reports presented on Friday mentioned it. It was fortunate for Israel that the news reached the Angel as well, who knew what it might mean, and whom to call for details. The result was that when he met Zamir that night, he had new, concrete intelligence to share—intelligence that would, once and for all, shatter the paradigm that had, for so many months, frozen Israeli intelligence in the conviction that war was unlikely.

AT 5:45 A.M. on Friday, October 5, IDF Military Intelligence sent out a report that, on the basis of reconnaissance air photography from the day before, presented Egyptian deployments along the Suez Canal. The final sentence said all that needed saying: "From the data we may conclude with clarity that the Egyptian military along the canal is arrayed in an emergency deployment the likes of which we have never seen before." Defense Minister Dayan saw the report just after it went out. "One can get a stroke," he said, "just from looking at the numbers." This report, as well as other intelligence that continued to pour in about the unexplained evacuations of Soviets from Syria and Egypt, was the main topic of the meetings that took place on Yom Kippur Eve.

In the early morning hours, MI chief Eli Zeira held a meeting in his office. Zeira was apparently more worried about the Soviet evacuations than about the deployments along the southern front—deployments that included equipment for bridging the canal. During this meeting, the question was raised about whether to activate the "special means of intelligence gathering" that were under the sole and direct responsibility of the MI chief. Their specific nature remains a secret, but according to Howard Blum in his book on the Yom Kippur War, these were "a series of battery-operated devices attached to phone and cable connections buried deep in the sand outside Cairo." They could pick up not only telephone and telegraph signals but also conversations taking place in rooms where the telephones and telexes were located. The problem was that ongoing activation would require the occasional replacement of batteries, a dangerous operation deep in enemy territory that MI was reluctant to undertake.[8] According to an Israeli source, these devices had been planted on February 16–17, 1973,

in Jabel Ataka, west of the city of Suez, near the headquarters of
the Egyptian Third Army, by a commando team that had reached
the location by four American-made CH-53 helicopters.[9] In the
meeting on the morning of October 5, Zeira, who still believed
war was unlikely, refused requests to activate the equipment.

At 8:25 a.m., a brief meeting took place in the office of the IDF
chief of staff, David Elazar. In light of the new information about
the Egyptian deployments and Soviet evacuations, Elazar decided
to put the regular army on Alert Level 3, the highest alert level
since the Six-Day War. He also put the air force on full alert, moved
the rest of the 7th Armored Brigade up to the Golan Heights, and
dispatched another tank brigade to the Sinai. To call up the reserves
would require cabinet approval, and this was not yet possible. But
Alert Level 3 meant that all the preparations were in place for a
full call-up. Zeira at this point evidently still had not mentioned
the warning Zamir had received from Marwan, and it is unclear
whether Elazar knew about it when he made his decisions.

At 9:00 a.m., the weekly security briefing was held in the office
of Defense Minister Dayan. Zeira presented an overview of the
intelligence, again focusing more on the Soviet evacuations than
on the offensive posture taken by the Egyptian deployment at the
canal, which he saw as reflecting Egyptian anxiety about a possible
Israeli preemptive strike like the one that had taken out Egypt's
air force in the opening minutes of the Six-Day War. This was
the meeting in which Zeira told the others present about Zamir's
emergency trip to London, saying that they were waiting for his
report that evening, and then "we will be wiser men."

During the meeting, Dayan asked Zeira whether the special
means of intelligence gathering had provided anything useful. Not
only did Zeira fail to tell him that they hadn't been activated, but
he also led Dayan to believe that they simply had failed to provide
any indication of war. The effect of Zeira's misleading statement

was to allay Dayan's fears about an imminent attack. Because he believed that the equipment had been activated but gave no warnings, it was not unreasonable for him to conclude that Egypt was not on the verge of attacking. As for Chief of Staff Elazar, who was present as well and knew all about the special equipment, Zeira's words merely confirmed what he had already heard three days earlier, on Tuesday. Then, and possibly on Monday as well, Elazar had asked Zeira if he had activated the special equipment, and he had answered, falsely, that indeed he had.

This was no simple misunderstanding. Zeira was under pressure from top officers in MI to activate the equipment, and he had refused since he had not felt that the circumstances warranted its deployment, as there was, in his view, no imminent threat of war. In lying to his superiors, however, he directly and significantly contributed to both Dayan's and Elazar's serious underestimation of the threat at hand.[10]

During the meeting, Dayan gave his approval to the various decisions Elazar had made. He also decided that a message should be sent via Washington to Moscow, Cairo, and Damascus, to the effect that Israel had no hostile intentions but was fully aware of the actions being taken on the Arab side, and that if the Arabs attacked, they would find Israel ready for battle.

The issue of calling up the reserves was also raised at the meeting, and again at the next meeting, at 10:00 a.m. in the prime minister's office at IDF headquarters in Tel Aviv. Here it was Elazar who took the lead, updating Prime Minister Golda Meir about the actions already taken to prepare for war. Elazar said there was no need for a full call-up yet, because if Egypt and Syria were about to attack, MI's intelligence-gathering capabilities, as well as those of the Mossad, would have given clear indications to that effect. "We'll prepare for war," he concluded, "and hope that the indications come early enough." Meir expressed her concerns but accepted his position and approved the message Dayan wanted sent to the Soviets, Egyptians, and Syrians through Kissinger.

The fifth meeting that day involved a much broader forum— the full cabinet. This unscheduled meeting started at about 11:30 a.m., and it included all available government ministers. After the MI chief gave an overall survey of the intelligence picture, which did not mention Zamir's trip to London, the IDF chief of staff spoke. Elazar agreed with Zeira's assessment that Egypt's and Syria's offensive postures, combined with the absence of anything that would clearly prevent them from attacking, had forced the IDF's hand, requiring that measures be taken in response, including putting the army on Alert Level 3 and rushing reinforcements to the Sinai and the Golan Heights. "As for calling up the reserves and other measures," he added, "we are waiting for further indicators" of war.

From Elazar's words, it was clear that his own position had evolved. If earlier that morning he believed that putting the military on full alert and deploying more forces along the fronts was sufficient to address the present threat, as the hours passed he started talking more and more about calling up reserves. In light of the possibility of a call-up during the Yom Kippur holiday, the cabinet formally empowered the prime minister and defense minister to make such a decision on their own, a decision that would normally have required the full cabinet's approval.

The final meeting of the day was an emergency meeting of the IDF General Staff, immediately following the cabinet meeting. There, Zeira told the IDF's top generals that "the likelihood of war initiated by Egypt and Syria is very low." More likely, he estimated, was a limited Syrian attack on the Golan Heights, or limited Egyptian fire, possibly a helicopter assault along the Suez Canal. Least likely was a broad, joint assault by the Egyptians and Syrians together, including a crossing of the canal with the aim of reaching the Mitla and Gidi Passes. This assessment, which was similar to the one he had given to the cabinet an hour and a half earlier, completely contradicted the assessment of MI's Research Department, where the IDF's top intelligence analysts were located. MI-Research had concluded that if Egypt were to attack at all, it would go for a full-blown assault on the canal rather than something limited, and that the present deployment by Egypt and Syria on both fronts pointed to just such an assault, in accordance with the Egyptian and Syrian war plans that had been in MI's possession for some time.

Elazar, however, was much more worried than Zeira. He still felt that the likelihood of war was not high, but it was certainly not "very low." His own relatively mild optimism stemmed from his belief that "if in fact they intend to attack simultaneously from Syria and Egypt, we will get the warning." This belief, it now seems, was based on his familiarity with Israeli intelligence's two strategic-level sources of information: the special means of intelligence gathering under the MI chief's authority, and the Mossad's Angel. But Elazar did not know that the special measures had not been activated. And though he had heard Zeira mention Zamir's trip to London, it was not presented with the urgency it demanded. Zeira hadn't told Elazar about the contents of his phone conversation with Zamir from the night before. As a result, the IDF chief of staff, according to the testimony of his own deputy, was unaware throughout Friday that Zamir had gone to meet the Angel because of a warning of immediate war. For the kind of warning that would justify calling up the reserves, Elazar's sights were set on the MI's "special intelligence-gathering measures."

One bit of intelligence that could have turned the tide that day was picked up by surveillance equipment, though not of the "special" variety. At 5:00 p.m. on Friday, members of Intelligence Unit 848 intercepted a message from Iraq's ambassador in Moscow to

his own foreign ministry in Baghdad. The ambassador reported
that he had checked with the Soviet Foreign Ministry to find out
the reason for the emergency evacuations that had begun the day
before and was told that Egypt and Syria had alerted the Soviets
that they were about to attack Israel. Under normal circumstances,
such a message would have been sent out within half an hour from
the moment it reached MI-Research. But despite the IDF's being
at Alert Level 3, most MI-Research officers were at home or in
synagogues for Yom Kippur. The officer on duty hesitated, for he
was reluctant to send out a message that might trigger a massive
call-up on Yom Kippur. He began consulting with other officers
and commanders, and after six full hours Zeira ordered that it be
withheld because he was waiting for further information.[11]

THAT "FURTHER INFORMATION" was, of course, the Mossad chief's
report from his meeting with the Angel. At that very hour—11:00
p.m. Israel time, 10:00 p.m. in London—Zamir and Dubi were
making their way to the rendezvous point. Zamir was unaware
of the latest developments back in Israel. He didn't know about
the reconnaissance photos from the day before showing the entire
Egyptian military on a war footing. Neither was he aware of the
string of meetings that took place that day in Tel Aviv, in which it
became increasingly clear how badly the Israelis needed just one
more piece of hard evidence showing that Egypt and Syria were
about to attack, in order to bring the IDF chief of staff to seek government approval of a massive call-up of reserves on the holiest day
in the Jewish religion. Neither was he aware that just such a piece
of information had reached MI six hours earlier but hadn't been
forwarded to the chief of staff; or that the latter was under the false
impression that the special surveillance equipment was operational
when it wasn't, and that he therefore had a completely misguided
impression of the overall intelligence picture.

He did, however, know that back in Israel, there was serious concern about the possibility of war and that they awaited his word. But Zamir was not fully prepared for the dramatic news that Marwan brought.

It was close to 10:00 p.m. London time when Dubi and Zamir reached the apartment where the meeting would be held. Mossad agents, who had been in place for several hours, gave the area around the building a final once-over. Dubi and Zamir went in and waited. It was a long wait. Marwan had rarely been late before. Slightly after 11:30 p.m., they finally heard a knock on the door. Dubi opened it, and in walked the Angel.

Handshakes and formalities were exchanged. Dubi took a seat near the large dining table, notebook open and pen in hand. Marwan sat in an armchair by the coffee table, facing Zamir.

THIS WAS THE first meeting between Marwan and his handlers since the failed attack on the El Al jet in Rome a month earlier. The Israelis wanted to make sure their source hadn't been compromised, and they wanted him to know they were concerned. This is why Zamir's first line of questioning was about whether any suspicions had been raised after the Italian forces raided the apartment in Ostia—a raid that clearly was based on advance warning—and whether Sadat had shown any interest in the question of how the Italians knew about the attack. Marwan reassured them that the episode had not caused him any trouble. Sadat probably figured that Marwan had tipped the Italians off; since the terror attack wasn't in Egypt's interest anyway, this in itself was unlikely to trouble the president. But nobody suspected he had said anything to the Israelis.

From the abrupt manner in which he deflected Zamir's questions, however, it was clear that Marwan had something more pressing on his mind.

Marwan was tense. "I have come here," he announced, "to talk about the war, and nothing else. I came late because I have spent the entire evening at our consulate in Kensington. I've been on the phone with Cairo, trying to get the most up-to-date information. He [Sadat] intends to go to war tomorrow." From the way Marwan expressed himself in what followed, one gets the sense that he thought the Israelis already knew about it. It was a belief held widely by the Egyptians that the Israelis would know about the attack two full days before it was launched. But it is also possible that he was trying to gloss over the fact that—despite presenting himself to the Israelis as the oracle of all knowledge worth knowing in Egypt—here he now was, less than twenty-four hours before the attack, having learned about it only a few hours earlier.

Zamir was taken by surprise. He had come to the meeting worried because from the latest information he had, especially the Soviet evacuations, he could see that Egypt and Syria were heading for war. But he had not imagined that the attack would be launched in less than twenty-four hours. And he was also worried that, just as with past warnings, this one, too, would prove a false alarm. So his immediate response was, "On what do you base your assertion?"

For Marwan, who had previously given false alarms of war, both his credibility in the eyes of the Israelis and his image as a central player in Cairo were obviously important. Nor is it clear where he got his information—to whom, in other words, he had made those phone calls throughout the evening. And because his information was based on telephone conversations rather than face-to-face meetings, it is fair to assume that what he heard had been phrased cautiously or even ambiguously. He had not spent the crucial days before the war in Sadat's presence, so he couldn't know what the atmosphere was like in the presidential offices, where there were people who already knew the secret. The dissonance between the information he had received, in whose credibility he had no doubt, and his intimate knowledge of Sadat's psyche—the president had changed his mind many times about the date of attack—had its effect on him. The more Zamir pressed him to give his own independent take on whether war would in fact erupt the next day, the more Marwan grew agitated, at least once raising his voice. "How should I know?" he shouted. "He [Sadat] is crazy. He can march forward, tell everyone else to march forward, and then suddenly march backward." Marwan was giving voice not only to his frustration at his inability to give a straight answer to the most important question of his career as a spy, but also to his personal aversion toward Sadat, his inclination to disrespect him and see him as unreliable.

Zamir was less worried about Marwan's inner conflict than about whether or not a war would start the next day. He had been a senior IDF officer in 1959, when a poorly thought-out military exercise involving an unannounced, emergency mass call-up of reserves instilled fear in an entire nation, triggered the call-up of reserves in Egypt and Syria in response, and ratcheted up tensions in the whole region. The affair, known as the Night of the Ducks, brought an end to the military careers of the commander of the IDF's Operations Branch, Maj. Gen. Meir Zorea, and the chief of Military Intelligence, Maj. Gen. Yehoshafat Harkabi. Images of that episode flashed through Zamir's mind as he spoke with Marwan. The Night of the Ducks, he realized, would look like child's play compared with a mistaken emergency mobilization for war in the middle of Yom Kippur. He could see the worldwide reaction to the IDF pulling tens of thousands of reserve soldiers out of the synagogues and sending them to the front to await an Arab onslaught that never came. The price would be incalculable. Now was the time, Zamir knew, to press his source as hard as possible, to make sure the warning was well grounded.

Marwan's discomfort did little to quell Zamir's concerns. He quickly realized that he'd have to rely on his own experience, which was much greater than Marwan's, to formulate his own opinion. Zamir didn't know what had happened in Israel since his departure to London, but he had no reason to think that the reserves had already been called up. He understood that a clear warning that war would be launched the next day would leave the decision makers without any alternatives to a full-blown emergency call-up. And so, despite his being the chief of the Mossad and not the prime minister and her cabinet, he suddenly felt the full weight of the government's decision on his shoulders. But Zamir was himself a former general, having previously served as the chief of the IDF Southern Command, and he fully understood the implications of trying to fend off an Arab assault without calling up reserves.

By the end of the meeting, he had already made up his mind. He would send back to Israel an unambiguous warning that Egypt and Syria planned on launching a full-scale attack the next day.

This decision would alter the course of the Yom Kippur War.

But he wasn't finished with Marwan. Next, he grilled him about the war plans. Marwan hadn't brought any documents with him, but most of the key details of the latest battle plans were burned in his memory and had just been reconfirmed by his contacts in Cairo. Nothing had changed since the last time he'd passed the most recent version of the war plans to his handlers several weeks before. Egyptian infantry divisions would cross the Suez Canal and move farther east up to six miles. He went into some detail about the air and commando raids aimed at blocking IDF reinforcements heading for the front. Marwan also confirmed that the Egyptian air force would send its Tupolev Tu-16 bombers armed with Kelt missiles to strike the IDF headquarters in Tel Aviv. This, too, had appeared in the plans he had previously passed along.

Zamir also asked about the precise hour of attack (H-hour),

though he didn't consider it such a pressing question. In all of the Egyptian battle plans that Israel had seen for years, H-hour was precisely sunset—a time that left just enough daylight to carry out a major air assault on the Sinai, before darkness came to preclude an effective response by the Israeli Air Force. According to Marwan's report, that would be the plan this time as well. On October 6, 1973, the sun would set at 5:20 p.m. Israel time.

What neither Marwan nor his handlers knew, however, was that two days earlier, the Egyptian war minister had met with the president of Syria and had agreed to launch the attack at 2:00 p.m., as a compromise between Syrian and Egyptian operational needs.

The meeting lasted more than two hours. Marwan returned to his hotel, with Mossad agents keeping tabs on him. The next day, Saturday, he went back to Egypt. Zamir and Dubi, who had spent the whole meeting writing down every word, went directly to the home of the Mossad's London station chief, a ten-minute walk. On the way, Zamir wondered aloud what would happen if he sent a warning of immediate war and the war never came. He didn't need to wait for Dubi's answer, however. He had already made up his mind.

They reached the apartment of Rafi, the station chief, who was waiting for them. Zamir took a few minutes to carefully craft, longhand, the coded message that he would send to his chief of staff, Freddy Eini, who waited at home in Israel. Also present was Zvi Malhin, who was responsible for security for the meeting with Marwan. When Malhin saw the message Zamir had written, he reminded him of the Night of the Ducks of 1959, as if Zamir needed reminding, and what happened to those responsible. But Malhin, too, was convinced that war was coming: A few hours before war started, he called his wife in the Afeka neighborhood of Tel Aviv, and told her to find a neighbor's house with a bomb shelter where she could take cover. Their own house didn't have one.

Zamir called Freddy Eini. By 1973, direct dial had been introduced between London and Israel, and there was no need for an international operator. It was now close to 3:00 a.m., exactly twenty-four hours after Eini had called Zamir to tell him that the Angel wanted an urgent meeting in London to talk about chemicals. It was extremely important to Zamir that Eini now understand every word he said, and that he move as quickly as possible to implement what was included in the message. When Eini answered, Zamir first told him, "Put your feet in cold water"—that is, be wide awake, right now. Once Eini had assured him he was fully alert, Zamir dictated to him the message as he had written it down. It read as follows, in full:

> The company, it turns out, intends to sign the contract today before nightfall.
>
> It is the same contract, with the same conditions with which we are familiar.
>
> They know that tomorrow is a holiday.
>
> They think they can land tomorrow before dark.
>
> I spoke with the manager, but he cannot put it off because of his commitment to other managers, and he wants to keep his commitment.
>
> I'll update you on all the conditions of the contract.
>
> Because they want to win the race, they are very afraid that it will be made public before the signing, for there may be competitors, and then some of the shareholders will think twice.
>
> They have no partners outside the region.
>
> In the Angel's opinion, the chances of signing are 99.9 percent, but then again, he is like that.[12]

Meanwhile Dubi prepared a communiqué about the meeting. When he was done, he went to the Israeli embassy at Palace Green in central London in order to send it via the code room. According to some accounts, because of Yom Kippur no one was on duty in the code room, and they had to wait for someone to show up. In truth, however, the station chief was there waiting for him, and the report was sent to Mossad headquarters in Tel Aviv during the early morning hours. The communiqué repeated Zamir's alert that war would commence later that day and added that the source had said that Sadat might change his mind at the last minute. Beyond this, the main message was that the Egyptian war objective was limited only to capturing territory up to six miles east of the Suez Canal, and that at this stage there was no intention to advance to the Mitla and Gidi Passes.

DUBI WENT BACK to his apartment. His wife, Ronit, was waiting. She was used to his unpredictable schedule, but his long absence in the middle of the night of Yom Kippur was unusual even for him, and it suggested something serious. She didn't have to ask many questions. With her, he could be explicit. "It's war. The bar mitzvah's off."

Their son Ofer had come of age, and his bar mitzvah celebration, which was supposed to take place soon after, was one of Israel's first, if least painful, casualties in the conflict that would begin in just a few hours. Later that morning, utterly exhausted, Dubi finally went to bed.

Ronit woke him shortly after 1:00 p.m. The war had begun.

Zamir, on the other hand, hadn't gotten any sleep at all. From the moment he'd finished his phone call with Eini, he had been overwhelmed with tension. When he heard that the Egyptians had attacked at 2:00 p.m. Israel time, he "leapt through the roof," he later recalled. In part, his relief was because he was confident that Israel would achieve an easy victory. But mainly it was because he could breathe easy now that his warning hadn't proved false. He stayed in London until Sunday, when he flew to Cyprus, and then was taken back to Israel by an airplane sent specially for him. He knew nothing about how the war was going and remained convinced that his message had allowed the Israelis a proper response. Only when he met Nahum Admoni, a senior Mossad officer who came to meet him at the airport, did he discover just how wrong he was.

Chapter 10

DOVECOTE: WARNING AND WAR

Freddy Eini didn't need coffee to get him going after hanging up with Zamir. He quickly began going down the list of calls he needed to make. As he'd promised the night before, the first was to the MI chief, Eli Zeira. Because MI was the central clearinghouse for all intelligence gathered by Israel's different branches, it made sense that its director should be the first to receive the message. Zeira listened carefully and told Eini to immediately call the head of MI-Research, Brig. Gen. Arieh Shalev, and to read it to him word for word. Before doing that, however, Eini continued down the list. He called Golda Meir's military secretary, Israel Lior, as well as the assistant to the defense minister, Arieh Braun. Then he called Arieh Shalev, as Zeira had told him. Years later, Eini would recall how Shalev, who was none too pleased about being woken up, told him to refer it to MI's reporting and dissemination center, and they'd take care of it. Clearly the head of MI-Research still hadn't recognized the magnitude of the crisis. After a brief and, from Eini's perspective, rather aggressive exchange, Shalev got the picture and wrote down the message that Eini dictated to him.

The IDF chief of staff was not on Eini's list. Instead he got the message from his aide-de camp, Avner Shalev, who had heard it from

Brig. Gen.Yehoshua Raviv, the defense minister's military secretary. Both Dayan and Lior called Eini back to hear the message a second time. By 4:30 a.m. on Saturday, the entire decision-making echelon of the Israeli government was wide awake and getting ready for an attack they expected to come the following evening.[1]

TO WHAT EXTENT did Ashraf Marwan's warning, the clearest warning of war that Israel ever received ahead of time, really succeed in dispelling the paradigm according to which Egypt would never launch a war so long as it didn't have long-range warplanes and operational Scud missiles? This is not merely an academic question. As the events of that day unfolded, every main player acted strictly according to his or her own view about how seriously to take the Angel's warning—sometimes even to the point of ignoring direct orders.

Beginning early in the morning of October 6, key Israeli decision makers and their aides held intensive meetings in the respective headquarters of the IDF chief of staff, the defense minister, and the prime minister—three buildings located just a few yards apart from each other at the defense complex in Tel Aviv known to Israelis as "The Campus" (hakirya). Two questions dominated their discussions. The first concerned an emergency call-up of reserves; the second was about a preemptive strike to be launched by Israel's air force, in order to keep the military initiative in Israel's hands, just as had happened so successfully with the start of the Six-Day War in 1967.

As far as IDF chief of staff David Elazar was concerned, Marwan's warning removed all doubt about war. From the moment his assistant woke him up at four thirty that morning, Elazar prepared for a conflagration that was to begin later that day. Within an hour and a half, he ordered the commander of the air force to ready a preemptive strike to be launched at 11:00 a.m., approved a partial call-up of reserves for the air force, made the necessary preparations for a broader call-up of army reserves, and ordered further preparations for war, both at the front lines and on the home front. At 6:00 a.m., he walked into his first meeting, with Defense Minister Moshe Dayan. There he made his case for approval of what he saw as two absolutely critical moves under the circumstances: a preemptive strike and a mass call-up of reserves.

Elazar, however, ran headlong into the skepticism of Dayan regarding the validity of Marwan's warning and the likelihood of war. As opposed to Elazar's fast pace of action, Dayan insisted on taking things more slowly. When their meeting began, Dayan first addressed less pressing matters, such as the evacuation of children (in the form of a "field trip") from the civilian settlements on the Golan Heights, and the Civil Defense Corps' preparations for the possibility of Egyptian Scud missile attacks. Only afterward did he turn to Elazar's two requests. He flatly turned down the preemptive strike and agreed to only a very limited call-up of a single reserve brigade to reinforce the northern front. The back-and-forth between him and Elazar, who demanded that at least four divisions be called up, reminded one of the people present in the meeting of the bargaining session between God and Abraham on the question of how many righteous people God would need to find in Sodom and Gomorrah to refrain from destroying the cities. In the end, Elazar and Dayan couldn't bridge the gap, and they agreed to let the prime minister decide.

Why did Dayan rebuff Elazar's requests? The reasons he gave were telling. He rejected a preemptive strike, he said, because "on the basis of the information we have right now, we cannot do it." In other words, what distinguished Dayan from Elazar wasn't the question of whether such a strike was necessary to thwart the Arab attack but whether that attack was actually coming or not. Elazar had concluded that war was a sure thing, and a preemptive strike

was therefore unavoidable. Dayan saw it as just one of many possibilities, so he opposed the strike. The same was true for calling up
the reserves. Dayan was a very cautious man, and he didn't believe
Israel could win a war with the standing army alone. Rather, his
denial of Elazar's request came from his assessment that the likelihood of war was still too low to justify a broad call-up. "You can't
call up the whole system," he told him, "just because of a few messages from Zvika."[2]

Dayan's skepticism about the war was based in part, apparently,
on the assessments of Eli Zeira. Zeira joined the meeting at 7:00
a.m. and reported that, despite further indicators that Egypt and
Syria were headed for a military initiative, he was still not prepared to accept that war was likely and added that from a strategic-
political standpoint, Sadat had no need for it. About fifteen minutes
later, at the beginning of a hastily assembled meeting of the IDF
General Staff, Zeira restated his thesis that starting a war would
be irrational for the Egyptians and Syrians, even though their
deployments justified the IDF's taking measures of its own. And
in the meeting with the prime minister that began just after 8:00
a.m., Zeira reiterated his belief that even though Egypt and Syria
were ready for war from a technical and operational standpoint,
Sadat had no compulsion to launch an attack and knew that if he
did attack, he would lose.

From all these statements it emerges that despite the fact that
Marwan's warning (as well as additional developments) may have
led him to raise his assessment about the likelihood of war to some
degree, the MI chief still clung to the same set of beliefs that he
had held since taking his post a year earlier, and continued to doubt
whether there would be a war that day. In this he was relying, in
part, on the contribution of the head of Branch 6 (Egypt) of MI's
Research Division, Lt. Col. Yonah Bandman, on whose expertise
and judgment regarding Egyptian intentions Zeira continued to
rely until the very last minute. In the late morning of that day,

Bandman believed that the Egyptians saw no reason to go to war, and even refused an order from the chief of MI-Research to prepare a report saying that the likelihood of war was high. In the end, that report was prepared by another officer, while Bandman wrote a dissenting report of his own, explaining why war was unlikely. Zeira, who received Bandman's report, considered having it distributed as well, but in the end chose not to. The very fact that he considered it, however, shows that in spite of everything, he still thought that war that day was far from certain.[3]

Elazar, on the other hand, took the Mossad chief's warning at face value. In his view, there was no time to waste. At about 7:45 a.m., after conducting the meeting of the IDF General Staff, he spoke for a few minutes, privately, with the commanders of the Southern and Northern Commands, Maj. Gen. Shmuel Gonen and Maj. Gen. Yitzhak Hofi, respectively. He ordered them both to ready their officers for a war that would begin later that day.

For her part, Prime Minister Golda Meir was not buying either Zeira's or Dayan's hesitation. Like Elazar, she expressed her complete faith in Zamir's message about his meeting with Marwan, and saw the question of war coming that day as a closed one. After arriving at her office in IDF headquarters in Tel Aviv, she asked to see the defense minister immediately. At first he refused to meet her before 10:00 or 11:00 that morning, and only agreed to meet earlier after she insisted.

The meeting in Golda Meir's office began just after 8:00 a.m. Elazar and Dayan each presented their positions. Again Dayan dawdled, raising issues of civilian evacuations and home-front preparations. Elazar, on the other hand, did not mince words about the possibility of war. "I read the message from Zvika [Zamir]'s man," he said. "The message is authentic. For us, this is very short notice."[4] He demanded that immediate and decisive moves be made.

Meir was quick to make her decision. She accepted Dayan's

position rejecting the proposed preemptive strike, out of fear that the world, and especially the United States, would see Israel as the aggressor. This, she believed, would make it harder for the United States to help Israel during the conflict, a significant loss that would outweigh any tactical gains.

On the matter of calling up the reserves, on the other hand, Meir accepted Elazar's position. According to the minutes of that meeting, she did not mention Ashraf Marwan explicitly, but in the days that followed, she said several times that her assessment had been based on the message from "Zvika's friend."[5]

By 9:00 a.m., the first order went out. By 10:00 a.m., phones were ringing in the homes of thousands of reservists. The call-up would gain momentum over the next few hours.

ONE MIGHT THINK that Zeira's opinion became moot as soon as the broad call-up of reserves had begun. But a careful look at the transcripts of the Agranat Commission's hearings, as well as other sources, suggests that in one immensely important matter—namely, the deployment of the regular army forces at the Suez Canal—his mistake had deadly and decisive consequences.

The IDF's regular-army tank division in the Sinai, the 252nd Armored, was caught unprepared when the assault came at 2:00 p.m. Only one tank squad, which was regularly stationed at Fort Orkal at the northern reaches of the canal, was at battle stations. The other tanks of the front-line 14th Brigade were in various stages of preparing to deploy for battle, while the other two tank brigades, the 401st and 406th, were heading to their forward meeting points.

The division had been on high alert since the day before, and its commander, Maj. Gen. Albert Mandler, believed, on the basis of the intelligence available to him, that war was likely. If he had been given the order to prepare for battle immediately after Elazar had given it to his commander, Southern Commander Maj. Gen.

Gonen, Mandler would have gotten his tanks into position opposite the Egyptian crossing points in time. Just how much this
would have changed the outcome on the Suez front is a matter for
speculation, but there is no doubt that it would have been vastly
preferable, from the Israeli standpoint, to what actually ended up
happening, which was that almost all of the Israeli tanks engaged
the fight while they were rushing to the front, and reached the
canal only after the Egyptians had already crossed and set themselves up on the eastern bank.

In the first phase of the crossing, 32,000 Egyptian infantrymen
were ferried in 720 boats, each one making twelve round-trips
across the canal over a six-hour period. The result of the 252nd Armored's tanks not being in position was that the Egyptians crossing
the canal met with no Israeli tank fire or any serious and concerted
counterattack.

Elazar gave the order to Maj. Gen. Gonen to prepare for war
that day, with the assumption of a 6:00 p.m. H-hour. The order
was given at 7:45 a.m. About twenty minutes later, Gonen called
Mandler, the commander of the 252nd, and ordered him to prepare
to carry out a plan called Dovecote, which would allow him to
defend the line at the canal using regular-army forces, but not to
move the forces from their positions. After 10:00 a.m., he spoke
to Mandler again. In direct violation of Elazar's orders, according
to which Gonen was supposed to prepare his forces for a war that
would begin at 6:00 p.m., Gonen said to Mandler: "What does [the
H-hour] mean? Is it the end of their big exercise? Opening fire?
Relaunching the War of Attrition? Maybe a full-scale invasion—
but that seems unlikely." In other words, Gonen scuttled Elazar's
order, leaving the forces in the field with a mixed message as to
what, exactly, they were preparing for. Even worse, Elazar's orders
spoke of getting the entire Southern Command ready for war that
very day, while Gonen ordered the brigades of the front line "not

to break routine before 1600 hours." The result was that when the attack was launched at 2:00 p.m., out of the division's three hundred tanks only three, at Fort Orkal, were in position.[6]

The Egyptian forces therefore crossed the canal virtually untouched. One exception was at Fort Budapest, where two tanks that were supposed to defend it reached their posts just minutes before the Egyptians launched their ground assault. They managed to destroy the Egyptian tanks and armored personnel carriers that were preparing to storm the fort, dispersed the troops arrayed to attack, and prevented the fort from being overrun.[7]

Because of the failure to implement the Dovecote plan, the Egyptians were able to carry out the most critical part of their assault, crossing the canal, with virtually no opposition or casualties. When the Israeli tanks approached their "swim fins," forward positions from which they were supposed to launch raids north or south along the canal to intercept Egyptian forces crossing as well as those still on the western bank, they discovered that many of these positions had already been taken by Egyptian commandos, who assaulted the tanks with antitank missiles. Scores of Israeli tanks were taken out during the night, as they tried to redouble the fortresses that were already surrounded by Egyptian troops. The final outcome of the initial battles was that by dawn on Sunday, Egypt had managed to cross the canal and establish itself on its eastern bank with almost no losses, while the 252nd Armored Division of the IDF lost fully two hundred of its three hundred tanks without having achieved any of its operational goals.

It was the IDF's worst military defeat since the failed attempts to occupy the Latrun police station during the battles of Israel's War of Independence in 1948. But as opposed to 1948, now the IDF had superior weaponry and training to that of its enemy. And its soldiers' morale was certainly no lower than it had been among the fighters in 1948. In 1973, the IDF's failures were entirely a failure of understanding, of intelligence, that prevented the IDF from recognizing the threat and preparing for it in the days before the attack, and specifically the confused and mistaken orders of Maj. Gen. Gonen in the hours before the battle.

How can we understand Gonen's behavior? How did a general reputed to be the biggest stickler for authority in the entire IDF fumble the chief of staff's explicit orders? Gonen later testified that he was thrown off by the assessment that the chief of Military Intelligence, Eli Zeira, had given him in the hallway before the meeting of the General Staff that morning—before Elazar had ordered him to prepare for war. Zeira had "explained that he still didn't think there would be a war, and that moving IDF troops could actually cause one."[8] From Gonen's words to Mandler at 10:00 a.m., moreover, we get a strong echo of Zeira's comments from the General Staff meeting on Friday, when he said that if the Egyptians did anything at all, it would be "either a [minimal] exchange of fire, or some kind of helicopter assault . . . least likely is an exercise to cross with the aim of capturing both banks of the canal."

From the wealth of evidence, it appears that the catastrophic situation that developed at the Suez Canal during the first day of the Yom Kippur War, and which had far-reaching consequences for both the battle on the Golan Heights and the bungling of the IAF's efforts to take out antiaircraft positions on both fronts, was the direct result of Zeira's insistence on clinging to the old paradigm even after all evidence suggested it should be abandoned. And since Gonen preferred to act in light of the assessments of the head of Military Intelligence rather than just follow the orders of the chief of staff, those seven hours that, because of the warning of Ashraf Marwan, could have allowed him to properly deploy the tanks of the 252nd Armored Division were wasted.

ALTHOUGH THOSE PRECIOUS hours were wasted in terms of rebuffing the initial assault on the Suez Canal, there is no doubt today that Ashraf Marwan's timely warning, and the emergency call-up of reserves that resulted, nonetheless prevented Israel from facing a far worse situation on the battlefield. This was felt most obviously on the Syrian front.

By midday on Sunday, October 7, less than twenty-four hours into the fighting, the Syrians were on their way to routing the IDF on the Golan Heights. The limited defensive line in the southern Golan held by the IDF's 188th Armored Brigade had collapsed the evening before, and during the night the full strength of the Syrian 5th and 9th Infantry Divisions had taken over the entire southern Golan. In the morning, Col. Tawfik al-Jahani, commander of the Syrian 1st Armored Division, gave the order to advance toward Nafah Junction, where the IDF's 36th Armored Division was head-quartered. If the Syrians could take Nafah, that would give them control over the whole central Golan and allow them to cut off the IDF's 7th Armored Brigade, which was defending the Golan's northeast. Moreover, taking Nafah meant that Syrian tanks could then make their way west, toward the Bnot Yaakov Bridge, where they could straddle the sources of the Jordan River and prevent IDF reservists from reaching the Golan.

Conquering Nafah, in other words, meant conquering the entire Golan Heights. Once taken, it would be difficult, if not impossible, for the Israelis to get it back.

At 11:00 a.m., following Al-Jahani's order, 250 Syrian T-55 and T-62 tanks made their way in two columns toward Nafah. At this point, Israeli commanders still had no idea what was happening on the ground. The battlefield chaos had prevented the officers in the IDF command center on Mount Canaan, responsible for running the show in the north, from realizing that the defensive line in the southern Golan had broken. Now that they knew it, they were still under the false belief that the Syrians would use their success to move directly west, toward the Sea of Galilee, when in fact they were heading north toward Nafah Junction. The fact that some initial reserve units had, since the early morning hours, managed to keep a hold on the roads leading directly west toward the Sea of Galilee had given the officers of the Northern Command a false sense of hope. The chief of the Northern Command, who hadn't slept in over forty-eight hours, allowed himself to believe that the worst was behind him. Now that reserve forces were entering the war, the tide of battle would turn in the IDF's favor.

Two hours later, when he finally understood what was happening, the general's optimism was replaced by a sense of foreboding and failure. At 1:10 p.m. on Sunday, the following note was made in the records of the Northern Command: "Syrian tanks at the perimeter of Nafah Base."

AT 1:30 P.M., Brig. Gen. Rafael Eitan, commander of the IDF 36th Armored Division defending the Golan Heights, left his bunker at the Nafah base, taking his staff with him. Under Syrian fire, they headed north to Tel Shiban. Within twenty minutes, the last soldiers defending the base were ordered to clear out as well. Crammed into two half-tracks, they headed west to the Bnot Yaakov Bridge. The base was abandoned, with only a few IDF tanks remaining in the area to try to keep it from being completely overrun. Most of them were hit within thirty minutes.

In the "Palace," the code name for the command center at Mount Canaan, it became clear now that only a miracle could save the Nafah Junction. All eyes turned to the 679th Armored Brigade, a unit of reservists under the 36th Division. The fate of the Golan Heights was in their hands.

THE CALL-UP OF the reservists of the 679th Brigade had begun at 10:00 a.m. the day before, on orders from its commander, Col. Ori Orr. The tanks were old British-made Centurions. They ran on unreliable gasoline engines that turned every tank into a potential firetrap, and their poorly designed transmissions failed repeatedly. Of the hundred or so tanks kept in emergency storage at the Yiftah base near Rosh Pina, fewer than fifty ended up making it into battle. Of the rest, some broke down before reaching the front, some never made it out of the base, and others were taken out by Syrian fire. And those that did make it to battle were not in any shape to fight. Because of the pressure of time, they were manned by teams that weren't the original ones assigned to each tank, but instead had been cobbled together according to the order in which the soldiers had shown up for duty. They were low on ammunition because there hadn't been enough time to load the shells that had to be brought from another camp. Much of their communications equipment either didn't work at all or hadn't been calibrated to the right frequency, and many of the tanks didn't even have time to adjust their sights, the minimal preparation for shooting straight. But thirteen hours after the war started, at about 3:00 a.m., a twenty-five-tank force of Brigade 679 started making its way up the Golan under cover of darkness. They took a position at around 10:00 a.m. in the Quneitra area, along the eastern border of the northern Golan. This was a mistake, since the Syrian armored fist was thrusting up the middle of the Golan, toward Nafah from the south.

By 10:30 a.m., another force of twenty-two tanks organized themselves and set out to the front. At around noon, when they were a mile south of Nafah Junction, they got an order to turn south toward Hushniya. Half an hour later, they encountered dozens of Syrian T-62 tanks from the 91st Brigade that were planning on going around Nafah and attacking it from the north. The Israeli tanks were caught by surprise, but within a few minutes they returned fire. Thus began one of the most important battles of the war.

Despite taking heavy losses, the Israeli tanks managed to slow the advance of the Syrians northward. But the latter nonetheless circumvented Nafah from the east. At the same time, Syrian tanks of another brigade entered the abandoned base from the south. The pressure from the Syrian tanks increased from minute to minute.

At this critical moment, three tanks from the IDF's 679th Armored Brigade, the very last tanks to leave Yiftah, reached the outskirts of the base at Nafah. There they saw ten Syrian tanks about 900 yards away, and started taking them out. Soon after, about fifteen of the IDF reservist tanks that had been mistakenly sent to Quneitra finally reached Nafah and began attacking some of the tanks of the Syrian 91st. At the same time, additional smaller reserve IDF units began putting pressure on the Syrian 51st. The number of disabled Syrian tanks grew steadily, as did the Israeli counterpressure. By about 4:00 p.m., the Israelis had gained significant momentum, which continued until the battle drew to a close at nightfall. The exhausted IDF reservists, mostly tank teams from the 679th Brigade who, twenty-four hours earlier, had been fasting and praying in their synagogues, managed to turn the tide of the battle. The Syrians lost about forty tanks and were forced to pull back from the Nafah base and its surroundings, including the crucial road from the Bnot Yaakov Bridge to Quneitra. The next day, the Syrians tried taking the central Golan Heights a second time. Again they failed, and the IDF readied a massive counterattack.

The battle for the Golan Heights had been decided in Israel's favor.

DESPITE THE MANY EFFORTS by historians and retired officers to reconstruct the battles of the first days of the Yom Kippur War, one question that has rarely been asked is this: What would have happened if the order to call up reserves had come not at 10:00 a.m. on Saturday but had waited until the war was launched four hours later, at 2:00 p.m.? What, in other words, if Ashraf Marwan hadn't warned Zvi Zamir about the war, if Zamir hadn't then gotten Freddy Eini to rouse everyone from bed, if the decision makers hadn't awoken at 4:30 a.m. and started meetings at 6:00 a.m., culminating in the prime minister's approval at 9:40 a.m., over the objections of her defense minister, of the full-scale call-up of the entire reserve force of the IDF?

The commander of the 679th Armored Brigade, Ori Orr, got his orders from the chief of the 36th Armored Division at 10:00 a.m. Later on, Orr would become the IDF Northern Commander and, after leaving the IDF, deputy defense minister of Israel. In his estimation, without Marwan's warning, the delay in Israel's ability to field any reserve units would have been a minimum of four to six hours. Nafah Junction, as well as the command camp of the 36th Armored Division at Nafah, would have fallen basically without a fight. It is highly likely, moreover, that by the afternoon of Sunday, October 7, the Syrians would have fully encircled and cut off the 7th Armored Brigade, which was positioned in the northeastern Golan. Other scholars have come to the same conclusion.

In retrospect, Ashraf Marwan was single-handedly responsible for enabling Israel to prevent the Syrian conquest of the Golan Heights in the Yom Kippur War. Retaking the Golan afterward would have required not only a prolonged and grisly battle but also redirecting major forces from the Egyptian front, increasing the likelihood of a more aggressive Egyptian push in the south. Israel would have sustained not only far more casualties than it did, but also a greater loss of territory by the time a cease-fire was called. On the northern front, at least, the "draw" at the end of the war would have looked a lot more like an Israeli defeat.

BEYOND THE DECISIVE impact of Marwan's warning on the battle for the Golan Heights, however, there were also two additional, crucial moments where Israel took huge advantage of the Angel's help.

In the first minutes of war, Egyptian Tupolev Tu-16 "Badger" bombers flying out of the southwest launched two air-to-ground Kelt missiles in the direction of Tel Aviv. According to the Egyptian war plans, these missiles were aimed directly at IDF headquarters, as a warning to the Israelis to refrain from attacking deep in Egyptian territory, as they had done during the War of Attrition. A pair of Israeli Mirage fighters had been scrambled from the air force base in Hatzor, in what was apparently the first sortie of the war, to patrol the Mediterranean near Ashkelon, southwest of Tel Aviv. At a certain point they received instructions to turn west— straight for the Egyptian bombers. When they approached, they saw the flames of the launching missiles. Maj. Eitan Karmi, who flew the lead plane, was ordered to go after the missiles rather than the bombers. One of the missiles, apparently, dropped into the sea. The other was taken out by Karmi's cannon and plunged into the water just off the coast of Tel Aviv. The plume of water that billowed up after the missile exploded was huge.[9]

The Egyptian war plans, delivered by Marwan, had explicitly revealed the intention to launch such missiles on Tel Aviv. Without that information, the second missile, carrying a one-ton ordnance, would likely have landed in central Tel Aviv. The effect of such a strike, both on the morale of the Israeli populace and on the way the conflict developed, would have been significant.

The other event concerns the fighting along the southern front in the days that followed the first day of war. Although the Israelis failed to take advantage of Marwan's warning during the opening hours of fighting in Sinai, the importance of his information would soon become clear. Military Intelligence had sent out, just a few minutes before the war began, a report that clarified, on the basis of Marwan's report from the night before, that in the first phase

Egypt did not intend to move its armored divisions across the canal
or to go for the Mitla and Gidi Passes. This was a confirmation of
intelligence he had passed along a few weeks before.

Yet from the moment that the attack was launched, the officers
of MI-Research ignored this crucial bit of information and went
back to assuming the war plans that they knew best, namely, that
the Egyptians planned on moving their two armored divisions,
and not just the five infantry divisions, across the canal; and that
their operational goal was the capture of the Mitla and Gidi Passes.
Stunned by the assault and by the initial results on the ground,
their intelligence assessments became hurried and confused. Over-
confidence was replaced with something close to panic. Thus, on
the basis of just one or two data points, MI mistakenly reported
to the IDF chief of staff a few hours into the fighting that the
Egyptian 4th and 21st Armored Divisions "have crossed and are
crossing" the Suez Canal. An MI compilation that went out at 1:30
a.m., nearly twelve hours into the war, included among the enemy's achievements the advance of the two armored divisions across
the bridges.[10] Only on the morning of Sunday, October 7, did MI
correct its assertion that the divisions had crossed, but it still continued to ignore consistently the updated war plan that Marwan
had passed along and assessed the enemy's moves according to the
older, outdated plan.

The intelligence unit of the Southern Command estimated at
around midday Sunday that the Egyptian intention was to move
the 4th Armored, as well as additional armored forces, eastward,
in order to launch the attack deeper into Sinai. The fear of such
an attack was the main reason why the defense minister proposed
withdrawing from the line that the IDF had held the morning of
October 7, and moving it farther back. According to Gonen's testimony, Dayan told him when they met in the war room at Um
Hashiba during the late morning that day: "This is not a local

battle, it is a war for the Land of Israel. Leave the forts, withdraw into the mountains."[11] Fortunately for Israel, Dayan's proposals to withdraw some twenty-five to thirty miles eastward were rejected by the chief of staff and the prime minister.

With the swift arrival of reserve forces during the afternoon of the second day of war, the question of withdrawing came off the table. Yet the damage caused by the incorrect use of outdated intelligence was far from over. One of the main factors in deciding whether to launch a quick counterattack was the fear that Egypt was about to send its armored divisions eastward. If they crossed the canal, it would be much harder for the IDF to recover lost territory. There were surely other considerations as well, such as the desire to save soldiers who were still stuck in forts along the canal. But if MI had recognized that the Egyptians' plan was to hold on to territory east of the canal without launching armored attacks into the Sinai, the IDF's one regular-army and two reserve divisions would have had time to organize themselves properly for a more effective counterattack. It is hard to say what the outcome would have been, but clearly it would have been better planned, the forces being given enough time to learn the battle plans and prepare to attack, and the chances of success would have been higher.

This didn't happen, however, and the counterattack of October 8 was the greatest failure of any ground assault in the whole war.

IT WAS IN the late hours of October 7 that Zvi Zamir reached Israel on a special flight from Cyprus. He rejoined the group of key decision makers in Golda Meir's office in Tel Aviv. Thoroughly familiar with the updated war plans that Marwan had passed along, Zamir saw that Egypt was, indeed, following them. He made this clear in a meeting that took place that night in the prime minister's office. When asked for his opinion about the counterattack that was being planned for the next day, he said that "the Egyptians are waiting for precisely this kind of retaliation from us." In another meeting the next day of the same forum, when the scale of the failure of the counterattack had become clear, Zamir repeated that "we know the Egyptian plan," and that the Egyptians were waiting for an IDF counterattack, in order to defeat it using infantry armed with antitank weapons. Therefore, he added, "if we continue to insist on fighting for the canal, the situation will be bad."[12]

Two days later, just before Maj. Gen. Chaim Bar-Lev was sent south to take his post as the new commander of the Suez front, Zamir met him and explained every detail of the Egyptian battle plan. He also gave Bar-Lev a telexed printout of the plan, so that he could read it on the helicopter ride to command headquarters at Um Hashiba. Zamir made Bar-Lev swear to destroy the document out of concern for the well-being of its source.[13] Bar-Lev read the plan carefully. From this moment on, the Southern Command began referencing it heavily. It was one reason why, from that point forward, Israel saw major improvements along its southern front.

Any fair analysis of the information Marwan provided will compel the conclusion that his contribution to Israel's conduct of the war was, in the end, decisive. If not for the chaos that characterized the first days of the war, at every level of decision making and along every front of battle, Israel would have taken advantage of that information to far greater effect and the IDF would have fared much better on the battlefield. Most important, however, was the warning that he gave about the start of war itself. It was the single piece of information that resulted in the call-up of reserves four hours before the attack—without which the Golan Heights would certainly have fallen.

After the war was over, the chief of the Mossad gave the order to pay the Angel a sum of $100,000 as a bonus in reward for that warning. It had been worth every penny.

Chapter 11

THE RISE AND FALL OF
ASHRAF MARWAN

If Egyptian intelligence had any inkling that Israeli spies had penetrated their deepest secrets before the war, the opening days of battle would have laid such fears to rest. Nobody could have guessed that Israel had seen the attack plans in advance. From Israel's perspective, the only good thing about the debacle was that now the Mossad didn't need to worry about the immediate safety of its agents in Egypt.

Ashraf Marwan returned to Egypt on October 6, the day the war began. Sadat, who ran the initial phases of the war from the Center 10 bunker, was far too busy running the war and managing ongoing relationships with Syria, the Soviet Union, and the United States to spend time with his special liaison for Libyan and Saudi affairs. The two barely saw each other.

This fact, of course, does not sit well with certain people, especially members of Marwan's family who, to this day, insist that not only was he a double agent but that he and Sadat together concocted the whole plan to deceive Israel. In their telling, Sadat actually spent much of the war in Marwan's home—for that was the only place he knew he would be safe from Israeli shelling.

The truth was far less dramatic.

Ashraf Marwan spent most of the war carrying out his duties as Sadat's liaison. There was a constant need to coordinate diplomatic positions with various Arab powers, and Marwan began traveling to Arab capitals soon after returning to Cairo, carrying written and oral messages from the Egyptian president—whose prominence had suddenly risen dramatically, both in the Arab world and elsewhere, because of his unexpected battlefield successes. Marwan met with other world leaders, as well: On October 13 and 14, during the war's critical phase, when Sadat was under tremendous pressure to launch a land assault into Sinai in order to take pressure off the Syrians on the northern front, Marwan went to Yugoslavia, where he handed a letter to Yugoslav president Josip Broz Tito and met with the country's vice president and foreign minister, Miloš Minić.[1]

Given everything we know about both Marwan's itinerary at the time and his method of operation, he could not have been the source of the most important piece of intelligence to reach the Mossad after the war began. On October 12, an antenna positioned atop Mossad headquarters in Tel Aviv picked up a signal from a source in Egypt saying that the Egyptian army was preparing a land assault in Sinai. Zamir's chief of staff, Freddy Eini, passed it directly to Zamir, who at that moment was sitting with the prime minister in one of the most dramatic cabinet meetings of the war.

Since the failure of the IDF counteroffensive four days earlier, no attempt had been made to get the Egyptian army out of the strip of about six miles along the canal, which it occupied at the beginning of the war. The IDF focused its efforts on the northern front, where it reoccupied most of the Golan Heights and started advancing toward Damascus. On October 11, the outskirts of the Syrian capital, including its international airport, were within range of Israeli artillery. Now Israel's leaders turned their attention to Egypt. The discussion started on the morning of October 12.

The chief of staff made his position clear: At present the IDF could not reoccupy the territory that was lost in the Sinai. The Soviets had been supplying arms to Egypt and Syria since the second day of the war while the Americans still refrained from shipping arms to Israel; hence, the balance of forces continued to favor the Arabs. The only development that could change the war situation was if Egypt initiated a second offensive in the Sinai. The chief of staff assured his listeners that if this happened, the IDF would repulse the attack, cause heavy losses to the Egyptian army, and use this momentum to cross the Suez Canal and cut off the Egyptian force of 100,000 soldiers in the Sinai from its logistical bases west of the canal. But without a renewed Egyptian offensive Israel would have to demand a cease-fire in place, that is, to admit its defeat in the war with Egypt. At this critical point, while Golda Meir, Moshe Dayan, and senior army generals debated the situation, Zamir was called out of the meeting to get the message from Eini.

When Zamir came back, he announced the news—and the mood suddenly shifted. The IDF chief of staff, David Elazar, said that he no longer favored a cease-fire. Now, he said, Israel should wait for the new assault, rebuff it, and then take advantage of the moment to mount a counteroffensive that would change the entire war. His proposal was approved.

The Egyptian assault began on October 14. This time, the IDF was fully prepared, devastating the attacking forces, handing Sadat his biggest blunder of the war. More than two hundred Egyptian tanks were destroyed, and the Israelis lost only fifteen. Just as Elazar had predicted, it opened the door for a shift in momentum. Within a week, IDF forces crossed the Suez Canal and advanced westward to Cairo, leaving Egypt's entire Third Army stranded in the Sinai desert.[2]

At this stage, however, Sadat showed no readiness to end the war. To the contrary. On October 16 he gave a defiant speech in the Egyptian Parliament and defined the road ahead as "a long, protracted war . . . a war of attrition." He also threatened to hit Israel's hinterland with missiles if Israel attacked Egypt's vulnerable heartland. On the basis of this speech, as well as intelligence the Israelis had gathered, Zamir told Golda Meir on October 18 that both Egypt and Syria intended to keep on fighting. These reports were bad news for Golda and her colleagues. Even though the IDF had gained the upper hand, the Israeli war machine was exhausted and needed a cease-fire as soon as possible. It was agreed that more information about Sadat's intentions was needed. Only one source could provide it. Dubi was instructed to arrange a meeting with the Angel and Zamir left Israel to meet him.

The meeting took place a day later in Paris. During its first part, Zamir had to calm down Marwan, who was highly frustrated by the fact that his warning on the eve of the war had not been immediately heeded by the Israelis. Then he described the way Sadat and his advisers viewed the situation when he left Egypt on October 17. In Marwan's view, they still believed Egypt was winning. Since the USSR started shipping arms to Egypt shortly after hostilities began, and since Egyptian losses were minimal, they now had more tanks than at the beginning of the war. By his account, the Egyptian army lost only 130 tanks in the battle of October 14, far fewer than the Israelis' estimate. Accordingly, he told Zamir, Sadat intended to prolong the war for at least a few months and would reject any cease-fire at this stage. He aimed to bleed Israel as much as possible, for as long as possible. Therefore, even if the IDF approached Cairo and Alexandria, the Egyptians would keep on fighting. Soldiers armed with antitank Sagger missiles would wait for Israeli tanks behind every bush.

Marwan also spoke about Sadat's missile threat, which worried both Golda and Dayan. He estimated that Egypt had four hundred missiles capable of reaching Israel. Again, this was much higher than the Israeli estimate of about two dozen Egyptian Scuds. Toward the end of the meeting, Zamir and his spy talked about how to get Sadat to agree to a cease-fire.[3]

Zamir reported to Golda the next day. By then, in both the military and diplomatic theaters the situation had started to change dramatically. Concerned about Israel's crossing of the Suez as well as the difficult situation of the Syrians, the Kremlin was now pressuring Sadat to accept a cease-fire. Prime Minister Alexei Kosygin landed in Cairo and briefed Sadat about the deteriorating situation on the Canal front. Nevertheless, when he headed back to Moscow on October 19, Sadat still refused to accept a cease-fire.[4] Indeed, at this stage the information that Marwan had given Zamir genuinely reflected Sadat's line of thinking. But as the IDF continued advancing into Egypt's heartland and emergency meetings were held between Secretary of State Henry Kissinger and Soviet leaders in the Kremlin, the superpowers agreed on an immediate cease-fire in place. Sadat had little choice but to accept it officially on October 21. This Israeli checkmate essentially ended the war. In the south, the Egyptian army held most of the territory it occupied at the beginning of the war, but half of it, the Third Army at the southern sector of the front, was cut off by the IDF, which now stood just sixty-three miles from Cairo. In the north, Israel regained all the territory it had lost at the beginning of the war and occupied additional Syrian territory that allowed the IDF to threaten Damascus. But Israel paid dearly for these military achievements. More than 2,500 Israeli soldiers were killed and 5,600 were wounded. This would have been proportional to a loss of more than 160,000 soldiers killed and more than 360,000 wounded in the United States in 1973. And the Israeli economy would have to recover from the shock of the unexpected war—which could hardly even begin as long as hundreds of thousands of reserve soldiers, the core of the country's workforce, were still in arms. The same was true for Egypt and Syria. Like Israel, they needed political agreements that would stabilize the situation and allow a return to normal life.

The political and the territorial outcomes of the war created a complex diplomatic powder keg that required creativity and tireless shuttle negotiations to enable the successful separation of forces and sheathing of swords, a process that continued until the disengagement agreement on the Syrian front in May 1974. The man who led this effort was US secretary of state Henry Kissinger. One of the key participants from the Arab side was Ashraf Marwan.

Kissinger's first priority was dealing with the problem of the besieged Egyptian Third Army. In exchange for Israel's agreement to allow the orderly transfer of nonmilitary supplies, Egypt gave up on its demand that Israel withdraw to the battle lines of October 22—the date that the UN Security Council had called for a cease-fire—which would have consolidated Egypt's gains. Sadat's capitulation was not taken well in the Arab world, and he sent Marwan to meet with leaders in an effort to clarify his position and calm their concerns. But one person with whom he met was not on Sadat's agenda. On October 28 the Angel conferred with Zamir, for the second time in less than ten days. This time the meeting took place in London. Marwan informed the Mossad chief that Sadat was not too worried about the military situation and was certain that the Soviets would not allow the Israelis to destroy the Third Army. He also told Zamir that the Kremlin promised Sadat that they intended to launch a diplomatic initiative that would ultimately bring Israel to the 1967 international border. Marwan also claimed that the Kremlin had American backing for this initiative.

Golda Meir was briefed by Zamir a day later, and on October 30 she left for talks with President Nixon. During these talks she held very firm positions and rejected any possibility of an Israeli withdrawal, at least in part because of her fear that such a move would pave the road to a withdrawal to the 1967 border.[5]

About three weeks later, in mid-November, Sadat found himself in the thick of a major diplomatic kerfuffle with Libyan leader Gaddafi. Gaddafi was furious about Sadat's decision to go to war without consulting with him. Sadat sent Marwan to Tripoli to assuage the leader's temper. It worked, and Gaddafi backtracked from his threat to expel 100,000 Egyptians working on Libyan soil. These and other diplomatic missions were undertaken by Marwan without any regard for proper channels or even alerting the Egyptian foreign ministry. In most cases, the local Egyptian ambassador knew nothing of the contents of Marwan's messages—or even of his arrival in the country.[6]

With the war's outcome as it was, and with Sadat's call to the United States to bring about some kind of agreement between the sides, the joint Syrian-Egyptian effort had run its course as a military operation and was now shifting to the diplomatic arena. Ministers of war and military chiefs now made way for the negotiators. Ashraf Marwan stepped into the limelight; in addition to liaising with Libya and Saudi Arabia, Sadat now put him in charge of the Syrian brief as well. So when Egypt, which had supported the creation of an international peace conference to be held in Geneva at the end of December 1973, wanted to put pressure on Syria to join, Marwan went to Damascus to meet with top Syrian officials; only later was he joined by Egypt's foreign minister.[7] Egypt's efforts came up empty in that case, and the Syrians were absent when the conference opened.

Six months later, at the height of armistice negotiations between Israel and Syria, Sadat made more effective use of Marwan's powers of persuasion. Marwan embarked on a series of secret missions to Saudi Arabia and Algeria, together with Kissinger aide Harold Saunders, in an effort to convince the leaders to support a draft agreement that neither the Syrians nor the Israelis had yet seen. On May 4, 1974, King Faisal received the two of them—surprising

Kissinger not only by the Saudi monarch's willingness to meet
with lesser officials but also by his willingness to cooperate on a
move led by Egypt and the Americans to pressure Syria. Both he
and Houari Boumediene, the president of Algeria, refrained from
publicly supporting the agreement, but they made it clear that they
would not oppose it.[8]

A few days later, against the backdrop of spiraling hostilities between Israel and Syria and a concern that a full-scale war would
flare up again, Marwan arrived in Damascus. His goal was to im-
press upon the Syrians that if they restarted the war with Israel,
they would do so on their own.[9] But there was something else
on his agenda, which very few knew about. Marwan had been
asked by the Mossad to find out what Assad was really thinking
about renewing fire. After returning from Riyadh to Cairo, he had
proposed to Sadat—who himself did not know what Assad was
thinking—that he go to Damascus, and Sadat agreed. Assad received Marwan and spoke with him openly, convinced that his
words would not go beyond the two of them and Sadat. But Marwan's report quickly reached Israel.

In Tel Aviv, the report was greeted with wild approval, mainly
because it represented an honest, clear, and authentic view of the
Syrian leader's thoughts about war with Israel—thoughts that were
far less belligerent than the Israelis had believed. The skirmishes
with Syria came to an end, and on May 31 the two governments
signed a disengagement pact at the Golan Heights, bringing the
Yom Kippur War to its formal conclusion.

MARWAN'S ROLE IN the negotiations reflected his rising position
in the Egyptian leadership. When he wasn't on a mission sent by
Sadat, he was by the president's side. One unforgettable example
took place on January 18, 1974, when Kissinger met Sadat at his
residence in Aswan, carrying a personal letter from Golda Meir,

in which she expressed her longing for peace. When Sadat had finished reading it, Marwan walked in and whispered into his ear that representatives of Egypt and Israel had just reached a disengagement agreement at the negotiations tent at Kilometer 101 on the Cairo-Suez road. Sadat was visibly moved. He stood up, kissed the secretary of state on both cheeks, and said, "Today I take off my military uniform. I do not expect to wear it again except on formal occasions. Tell her that *this* is my answer to her letter."[10] Kissinger reported back to the Israelis—and so did Marwan. Although Marwan's report only confirmed Kissinger's, this in itself was no small matter. "Governments, like anyone else," John le Carré has his character George Smiley telling his students, "trust what they pay for, and are suspicious of what they don't."[11] If nothing else, Marwan's report raised Kissinger's credibility in the eyes of Israeli leaders.

Marwan's position improved on a formal level, as well. On February 14, 1974, he was made secretary to the president of the republic for foreign relations, a new position that turned him into a direct competitor to Foreign Minister Ismail Fahmi. The already tense relations between the two worsened in the months that followed, especially in light of reports that Sadat had been disappointed by Fahmi's failure to improve the complicated relations between Egypt on the one hand, and Jordan and the Palestine Liberation Organization on the other. Reports from "diplomatic sources in Beirut"—often a code word for one high-level figure or another in the Middle East—said that he was also disappointed by Fahmi's failure to find an effective balance for Egypt between the two superpowers, stirring dissatisfaction among leftists in Egypt who wanted to see a greater Soviet role in the country. Given the fact that both Sadat and Marwan were sharply anti-Soviet, the idea that Marwan would be promoted at Fahmi's expense in order to improve relations with Moscow seems unlikely. Yet there he was,

Sadat's right-hand man, the rising star in the Egyptian political arena, climbing the ladder.

On August 18, 1974, he took another step up when he was appointed to head up a new department in the President's Office dealing with Arab affairs. In the wake of this move, which formally excised some of the functions of the Foreign Ministry and transferred them to Marwan's office, "diplomatic sources in Beirut" reported that Sadat was planning on firing Fahmi in the near future and appointing Marwan in his place.[12] This never ended up happening, but there can be no doubt that Marwan's position in the Egyptian pantheon was on the rise—at Fahmi's expense.

Marwan's centrality to Egyptian diplomacy was reflected in a string of sensitive missions he carried out for Sadat to advance an interim agreement with Israel. As opposed to Fahmi, who was much more interested in the favor of the Arab world than in advancing his own president's policies, and therefore continued to oppose any agreement with Israel, Marwan was relatively independent and had a clear pro-American attitude, which made it much easier for Sadat to work with him. Marwan's closest friends in the Arab world, people like Kamal Adham, were similarly interested in ridding the region of the Kremlin's influence, and together they created a whole sphere in which active opposition to the Soviets could be expressed and put into practice.

And so, Marwan found himself taking a leading role in the most sensitive, minute, manipulative diplomatic dances that defined the Middle East in the 1970s. One of the most interesting of these brought together two complex relationships, that of the Israeli-Arab conflict and that of Iran and Iraq. In 1974, at the height of American-Egyptian efforts to reach a new interim agreement with Israel, Kissinger and Sadat tried to garner Iraqi support, which they saw as critical in the face of ardent Syrian opposition to an agreement. Like other Arab states, Iraq publicly took a fiercely anti-Israel position. But beneath the surface, the Iraqis had other interests, and by playing on those interests they believed it was possible to effect a change in Iraq's stance. The most obvious of these was Iraq's need to stop the Kurdish rebellion in the country's north, which had been going on for years and had already claimed heavy casualties in the Iraqi military. The Kurds received both financial and logistical support from Iran and the United States, and a sizable contingent from the Mossad had spent years training the Kurdish fighters to take on the Iraqi army. After repeated failed attempts to quash the rebellion by military means, Iraqi strongman Saddam Hussein had secretly turned to the shah of Iran and other leaders to try to end the rebellion through diplomacy. Kissinger and Sadat thought that if Egypt and the United States were to agree to get Iran to stop helping the Kurds, Iraq might be convinced to support an interim agreement with Israel in exchange.

Ashraf Marwan, who was perfect for these kinds of sensitive negotiations, traveled to Tehran and Baghdad in September 1974 to sound out the leaders on such a deal. In at least some of the talks, as with the shah of Iran on September 2, there were also top-level Saudi officials taking part, including Crown Prince Saud, as well as Kamal Adham. The three of them expressed their sense that Saddam wanted to ratchet down Soviet influence in Iraq, so there was a good chance he'd be willing to agree to a deal if it included the Americans displacing the Soviets in helping the Iraqi military.

The mission was a success. By the end of it, Iran announced it was willing to stop helping the Kurds in exchange for Iraqi territorial concessions in the Persian Gulf. Iraq, for its part, let it be known that it would tone down its anti-Iranian policies and give its tacit support to an interim agreement between Egypt and Israel, in the process isolating Syria as the only major opponent. And indeed, Iran brought an effective end to the Kurdish revolt in Iraq in 1974.[13]

In other cases, Marwan took part in strategic initiatives that, even if they didn't bear fruit, nevertheless still underscored his growing status. On August 13, 1974, he and Fahmi met with Kissinger at the State Department. They covered a range of subjects, including American economic aid to Egypt, military aid to Egypt despite internal opposition in the United States, the price of oil, and the interim agreement with Israel. They also talked about tensions between Egypt and Libya. Kissinger asked why, despite Gaddafi's hostility toward Egypt's peace strategy that led to Libyan border provocations, Egypt had not gone to war against Libya—and even promised that America would support such a move. Marwan, who was known as a friend to the Libyan leadership, offered no opposition to Kissinger's idea and even went as far as declaring the Libyan military to be a paper tiger, which, despite having thousands of Soviet tanks, had only enough manpower to field a single tank brigade. Yet he nonetheless repeated that there was no point in discussing such a move before signing a new interim agreement with Israel, which would both stabilize the region and spell the end of Soviet involvement in Egypt.[14]

THE SOVIETS WERE not going quietly, however. The combination of Marwan's ascent and the rise of anti-Soviet policy in Egypt led the Kremlin to conclude that the president's aide had to be neutralized. According to Vasili Mitrokhin, a senior archivist in the KGB's foreign affairs division who defected to Britain in 1992, taking with him a large portion of his archive, what most angered the Soviets were reports of a secret visit to Cairo by CIA chief William Colby. The KGB's central command decided to take "active measures" against Marwan, who Moscow believed held overall responsibility for Egyptian intelligence, including relations with the CIA. The KGB's Section A prepared a psyops campaign painting Marwan as an American spy. This operation was given high priority, and the agency even sent the head of its North African division, Vladimir Kazakov, to Cairo in May 1975 to oversee the final preparations.

In the operation, KGB officers prepared a series of articles to be planted in newspapers in Lebanon, Syria, and Libya, portraying Marwan not only as working for the CIA but also as having taken massive bribes and kickbacks in Egyptian deals with Saudi Arabia and Kuwait. The KGB's Cairo station also spread rumors that Marwan had a romantic affair with Jehan Sadat—and that the president knew about it.

The fact that Ashraf Marwan, a young, handsome, and successful man, was close with the Egyptian republic's first lady, was well known; sometimes he even accompanied her when she traveled abroad with her daughters. In one such case, when she stayed at the George V in Paris, he asked the Mossad to bug her suite so that he would know what she said about him. The Mossad agreed but Jehan hardly spoke about him.

Marwan's sensitivity to his relations with the first lady was also connected to her marital life. Many people knew that the Sadats' marital relationship was far from ideal. Sadat did not trust his wife, who, as we have seen, tended to intervene in affairs of state even against his will. Sadat rarely stayed at his official residence in Giza, so the couple lived apart most of the time.[15] So while we may not have any evidence that Ashraf and Jehan actually had an affair, there was nonetheless fertile ground for the growth of these rumors. They definitely embarrassed Sadat and began driving a wedge between him and the man who only recently had been his most trusted aide.

Even after Marwan was dismissed from his role in the President's Office in March 1976 and installed to lead an industrial consortium far away from Sadat's inner circle (a development for which the Soviets, typically, took undeserved credit), the KGB continued to see him as a major threat. Oleg Gordievsky, a KGB officer who later defected to the West and wrote his memoirs, reported that he heard hallway conversations about the possibility of assassinating Sadat. Though there is no evidence that the KGB ever planned such an attack, there were a number of Soviet-linked organizations that did. In December 1977, Gordievsky learned that in a secret meeting in Damascus between leaders of Syrian intelligence and members of the Popular Front for the Liberation of Palestine (PFLP), plans for killing Sadat were discussed—plans that also included killing Ashraf Marwan. As far as we know, the KGB never tried to advance the plan but also did nothing to stop it.[16]

But aside from Marwan's pro-American stance and excellent relations with leading American officials—especially Kissinger—the Soviets may have had another reason to see him as a serious threat. Marwan's name was linked to a secret multilateral project aimed at limiting the spread of Soviet influence in the Middle East and especially in Africa. This project, known as the Safari Club, was named after a Parisian nightclub where its members often met. According to the best account we have of how the group worked, including interviews of Kamal Adham and his successor as head of Saudi intelligence, the Safari Club was established by Count Alexandre de Marenches, who was at the time the head of the central French intelligence agency, the Service de Documentation Extérieure et de Contre-Espionnage (SDECE), and was known as an anti-Soviet hawk. The initiative came at the heels of two specific developments. One was the spread of Soviet influence in Africa, especially in Mozambique, Angola, Ethiopia, and Somalia; the other was a series of scandals in Washington, especially the Watergate affair that brought about the resignation of President Nixon in the summer of 1974, as well as the congressional hearings on the activities of the CIA in 1975, which significantly weakened the agency's ability to address Soviet expansion. Against this background, Marenches, with the support of French president Valéry Giscard d'Estaing, turned to the leaders of Iran, Saudi Arabia, Egypt, and Morocco, asking that each take upon itself some of the responsibility for halting the spread of communism in Africa and the Middle East. The four leaders agreed, and the Safari Club was formally launched on September 1, 1976.

The organization's command center was located in Cairo, and it included both planning and operations branches. France provided the technical means, including secure communications, and Saudi Arabia provided principal funding. Professional parleys were held in France, Egypt, and Saudi Arabia, in which the main operations were coordinated in three major areas: financial and military aid to anti-Soviet forces in Africa; intelligence cooperation; and covert or "black" operations, such as psyops or assassinations. As part of the Safari Club's operations, which continued up until the Iranian revolution in 1979, Morocco and Egypt sent, with logistical help from France, an expeditionary force to Zaire in an effort to help its pro-American leader, Mobutu Sese Seko, fend off external threats to Katanga, the country's richest mining strip. At the same time, members of the club assisted the anti-Communist rebels in Angola and Mozambique who fought their pro-Soviet regimes, and supported Djibouti in its effort to prevent Ethiopia from invading it and to help stabilize the Horn of Africa. The club acted under the constant watch, and approval, of Washington.[17] According to some sources, the close congressional oversight of the CIA beginning in the mid-1970s required that the Saudis effectively fund the covert operations of an organization built by ex-CIA officials outside of American soil and, therefore, beyond congressional supervision. The organization carried out activities that would never have been approved for the CIA—some with direct CIA cooperation.[18]

Marwan was chosen by Sadat to represent him in the Safari Club.[19] Otherwise, very little is known about his involvement in its activities. What is certain, however, is that by the time the Safari

Club was founded in September 1976, Marwan was already out of Sadat's inner circle, no longer in the President's Office or carrying out his "special" missions. It is entirely possible that he had nothing whatsoever to do with the group—and that all the rumors to the contrary were just KGB propaganda. Despite the overwhelming number of such rumors connecting Marwan to global-scale anti-Soviet events, it is very hard to know how seriously to take them. It is, however, fair to assume that the KGB did see him as someone worthy of neutralizing or at least reducing his effectiveness, not so much because they thought his activities would, for example, bring the downfall of Mozambique's socialist president, Samora Machel, or rock the balance of power between Ethiopia and Djibouti, but rather out of their desire to weaken the anti-Soviet camp in Egypt itself.

THE KGB'S DEPICTION of Marwan as a CIA spy was fundamentally inaccurate; although he had excellent relations with the Americans, especially Henry Kissinger, he did not actually work *for* them before the mid-1980s. But their portrayal of him as corrupt, on the other hand, was quite close to the truth. Marwan began accumulating his wealth through graft soon after his rise to prominence in the wake of the Corrective Revolution in 1971. By the mid-1970s, when the Soviets started propagating reports of his corruption, he was already quite wealthy. Some of his money came from the Mossad, but the Soviets didn't know that. Most of it came from other illicit sources, especially percentages on various deals he brokered, taking full advantage of his political status. In other cases, Marwan used his position to get better prices on profitable purchases of his own. One example was the June 1974 purchase he made of a parcel of land, in his wife's name, in the town of Kardassa, on the desert road between Cairo and Alexandria. To secure it, he sent a request to the Egyptian minister of agriculture, claiming that the act reflected the will of the president. In a later investigation, it emerged that Sadat knew nothing about it. Similarly, the question was raised as to where Marwan got the money for the purchase.[20] In other cases Marwan needed no capital at all to make his money. His closeness to Sadat was far more useful. This was most evident in an affair involving the Coca-Cola Corporation.

Since 1968, when Coca-Cola began bottling operations in Israel as a result of pressure in the United States, it was a target for the Arab boycott, an organized effort of the Arab states, beginning in 1948, to refuse to deal not only with Israel directly but also with any company that did business with Israel (the "secondary boy-cott"). In 1974, Coca-Cola began a campaign aimed at removing its products from the boycott list. Egypt, the leader of the Arab world and a fledgling ally of the United States, a country whose leader spoke openly about ending the conflict with Israel, was the natural target of the company's efforts. The campaign was led by Sam Ayoub, a senior Coca-Cola executive who was a native of Al-exandria, Egypt, and knew his way around the Arab world. When he looked into the question of who could influence Sadat into re-moving Coca-Cola from the boycott, the man he found was Ashraf Marwan. Marwan turned to Sadat, and Sadat opened the doors to the Egyptian market. Part of the payment came in the form of investments that the company made in the Egyptian economy; but according to Ayoub, Marwan earned a heavy financial benefit in exchange for greasing the wheels.[21]

Other questions surround Marwan's academic achievements. Alongside his intensive diplomatic efforts, his wealth-building ef-forts, and his espionage efforts, Ashraf Marwan also claimed to have found the time to complete his doctorate—an effort that, accord-ing to his friends, he had begun immediately after finishing his master's degree. He claimed that in 1974 he submitted his thesis to his adviser, Dr. Ahmed Mustafa, who later became Egypt's science

minister.[22] This seems highly unlikely. From the time he purportedly completed his master's studies, around 1970 or 1971, until 1974,
he was incredibly busy with affairs of state, business, and treachery.
The man was admittedly talented; yet it is very difficult to imagine
his adding a major act of scholarship into the mix. And though for
the rest of his life he brandished the title of "Doctor," quite a few
people called his degree into question. Muhammad Tharwat, for
example, in his biography of Marwan, wrote that he failed to complete his studies because of his intensive involvement in Egyptian
politics. According to another source, Marwan paid his adviser off,
and the latter not only approved the doctorate but also wrote it.
Mohamed al-Fayed, the Egyptian businessman who became one
of Marwan's most bitter rivals in the 1980s, claimed that Marwan
never wrote the dissertation and received the degree only because
his father was the president of Cairo University. Fayed, who could
spin a yarn with the best of them, was wrong about Marwan's
father, who was an army general and never held that position. But
he may have been right in challenging the legitimacy of the degree.

ON MARCH 1, 1976, a presidential order decreed the termination of
Ashraf Marwan's service in the President's Office, and his appointment to the position of chairman of the Arab Organization for
Industrialization (AOI)—a new international consortium aimed
at establishing an independent Arab arms industry. On the face of
it, this was a promotion, giving him responsibility over a budget of
hundreds of millions of dollars and factories employing thousands
of workers. In practice, Marwan had been sacked. It was more or
less the end of his political career.

The same factors that underlay previous attempts to bring
Marwan down four years earlier became the cause of his downfall
now. One was jealousy. Marwan succeeded, in just ten years, in
becoming one of the closest people to Sadat, a key player in the

leadership, and a realistic candidate for foreign minister. In a society like Egypt's, where age and experience mean so much, his youth (he turned thirty in 1974) and rapid rise were enough to earn him many enemies. His crass behavior and his transparent contempt for colleagues only fanned the flames. The fact that he carried out the most sensitive of Sadat's missions without bothering to alert the diplomats alienated much of the Foreign Ministry, as well. His most important rival was Foreign Minister Fahmi himself. They had been close when Marwan was just starting out, and Fahmi had invited him to exclusive dinners with leading Americans, including Kissinger. But as Sadat's upstart aide took on ever greater responsibility in Egyptian foreign affairs, increasingly keeping Fahmi out of the loop, the foreign minister grew more and more alarmed.[23]

Another group of rivals were the remaining Nasserites who still held positions of power in Egypt. Marwan's assistance in helping Sadat eviscerate the "centers of power" in 1971, as well as his anti-Soviet stance and his influence on Sadat's new foreign policy—all of these turned him into a red flag in the bullish eyes of anyone who still revered Nasser's legacy, especially Nasser's own family. To this group were added, over time, various figures in the President's Office, in the military, and in the media. Some had been personally offended by Marwan; others were worried about his rise to power because of his debauchery and the stench of corruption that seemed to follow his every move. He was young, he had family connections, he was brazen, and he seemed to accumulate and squander his wealth with breathtaking speed. He seemed incapable of keeping his mouth shut. And to top it all off, the KGB ran a vast and effective smear campaign against him.

"Friends may come and go," the old saying has it, "but enemies accumulate." As time passed, an ever-widening circle of influential Egyptians saw Marwan's elimination from the public arena as a critical interest.

And so, after a hiatus of two years, a series of articles appeared cataloging his corruption. These triggered repeated appeals for an investigation. Sadat eventually capitulated and, as discussed earlier, he appointed Marwan's nemesis in the President's Office, Ahmad al-Masiri, to lead the inquiry. Al-Masiri was faithful to his mission. The investigation revealed, among other things, that Marwan had many millions of dollars invested in London. Neither Marwan nor his wife could offer a plausible explanation for the money. The findings were brought to Sadat and left little room for maneuver. Sadat announced that Marwan was out. From now on, the president's former right-hand aide would take charge of an entirely new organization, far removed from political power.[24]

THE ARAB ORGANIZATION for Industrialization was founded in April 1975 as a typical expression of the Arab world's attempts, throughout the mid-1970s, to reinvent itself. The oil crisis precipitated by OPEC (Organization of Petroleum Exporting Countries) during the 1973 Yom Kippur War brought tremendous profits to oil-producing states, especially Saudi Arabia and the Gulf states. These helped fund cooperation within the Arab world in order to make it a dominant player not just in the global energy market but also in other key areas, including the production of arms. The AOI was meant to lay the groundwork for an Arab military-industrial complex that would supply the lion's share of the region's arms through its own independent production of weapons and munitions. Participants in AOI included the governments of Saudi Arabia, United Arab Emirates, and Qatar, which offered funding; and Egypt, which offered the human capital and industrial capability required to produce weapons, an infrastructure Egypt had been developing since the 1960s. With an opening budget of over a billion dollars, AOI employed more than 18,000 people at its height. The project was overseen by Ashraf Marwan, who was chairman of the board, and the defense ministers of the four member states.

Given his age and lack of relevant experience, Marwan was not a natural choice to head up so huge and ambitious an operation. Yet the field was not entirely alien to him: He had a degree in chemistry and had gained some work experience in the production of explosives; more important, Marwan had become a master at weapons procurement, not just before the war—when he played a key role in helping Egypt acquire fighter planes via Libya—but also afterward. In the fall of 1975, for example, he held talks in France about a plan to build a factory in Egypt to assemble Mirage F1 planes for Marcel Dassault, and to provide maintenance for Mirages in the Saudi and Kuwaiti air forces, a negotiation that had resulted from a conversation initiated with Giscard d'Estaing, in which he also brought him up to date about efforts to reach a diplomatic agreement between Egypt and Israel.[25]

So Marwan's experience was in fact more relevant than it may have seemed on paper. And yet, it did not justify choosing him over experienced managers of major industrial concerns. The decision was obviously political, a result of pressure brought by Marwan's friends in the oil-rich states who wanted to make sure the project would be run by someone who understood their needs; and of Sadat's own need to find a new job for his former aide that would smooth his transition out of the President's Office and make his dismissal less embarrassing to Sadat. The president sweetened the package by awarding Marwan, just days later, a medal for his "wondrous achievements for Egypt in the most critical phases of the October war."[26] Marwan's public status, if not his political career, had been preserved.

The result, however, was that while many of his rivals were satisfied by his disappearance from Sadat's circle, quite a few others worried that the move gave Marwan a step up the ladder rather than down. "The marriage of Ashraf Marwan to Mona Abdel Nasser was the first step to [Marwan's] success," said one Egyptian politician, "and Sadat's desire that Arab states would provide their own weapons was the second."[27]

The consortium was headquartered in a modern office building in a suburb of Cairo. The building appeared on no maps, and its massive, dark, one-way windows, state-of-the-art air-conditioning, closed-circuit television, and uniformed guards carrying chrome-plated pistols made it stand out starkly against the Cairo cityscape. It was, for all intents and purposes, an imitation of industrial head-quarters in far wealthier places in the world. The consortium's managerial methods were also taken straight from the Western cap-italist playbook. In sharp contrast to the Egyptian norm, AOI ran a fairly tight ship, freed from government bureaucracy and other ex-ternal constraints. One of Marwan's first moves upon entering the position, a decision in which he took pride, was laying off sixteen hundred nonessential workers—almost unthinkable in the socialist climate of Egypt at the time.

Yet despite all this, AOI was a flop. In its first years, the in-frastructure was built and contacts made with Western weapons manufacturers to attain licenses and know-how for building criti-cal weapons systems in Egyptian factories. According to one con-tract with Westland Helicopters and Rolls-Royce of Britain, the consortium was supposed to start producing Lynx helicopters in a factory in the Helwan region. Another contract with the British aerospace industry arranged for the production of Swingfire anti-tank missiles; still another, with various French companies, called for the production of air-to-air and ground-to-ground missiles in factories in a Saudi military complex being built near Riyadh. An-other contract, worth $2 billion, was signed with Dassault and the German company Dornier to assemble Alpha Jet training planes in Egypt. Longer-term plans called for the assembly of France's most sophisticated fighter jet, the Mirage 2000, which was supposed to compete with the American F-16. The consortium signed a contract with American Motors for the production of twelve thousand jeeps per year in Cairo. In an interview Marwan gave to *Business-Week* a short time before Sadat publicly announced his intention to visit Jerusalem and reach a peace agreement with Israel, Marwan guessed that the consortium had signed something like $4 billion or $5 billion worth of contracts with Western weapons manufacturers for the production of arms in Egypt.[28]

But the true value of almost all these contracts, in the end, was little more than the paper they were written on. In late 1977, after hundreds of millions of dollars had been spent, AOI's total revenues amounted to $41 million. The only actual armament it produced was a West German armored personnel carrier capable of carrying ten soldiers a distance of four hundred miles. It is unclear exactly how many of the APCs were produced, or whether they were ever deployed in any army.

One of the central problems with the project was the poor state of manufacturing in Egypt. Experts assessed that the country lacked the qualified personnel needed to carry out AOI's ambitious plans. Marwan failed to prove otherwise. But what finally brought AOI down was the peace treaty between Egypt and Israel. In the wake of Sadat's initiative in October 1977, Egypt found itself suddenly isolated in the Arab world—and all the more so after the Camp David Accords were signed in 1979. In March 1979, Egypt's partners in the consortium announced their decision to cease all funding for the project—resulting in the immediate layoff of sixteen thousand employees in Egypt.

Marwan was not one of them. He had already quit in October 1978. Not, of course, because of the failure of the consortium or of his poor performance. On the contrary—he proved himself more than capable as a manager, and had the backing of the Saudis and the others. Rather, the reason was, as always, the incessant efforts of his rivals in Egypt and abroad to bring him down. And as always, it was his appetite for corruption that gave them exactly the ammunition they needed.

THE MEN WHO led the decisive battle against Ashraf Marwan were Foreign Minister Ismail Fahmi and Musa Sabri, editor of *Al-Akhbar* and one of Sadat's most ardent supporters and longtime friends. They were joined by a number of other important players in Egypt, including journalists who published accounts of Marwan's affronts and who were deeply worried about the prospect of his continuing to play a major public role—or even returning to the political arena.

Some of the charges were probably unwarranted. One day, for example, the editor of the newspaper *Akhbar al-Youm* placed a call to the foreign minister on a certain matter. Fahmi told him that instead of asking about that, he should be focusing on a story about the theft of diamonds worth tens of thousands of dollars from a certain hotel in London where, as it happens, Marwan was staying. Fahmi's aim was to foment a scandal by making it seem that Marwan, the public servant, was wealthy enough to have the diamonds in his hotel room. He told the editor to publish the item, adding that it came from a "secret and official" source. The report appeared not only in *Akhbar al-Youm* but in a number of other papers as well, and even though Marwan's name was not mentioned explicitly, there were enough hints to make it clear who was implicated. The affair, which became known as the *fadikha*, or "scandal," was brought to the attention of Sadat, who insisted on being told precisely whom it was about. When Musa Sabri identified Marwan, Sadat ordered a thorough investigation.

This time, the charges turned out to have been completely fabricated.[29] But that didn't stop the rumor mill from putting more and more pressure on Marwan. One of AOI's main offices was in

London, and Marwan traveled there often. Rumors soon reached
Cairo about weapons deals being hatched by Marwan and his old
friend Kamal Adham. In some cases, Jehan Sadat's name was mentioned as well. Marwan, it was said, had an apartment in London
and had lost a fortune playing roulette at the Playboy Club. It was
also said that Marwan worked hard to close a huge deal in which
EgyptAir purchased airliners from Boeing, knowing that Adham
would get a sizable fee for every plane sold. At the same time, there
were published reports that Marwan gave expensive gifts, including
color televisions, to senior figures in the Egyptian government and
in the military industry in order to dampen the accusations against
him.[30]

This string of revelations, many of which originated with
people most loyal to Sadat, increased the pressure on the president to remove Marwan from his position as head of AOI. Sadat
resisted, offering a number of excuses: Marwan was irreplaceable
in carrying out important and sensitive missions abroad on behalf
of the president; his special relationship with the leaders of the
Libyan regime had enabled him to solve the thorniest crises between Libya and Egypt; and the Saudi monarchy regarded him as
a highly effective link to Egypt, especially in delicate business, thus
making it possible for Sadat to conduct a productive dialogue with
the king. And then there was the debt Sadat owed Marwan for his
important contribution to the war effort, especially the acquisition
of Mirages from France via Libya.[31]

But the pressure on Sadat continued to mount. If, in the past,
it had been relatively painless for him to accept Marwan's flat-
out denials and claims that Nasserites were looking to do him in,
this time the clamor for Marwan's head was coming from Sadat's
own friends, including Sabri and the media moguls, the brothers Mustafa and Ali Amin. When media pressure combined with
intelligence reports describing Marwan's behavior, Sadat realized
that he had to act. What probably tipped the scales was not just

the incontrovertible evidence of Marwan's corruption, but record-ings of his conversations with various Gulf potentates, in which he sounded dismissive of Sadat, even antagonistic. And the moment Marwan appeared disloyal, he became a sitting duck. Soon there-after, he complained to Sadat that his office had been bugged, and Sadat ignored the complaint. Marwan heard the president's message loud and clear. Sadat had decided to remove the protective cover that had kept Marwan safe for so long, and he wanted Marwan to know it.[32]

As on so many other occasions in the life of Ashraf Marwan, the announcement on October 12, 1978, that he was leaving his position at AOI was accompanied by drama. Sadat wanted to play down the whole affair. Yet the decision reached the ears of Musa Sabri, and his *Al-Akhbar* paper ran a story with the headline, "An End to the Legend of Ashraf Marwan: Presidential Order to Fire Him from the Arab Organization for Industrialization and Transfer Him to the Foreign Ministry."[33] This angered Sadat—not least because within a few hours' time he found himself standing before Marwan's wife, Mona, in tears, who claimed that the arti-cles implied that Nasser's daughter was married to a thief. Sadat called Sabri and insisted that he bury the story. And indeed, in the paper's later editions on the same day, Marwan was described as having "resigned" and being given a senior appointment at the Foreign Ministry. Not long after, Sadat sent him on several new diplomatic missions, in order to make it look as though Marwan still had his favor. Sabri wound up feeling more than a little hurt by it all—a feeling that certainly increased when it turned out that Sadat, his longtime friend, had stopped taking his calls and re-fused to meet. Sabri, in response, announced his own resignation as editor of *Al-Akhbar*, and though he eventually was persuaded to withdraw his resignation, relations between the two never fully recovered.[34]

And as with the last time Sadat found himself dismissing Marwan, this time, too, he gave his former aide all the pomp and honor due a national hero. In a public ceremony covered widely by the media, he gave Marwan the highest medal of the Republic of Egypt and emphasized the man's achievements during the October War. Thanks to Marwan's efforts, Sadat concluded, "our air forces could complete their battle missions as necessary."[35] Later on Marwan made good use of his two medals to prove his loyalty to Egypt and, before the press, to bolster his claims that he had been a double agent working for Egypt against Israel.

Outside of Egypt, Marwan's dismissal was taken as a significant development in the Egyptian political leadership. Several days earlier, before the annual military parade on October 6, it was announced that another major figure, the army's chief of staff, Mohamed Abdel Ghani el-Gamsy, had also been retired. So Marwan's departure was taken to signify an effort on Sadat's part to clean house in a way that showed balance among competing camps in the regime.

The man who benefited most from the shake-up was Sadat's vice president, Hosni Mubarak, whose two main competitors had suddenly been eliminated.[36]

EVEN BEFORE MARWAN had been booted from the Egyptian public arena, his status with the Mossad had begun to decline. There had been no rupture in the relationship, and he continued passing information to his handlers whenever he traveled to Europe. During negotiations with Israel over the disengagement of forces following the Yom Kippur War, for example, Marwan gave over crucial information that led to the successful conclusion of the armistice on the southern front. And when Israel needed to conclude a similar agreement with Syria months later, Marwan, as we have seen, provided an invaluable portrait of the Syrian president.

But the war also brought about a shift in the relationship. Part

of it was personal. Egypt's great successes in the first few days of
the war, especially raising the Egyptian flag over the Bar-Lev Line,
gave the Arabs back much of their lost honor in the wake of 1967.
Part of Marwan's original motivation to spy for Israel came from
his innate desire to be on the winning side of the conflict. In his
meetings with his handlers immediately after the war, he expressed
his frustration that Israel had been surprised despite his warnings
and that the IDF had taken heavy losses without making effective
use of the detailed plans he had provided. Suddenly, the Israelis
were no longer the perfect, indomitable force that they once were,
and the Egyptians were no longer the humiliated bums that he had
been loath to ally himself with.

Other aspects of his original motivation had been undermined
as well. He was now a wealthy man, and the payments he received
from the Mossad no longer meant what they once did. And he
also had received great honor from the Egyptian government and
continued to be welcomed in capitals all over the world, sooth-
ing the wounds to his ego that his father-in-law had inflicted—
wounds that had surely contributed to his initial decision to betray
his country.

Another change had to do with the shifting relations between
Israel and Egypt. The end of the war, the armistice agreements, and
Egypt's shift from the Soviet to the American camp, opened the
doors to a genuine peace process, and the likelihood of a new war
initiated by Egypt had lessened considerably. As a result, the Angel's
most important role as far as the Mossad was concerned—to sound
the alarm if Egypt were about to attack—was no longer nearly as
important.

Yet despite this, Marwan still continued giving Israel crucial ongoing intelligence on Egyptian foreign policy. Beginning in the
mid-1970s, he repeated a single message to his Israeli handlers:
that Sadat was looking to end the conflict with Israel and instead

focus on "building Egypt." But the president's thoughts about peace concerned the Mossad and the rest of the Israeli intelligence community far less than did his thoughts about war. And so, the intelligence Marwan delivered garnered far less attention among Israeli decision makers than it had in the past. After Sadat launched the peace process, and especially after the Camp David Accords were signed, Egypt was suddenly a far lower priority for the intelligence community—and so was Ashraf Marwan.

Marwan's dwindling stature in Israel was also reflected in a drop in the caution Israelis were exercising with his intelligence. A CIA friend warned him one day that information only he knew was somehow getting to the Israelis—suggesting that the Israelis had neglected their long-standing practice of "paraphrasing" Marwan's intelligence in a way that made it impossible to know who the source had been before passing it to the Americans. Marwan complained bitterly to Dubi. An inquiry was made, the cause of the slip identified, and steps taken to ensure it didn't happen again. But clearly keeping Marwan a secret no longer held the same urgency for Israelis as it once did.

There were other indicators as well. Zamir finished his tour as chief of the Mossad in the summer of 1974. His replacement, Maj. Gen. (res.) Yitzhak Hofi, did not see a need to participate in Marwan's handling, and Dubi became the Mossad's only direct link with him. Their meetings also became less frequent. If prior to the war they would meet at least twice a month, and sometimes more, now they met only once every month or two. In the mid-1970s, Dubi left London and relocated back to Israel. Now he could no longer meet Marwan without notice whenever the Angel came to town. This, too, would never have happened when Marwan's importance for the Mossad was at its peak.

Even Marwan's payments were scaled back. Around the Yom Kippur War, his occasional payments reached $50,000 apiece. After the war, he received a fixed annual sum of $100,000—far less than before. Not that he really needed the money. Indeed, at one point he informed his handlers that he no longer wanted compensation at all, and for a number of years he continued to supply information without receiving payment. In the late 1970s, however, he fell on hard financial times and asked for help from the Mossad. Hofi agreed to forward him a onetime payment of over half a million dollars for all the years he had continued supplying information for free. That was the last time the Angel received any money from Israeli taxpayers.

All this brings to the surface, again, the question of Marwan's motives. Why would he continue to work for Israel for years, at considerable risk to his career and life, even after 1981, when he would leave Egypt for good? It clearly wasn't the money. It wasn't about his personal honor in Egypt; he had kept on helping Israel even when he was at the height of his glory. Nor was he coerced: We have no reason to believe that the Mossad ever attempted to get Marwan to do anything against his will.

Only one conclusion makes any sense. His role as a spy fulfilled some need, and he was reluctant to give it up. Perhaps it was the excitement and risk inherent in espionage. Once he had tasted it, going back to "normal" life was no longer an option. Somewhere in the recesses of his soul, he had a Hollywood-inspired passion for the life of a spy. At a certain stage he came to believe that if he stopped working for Israel, the Mossad would try to kill him. Exactly why he believed this is far from clear. But he continued to fear their vengeance many years later. Finally, part of the motivation may have had to do with a very special relationship he developed with Dubi, whom he still knew only as "Alex." Even someone as crafty and deceitful as Marwan needed somebody, somewhere, in whom he could confide, someone steadfast. Dubi was the only person on earth who could provide this, and their meetings became a kind of confessional for Marwan. Everybody, even the darkest criminals, needs a confessional. That is why he refused, repeatedly, the Mossad's efforts to replace Dubi with a different handler or even to add a second one.

The only occasion when Zamir's successor agreed to meet with Marwan was in order to convince him to agree to a second handler. Hofi explained that the new handler would stand in for "Alex" only when the latter was ill or unavailable for personal reasons. But Marwan was adamant that any effort to add anyone else to his operation would result in the Israelis' never seeing him again. Hofi capitulated, and Dubi continued to be Marwan's sole handler for years to come.

EVEN AFTER MARWAN left public life, he never left the public eye. Sensing that he no longer had the president's backing, the Egyptian press went after him like sharks after blood, publishing endless reports, true or false, of his corrupt real estate dealings or wild exaggerations about his wealth. They reached their peak in 1981, when the businessman Osman Ahmed Osman published his memoir in Egypt. He was close with Sadat, even marrying off his eldest son to Sadat's daughter. In the book, Osman attacked Nasser's policies but also claimed that Ashraf Marwan and his wife, Mona, accumulated 400 million Egyptian pounds by illicitly taking advantage of their status as family members of the revered leader. Painting himself as defender of the Nasser family, Marwan flatly denied Osman's accusations. "If only God were to grant me a few hundred years to live," he added, "could I struggle to earn one percent of that amount." Marwan's efforts to debunk Osman's claims, as well as those that Musa Sabri published in *Akhbar al-Youm*, were futile. A rare and detailed interview conducted with Marwan for the paper was never run, despite Marwan's repeated pleas for Sabri to publish it.[37]

At the same time, and in spite of everything, Marwan contin-

ued carrying on an informal relationship with Anwar and Jehan
Sadat. He was seen more than once in their home, updating the
president about various meetings he had held in the Arab world.
On other occasions he accompanied Sadat on trips abroad. Part of
this was due to the fact that Sadat clearly had a soft spot for Mona;
according to some, he saw in himself a kind of father figure for her,
perhaps because of the estrangement between her and the rest of
Nasser's family. Ashraf certainly gained from the continued connection, if for no other reason than that it showed the world that
he had not fully lost his influence. Dismayed that the connection
between Sadat and Marwan had not been fully severed, Marwan's
rivals feared that he might, one day, return to the political stage.
And so they saw to it that articles attacking Marwan continued to
appear in the press.[38]

Whether or not their fears were legitimate, the possibility of
Marwan's return evaporated completely on October 6, 1981, when
Sadat was gunned down during a military parade marking the
eighth anniversary of the October War. Sadat, who had protected
Marwan, promoted him, needed him, and never fully lost faith in
him, was gone. He was replaced by Hosni Mubarak, neither rival
nor friend. For Ashraf Marwan, a man whose thirst for wealth,
honor, and success could never be fully slaked, Cairo had little to
offer. He continued to keep a home there and spent quite a bit of
time there, usually with his family. He did not neglect his business affairs in Egypt, especially in real estate. But Sadat's passing
was, for him, a signal to begin again, to start a new chapter in his
story. Soon after Mubarak was sworn in, Ashraf Marwan moved to
London, which became the center of his new life.

Chapter 12

AN ANGEL IN THE CITY, A SON-IN-LAW EXPOSED

England was not a foreign country for Ashraf Marwan when he moved there in 1981. London had been something of a second home for him ever since he first visited to pursue his master's degree in the late 1960s. For him it was a place of refuge, a vacation hub, and the base of operations for a number of his businesses. Of course, it was also the center of his life as a spy.

Yet despite his love for London, he did not immediately bring his family along. Mona and the children, now on the brink of adolescence, moved into a posh Paris flat that Marwan bought them on Avenue Foch, in one of the most expensive neighborhoods in the world, which counted the Rothschild and Onassis families among its residents. For the first few years, Marwan saw his family mainly on weekends.

The ensuing quarter century of Marwan's life was dedicated to building his wealth. Like other aspects of his life, this, too, remains shrouded in mystery and conflicting accounts. Even people closely familiar with the London business scene have a hard time explaining how Marwan made his money and how much he made. Part of it has to do with the character of the man and his dealings. But it also has to do with the culture of "the City," as the financial core of London is known, a culture that until the 1980s handled itself according to a strict code based on collegiality, discretion, restraint, and tradition—in contrast to the American business world with its excessive legalism and emphasis on hardball competition, rapid growth, and jostling for control at almost any price. The London business culture was, at its heart, aristocratic, in many ways reminiscent of cricket, a game where ineffables were no less important than rules. This meant, however, that until recently there was very little of what is today called "transparency." Little was overseen by government, little known about what went down, because it was understood that the London business scene would keep its own tabs through its set of unwritten rules no less strict than the law itself.

Marwan was not part of this gentlemen's club. Even if he owned an apartment in the most luxurious part of town, even if he was driven around in a stretch limousine, he remained an outsider in the City. He had never attended the right boarding schools, but he knew full well how closed a world it was, with its clear share of racism as well. And so, when he did make his connections in the City, it was mainly with other outsiders like himself—people who, by virtue of being outcasts, felt no need to follow the unspoken rules of the game. This fact, while offering them both the limitations and the opportunities that others lacked, also makes it all the harder to reconstruct their moves decades later.

Marwan's first main link to the London business world was established before he left Egypt. In 1979 he purchased 40 percent of a small air-shipping company called Tradewinds. Founded in 1969, the company was sold in 1978 to one of the biggest concerns in Britain at the time, the London and Rhodesian Mining and Land Company, or Lonrho. The chairman of Lonrho was the British tycoon Roland "Tiny" Rowland—to whom Marwan had been introduced back in 1971 by his close friends Abdullah al-Sabah and his wife, Souad. Another connection was Subhi Rushdie, the chairman of the Allied Arab Bank. The connection with Rowland became the core of his London business operations until Rowland's death in 1998.

Rowland and Marwan first met in 1970, when the former came to Cairo to inquire about Egyptian cotton. Introduced to Marwan by Sadat, Rowland was taken by the young Egyptian's connections throughout the Arab world, and the sense that Marwan knew how to get him anything he needed to advance his interests. The two quickly hit it off, based in part on their similar approaches to business reflecting their similar life stories. Both shared a limitless thirst for money and power, an extreme egocentrism, and a need for honor and the taking of risk. They both knew how to identify and take advantage of the weaknesses of others. They were both born outside of the UK (Rowland in a detention camp in India where his parents, Dutch-German nationals, were held by the British during World War I), and both were outsiders to the City who flouted its rules. Rowland, for example, offered to Sir Angus Ogilvy, who had previously owned Lonrho and was married to the queen's first cousin, that he join the company's board of directors. They agreed that certain remunerations that Ogilvy received would be transferred to a Swiss bank account, routed via Canada, so that Ogilvy could avoid paying taxes. From Rowland's standpoint, the whole point of this illegal transaction was to make sure that Ogilvy faithfully represented his interests on the board. But when it came to light that the company had violated British-imposed sanctions on the white regime of Rhodesia, the entire board, including Ogilvy, voted against Rowland. In response, Rowland leaked Ogilvy's tax evasion to the press—a shocking violation of the accepted code of conduct in the City, causing embarrassment not only to Ogilvy but to the royal family, which in turn made Rowland himself into a pariah among the British aristocrats.[1] Indeed, neither Rowland nor Marwan was a big fan of the rule of law. They had no problem either giving or taking bribes, making threats, or conducting business in flagrant violation of the law. So when Marwan moved to London after finding himself an outcast in Cairo, the two found each other to be convenient company.

It was at a luncheon meeting the two shared at the Ritz on May 10, 1983, that Marwan involved himself in what would eventually become the most controversial business scandal in the City's modern history. The affair centered around Rowland's effort to commandeer the House of Fraser, and would likely have been much less of a scandal if not for the fact that the House of Fraser was the parent company for the Harrods department store, which was the favorite shopping venue for the British elites—including the royals.

Tiny Rowland first tried taking over the House of Fraser in 1977. He took advantage of the difficult financial straits of its owner and chairman, Hugh Fraser, which had resulted from the latter's gambling debts, in order to buy via a number of channels 29.9 percent of the company. At that point the chain included sixty-two stores, most of which were in a bad way. After Lonrho took a few more steps that indicated its intention to take over the company, the British authorities got involved, specifically the Monopolies and Mergers Commission, which decided to open an inquiry as to whether such a bid would put the public interests at risk. In March 1981, the commission concluded that while a merger between the two companies did not inherently pose such a risk, a takeover of Fraser by Lonrho would.[2]

Not long passed, however, before Rowland successfully engineered the ouster of Hugh Fraser from the position of chairman and resumed his takeover bid. This time he simultaneously made an offer to purchase the *Observer*. The Thatcher government approved the purchase of the newspaper but not a takeover of Fraser, and because they were by now used to Rowland's antics, the trade minister ruled that Lonrho may not purchase any further shares in the House of Fraser. While the formal reason given for this was that Lonrho already owned a textile factory and that its purchase of the House of Fraser might unfairly discriminate against other manufacturers, everyone knew that the real reason had more to do with the reluctance of the British elites to allow the country's greatest chain store, patronized by princes, to fall into the hands of someone as disreputable as Tiny Rowland. His support for the regime in Rhodesia, coupled with extensive questionable dealings across Africa and the damage he had caused the royal family in the Ogilvy affair, created a sense that was summed up by Prime Minister Edward Heath, several years earlier, when he called Rowland and Lonrho "the unpleasant and unacceptable face of capitalism."

Rowland was far from deterred. Though he agreed not to buy any more shares of Fraser, even making a public announcement to that effect in September 1982, it was but a diversion. His next move was to find more clever use of his nearly 30 percent stake to convince shareholders to sell off Harrods, enabling him to buy control of the rest of the company. When efforts to persuade the other shareholders failed, he decided he would do everything he could to gain hold of a majority stake before the next meeting of the board of directors—in clear violation of the Trade Ministry's ruling. To make this happen, he needed the help of Ashraf Marwan.

A few days after their lunch at the Ritz, Marwan bought two million shares of the House of Fraser, and then another 1.2 million. Rowland helped Marwan fund the purchase. All told, by mid-June 1983, Marwan held about 2 percent of the company. At the same time, other people connected with Rowland made similar purchases. By the time of the board meeting, Rowland had enough shares under his belt to pass a vote in favor of selling off

the department stores. And yet, it was thwarted by various technical bylaws that opponents of the move had managed to pass.

Rowland, ever the clever one, found a way around this through a
trick known in the City as "concert parties"—people who illegally
coordinate business moves but do so without ever actually discussing it, or at least without leaving any paper trail, so as to make
it nearly impossible to prove their collusion. Rowland had used
Marwan as a concert party, but it was far from enough. To make his
really big move on Fraser, he used a combination of tactics. First he
diverted attention by making it seem as though his own financial
difficulties had caused him to lose interest in the company. And
then he started looking for a major businessman who would buy
off Rowland's entire stake, with the tacit understanding that the
purchase was on some level fictitious. After selling off his portion,
he could freely buy more shares on the open market, enough to
combine with the old ones to give him a majority in the company.
Such a man would need to be wealthy enough to make the purchase on his own, yet *not* wealthy enough to turn around and buy
the other 20 percent needed for him to take over Fraser himself.
The man who helped Rowland identify the right businessman was
Ashraf Marwan.

And the man Marwan found for him was Mohamed al-Fayed.

MOHAMED AL-FAYED WAS born in 1933 to a middle-class Egyptian
family. His first wife, Samira Khashoggi, to whom he was married
from 1954 to 1956, was the sister of the multimillionaires Adnan
and Essam Khashoggi, themselves alumni of Victoria College and
personal friends of Ashraf Marwan. Samira was the mother of Al-
Fayed's firstborn son, Dodi, who died in 1997 in the same Paris car
crash that killed Princess Diana.

Mohamed himself was a successful businessman. In the 1950s he
started a shipping company together with his brother, and in the

1960s he moved to Dubai where he built his fortune. In 1974 he relocated to England and shifted most of his dealings there, and to France. In Paris he bought the famed Ritz Hotel, which he renovated at great cost—an investment for which he received high honors from the mayor of Paris at the time, Jacques Chirac. In 1975 he was introduced to Tiny Rowland and briefly joined the board of directors of Lonrho. Although they hit a rough patch because of Rowland's endemic inability to deal effectively with Arab businessmen, the two reestablished contact in 1983.

Rowland's biggest fear was that whoever became his new partner in the Fraser venture would take the opportunity to buy up another 20 percent and take over the company himself, instead of holding on to the 30 percent merely on Rowland's behalf. Before approaching Al-Fayed, he had Marwan do a thorough check of his finances to make sure that he did not have the capacity to make such a move. Marwan was a natural choice, both because he was already in on the scam and also because he was Al-Fayed's countryman, deeply connected in Egyptian intelligence, close with the Khashoggi brothers and therefore with intimate access to the details of Al-Fayed's life. It didn't hurt that Marwan had developed a reputation of being a man of mystery, all-powerful and all-knowing in Egypt. This reputation, which Marwan did everything to foster, accorded him much more power than he really had. A member of the British parliament expressed the typical exaggeration of Marwan's qualifications when he described him as "the son-in-law of the late President Nasser, [who] had been head of security, intelligence and information in Egypt. He had been trained by the KGB. He was therefore a man of great skill in intelligence, counter-intelligence and disinformation techniques, and of the utmost influence and power."[3]

Mohamed al-Fayed and his brother Ali had worked hard to create the impression that they were vastly wealthy, although in

practice their £100 million estate was mostly in hock to the local
banks. In late June 1984, Rowland spoke with Al-Fayed about selling him his holdings in the House of Fraser, insisting that the profits
would be significant. Al-Fayed loved the idea and wanted to close
the deal immediately, but Rowland stalled. Then Al-Fayed invited
Marwan for a chat, asking him to convey his intense interest in the
deal. Marwan told Rowland that in his estimation, Al-Fayed was
worth no more than £50 million. The implication was that while
he might be able to pull together the necessary money to purchase
Rowland's stake, he wouldn't be able to purchase anything beyond
that to take over the company, which at the time had a market
capitalization of about £600 million. And so, when the Al-Fayed
brothers showed Rowland a letter from their bank affirming that
it was putting £132 million at their disposal to purchase Lonrho's
stake in Fraser, both he and Marwan assumed that was pretty much
all they could afford.

They were wrong. For Mohamed al-Fayed had, precisely then,
earned the trust of the sultan of Brunei, at the time the wealthiest
man on earth. With his help, he created a fund in banks in England
and Switzerland containing an additional £350 million. It would
enable him to buy up the remaining shares he would need to take
over the House of Fraser.

On October 29, 1984, Rowland and Al-Fayed met together
with Marwan, and together they agreed that Lonrho would sell its
entire stake to Al-Fayed. It was further agreed that the deal would
remain a secret until it was completed, that the payment would
be in cash, and that Rowland would keep his position on Fraser's
board of directors.

Three days later, the deal was officially announced. For the first
time, the Al-Fayed brothers entered the spotlight, and they made
a sterling impression on the British press. They had, after all, saved
Harrods from the "unpleasant and unacceptable face of capitalism."

It was enough to earn them dinner with the prime minister, together with the sultan of Brunei, at Number 10 Downing Street—a
place where Rowland had been persona non grata for years.

Violating the terms of the agreement, the Al-Fayed brothers
suddenly demanded that Rowland relinquish his seats on the board
of Fraser. Rowland sensed that something was afoot, and if he had
any chance of acquiring Fraser, he had to move fast. He bought
back many of the shares he had sold to smaller buyers, including
Marwan's stake. The battle against Al-Fayed was on, and it became a
public one—though Rowland still didn't know how much money
his rival really had on hand.

In the turmoil that ensued, Marwan played a key role, as go-
between delivering messages from one tycoon to the other but also
as chief sleuth working for Rowland. He discovered, for example,
that the money the Al-Fayed brothers had used to purchase Lonrho's shares in Fraser had come from the sultan of Brunei and not
their own funds. Through his intelligence contacts in Egypt, moreover, he established that the Al-Fayeds had come from a middle-
class family and that all the stories of their wealth were false.
Marwan's discoveries found their way to the press, which fed on
them with abandon. But as opposed to Rowland, who battled with
his adversaries—especially the management of Fraser—through
threats and intimidation, the Al-Fayeds used soft persuasion, buying
support in Fraser with promises of cooperation, of massive investment in Harrods, and of higher wages. During the Christmas vacation, when Rowland and Marwan traveled together to Acapulco,
the Al-Fayed brothers held receptions for the executives of Fraser
in their posh apartment in London, showing a compelling facade
of vast wealth that convinced government officials to give their
blessing for a complete takeover of the company.

And indeed, on March 4, 1985, Mohamed al-Fayed publicly announced his intention to buy the House of Fraser. To Rowland

and Marwan's surprise, it turned out that he had £435 million
at his disposal. The two flew off to the Spanish coastal town of
Marbella, where they met Adnan Khashoggi, who insisted that all
the stories of Al-Fayed's vast family wealth from Egyptian cotton
were false and that their father was a mid-level inspector in the
Education Ministry. But when Marwan attempted to bring to the
British authorities proof that Al-Fayed had lied about the source
of the purchase, and that it was really the money of the sultan of
Brunei, he was roundly ignored. Marwan's reputation of being an
untrustworthy manipulator had caused his pleas to fall on deaf ears.

Rowland then turned to the press, mounting a public campaign
to discredit Al-Fayed that would go on for seven years and cost him
over £20 million. Hiring the services of lawyers, accountants, in-
vestigative reporters, and private investigators, he dug under every
rock to uncover wrongdoings of the Egyptian family in Haiti,
Brunei, Dubai, Switzerland, France, England, and, of course, Egypt.
His tactics included illicit wiretapping, bribery, and threats. And
the man who directed and implemented the campaign was Ashraf
Marwan. So effective had been Marwan's projected image of mystery and dubious friends that he frightened the Al-Fayeds into in-
vesting increasing resources into defending themselves from the
onslaught—including hiring personal bodyguards.

In the first phase, Marwan tracked down copies of the Al-
Fayeds' birth certificates, which proved their middle-class origins and therefore undermined their claim that the purchase was
made with family money. Though a translation of the certificates
was published in the British press, no one seemed to care that
much. The effort shifted to proving that Al-Fayed had illegally
taken advantage of his signatory power over the sultan's accounts.
Rowland paid £2 million to an Indian guru frequented by the
immensely wealthy, in exchange for a poor-quality recording of a
conversation between him and Al-Fayed, in which the latter was

purportedly caught admitting that the money had belonged to the sultan of Brunei. In eighteen hours of recordings, however, nothing really useful turned up. Marwan hired a private investigator to tap the home phones of Al-Fayed. He also offered the Haitian ambassador to London a sum of £2 million for embarrassing information regarding his dealings there, since Al-Fayed had fled Haiti after getting into an argument with the local strongman, François "Papa Doc" Duvalier. But this effort, too, led nowhere.[4]

Chris Blackhurst, an experienced journalist and a former editor of the *Independent*, shed some light on Marwan's method of operation. According to one account, which he heard from Al-Fayed's assistant, in late 1986 someone knocked on the door of the company's offices and asked to speak with the Egyptian millionaire. When asked what his business with Al-Fayed was, he explained that he was a private investigator, hired by Ashraf Marwan to install surveillance devices in the investment fund's telephones. The investigator had become terrified, however, when he learned the fate of someone else whose phones Marwan had hired him to tap: Gérard Hoarau, the exiled opposition leader of the Seychelles Islands who, just days earlier, had been gunned down at the entrance of his London home. The investigator was now asking Al-Fayed to protect him against possible threats from Marwan. Al-Fayed agreed to meet him, on condition that he tell him all the details of who had hired him. The investigator agreed, and a time was set. But before the meeting could take place, he was severely beaten in the Primrose Hill section of London. The meeting was canceled.[5]

Blackhurst had his own creepy dealings with Marwan as well. In one case, Marwan granted him an interview, telling him to show up at Heathrow Airport with passport in hand. Without even going through border control, he was put on a private plane headed for the tiny island of Majorca, together with Marwan— who owned a luxury hotel there—and two other businessmen who spent the entire flight ignoring Blackhurst and speaking only in Arabic. When they finally arrived in Majorca, Marwan ignored him for the better part of a weekend, and when he finally did allow the interview, it was brief and trivial in its contents. Marwan did, however, take the opportunity to drop names of dubious and violent figures in the Arab world with whom he was well acquainted, including Gaddafi. Blackhurst's impression was of a man bent on showing you that he wasn't just any businessman of the City but rather mysterious and dangerous, someone who could take you out of your world and exercise complete control over your life. If he had just vanished that weekend, Blackhurst mused afterward, no one would have had a clue where to look for him. This is how Blackhurst began his piece:

> Ashraf Marwan frightens people. The Egyptian multi-millionaire who made a fortune trading shares in House of Fraser, Fleet and Extel is now stalking a sleepy Yorkshire company, Bridon. He won't make a bid. He never does, but he might sell the shares to fellow predators such as Tiny Rowland—who will.
>
> Nobody knows where Marwan will strike next. The City can't keep up, for he is always one step ahead—on the next deal, the next million. When he does make a move, he does not tell the City. He hates its stuffiness, its unwritten rules. . . .
>
> Mysterious, shadowy, and sinister are the favorite descriptions of Marwan elicited in the City. His choice of friends does not help. He is close to Libya's Colonel Gaddafi and his cousin, security adviser Ahmed Gaddafadam. "Just because I am their friend does not mean I am a terrorist."[6]

Marwan was also one of the few people in the City who was publicly known as a liar. John Griffiths, who was appointed to lead the formal inquiry regarding Tiny Rowland's efforts to take over the House of Fraser, concluded in a March 1984 report that "Dr. Marwan's evidence did not carry to me the ring of truth. I certainly felt I cannot rely upon it as the whole truth . . . he was not frank." Tom Bower, who wrote unauthorized biographies of Al-Fayed and Rowland, asserted that this was Griffiths's way of saying Marwan's testimony was an outright lie.[7] And so it was received at the time. No other witness among the many who appeared before Griffiths was described that way. Marwan clearly was trying to cover up the fact that he had purchased the shares of Fraser in order to help Rowland take over the company. He told Griffiths instead that he bought the stock after reading an article about the company in the *Sunday Telegraph*. For proof, he brought a copy of the article. But Rowland's secretary testified that she had sent the article to Marwan on his request, and Griffiths concluded that the copy he held was a photocopy of the very clipping that Rowland had.[8] It is worth noting, in this regard, that Rowland himself, in denying that he had asked Marwan to buy shares on his behalf, said that he "would not want to do business with Ashraf Marwan . . . who is totally unreliable when it comes to business. . . . In terms of business Dr. Ashraf Marwan is totally unreliable."[9]

IN THE LATE 1980s, the Harrods affair faded from the public eye, and so did Ashraf Marwan. His behavior helped this along. He never really involved himself in the London business world and had no English friends. As opposed to other London businessmen, who built themselves lush offices in the financial district, Marwan kept a relatively modest office on Hill Street in the aristocratic Mayfair district. Other than a few pieces of East Asian art, his office had just a desk with a computer screen ferrying financial data from one side to the other, mostly about equities on the London exchange. Even when he received visitors in his office, one eye was always following the numbers on that screen. He insisted that this was how he worked: He collected information, waited for opportunities, and made quick decisions. That was how he purchased the hotel in Majorca. As he told it, he was having dinner in Spain, and the hotel's owner was describing the hotel, and mentioned he was interested in selling it. Marwan asked him how much he wanted and verified that that was the final selling price. The next morning, he called the owner up and closed the deal. In another case, in the late 1980s, he purchased 3.2 percent of the stock in the Chelsea soccer club after receiving a tip that a very wealthy businessman was looking to buy the team. He always kept abreast of developments on the team after that, and in 2003 he sold his holdings to the Russian oligarch Roman Abramovich in a deal that would later draw attention of the authorities. Marwan's investment in Chelsea was unusual for the length of time he held it. Usually he tended to buy companies or real estate holdings, mostly hotels, not as "buy-and-hold" investments, but to realize a significant gain in a short period of time.[10]

There is no doubt that Marwan became a rich man in London, but the information as to just how he did it, and just how wealthy he became, is far from clear. In the few interviews he granted, he claimed that he became wealthy from successful business deals, mostly in real estate, and chalked his successes up to a combination of wit and luck. Undoubtedly, the source of at least some of his wealth was in illicit weapons dealing undertaken together with top people in Libya, and presumably he knew how to take percentages on deals in which he served merely as broker rather than investor. Nor is there any clarity as to his net worth. According to reports whose provenance is unclear, by the time he left Egypt he had accumulated more than £300 million, mostly from buildings and hotels he had acquired in London.[11] But even if these reports are wildly exaggerated, he did not arrive in the UK penniless. Again, one inquiry in Egypt revealed that as early as 1972, he held equities on the London exchange valued at £2 million, and we may assume that his wealth only grew after that. His payments from the Mossad, through all the years, totaled about $1 million, and it seems clear that early on he used that money as a basis for making more money through various deals. In the summer of 1983, Marwan estimated, in testimony he gave in the context of the Fraser affair, that his net worth was around £20 million. After his death, the headlines consistently referred to him as "Billionaire Ashraf Marwan," though there is no reason to take that literally.

ALONGSIDE HIS PRODIGIOUS business efforts, Marwan continued, even if on a low profile, with his secret career as a senior source for Israeli intelligence. His connections with top Egyptian officials were never severed, and he made a point of spending some of his time in Cairo, where he continued nurturing his relationships among Egyptian elites, and where his wife and two sons continued living for some time as well. Neither did Marwan stop visiting Saudi Arabia and the Gulf states as well as Syria. In these visits, he met with top government officials, and he was always eager to gather new information that might be of interest to Israel.

Despite the lower priority that Egypt held for Israeli intelligence in the wake of the peace treaty, Marwan still remained important to the Mossad. Because of the nature of his connections across the Arab world, most of the intelligence he could provide was of a nonmilitary, political variety. And yet, the lack of high-quality sources in the Arab political arena made him, even twenty years after he first called the Israeli embassy in London, one of the Mossad's most highly regarded agents.

Dubi continued serving as his handler through the 1980s and into the 1990s. As in the past, their connection was based in London, Rome, or Paris. Once Marwan had bought the hotel in Palma de

Majorca, where he also kept a home, some of the meetings took place there. In one of these, when "Alex" and "the Angel" met next to the local golf course, Mona suddenly appeared, on her way out. Marwan, always unflappable, introduced Alex as one of his old friends, and the two exchanged pleasantries. The relationship between handler and agent stayed on an even keel during these many years. In some sense, it took on the shape of a relationship between husband and wife over decades, with both parties getting used to each other's foibles. But this relationship did not live in isolation, and eventually it came to an end for purely external reasons.

Two events, to be precise, brought it to an end. One was the Yehuda Gil affair. The other was the exposure of Marwan's secret life in the Israeli press.

IN LATE 1997, after a prolonged investigation, one of the most revered intelligence officers in the Mossad admitted that for years he had been supplying false information from a top Syrian official whom he had supposedly been handling. The revelation about Yehuda Gil, who exceeded Graham Greene and John le Carré in the license he gave his imagination,[12] was a bombshell for the agency, triggering a maelstrom of investigations across the whole Mossad to make sure there were no similar cases.

When the story emerged, Dubi had been Marwan's handler for twenty-seven years. Since 1974, the year Gil had claimed to have recruited the Syrian officer, Dubi had been the only person in the Mossad—with the exception of a single meeting with Zamir's successor, Yitzhak Hofi—who had had any contact with Marwan. In the new, tense environment that now emerged in the wake of the scandal, this kind of relationship drew intense scrutiny. Many remembered how adamant Marwan's refusal to consider any replacement for Dubi or even to add a second handler had been. The pressure suddenly mounted on Dubi, who was considered a straight shooter, meticulous, and reliable. While no one doubted the existence of Marwan or the quality of the intelligence he had given, the fear of future debacles like this one resulted in an intense effort to prevent anything like it from happening again.

It was decided, again, that Marwan needed another handler.

Dubi made it clear that in his opinion, if the Mossad pushed the point too hard, Marwan would prefer to cut off relations. But the Mossad's senior officers remained unconvinced, and on their orders Dubi prepared a new handler to meet Marwan. The meeting was to take place in one of the fancy hotels on Via Veneto in Rome. Dubi waited for Marwan in the hotel room as planned. He had the officer wait elsewhere for Dubi's green light indicating that Marwan was ready for him to join. But Marwan never showed. It was not the first time that he had stood Dubi up. His tight schedule and external, unavoidable pressures occasionally made it impossible for him to show, or even to notify him. Dubi waited in the room. Suddenly there was a knock on the door, and the other officer entered without waiting for Dubi's signal. This was evidence of the level of distrust that had permeated the Mossad in the wake of the Yehuda Gil affair.

Given the failure to add a second handler, the new Mossad chief, Danny Yatom, gave the order to inform Marwan that their relationship had run its course. It was the first time, in nearly thirty years of contact, that either side had cut off ties.

Soon after that, when it became clear that the Mossad still needed a source at Marwan's level after all, and when Danny Yatom had been replaced in 1998 by Efraim Halevy, an attempt was made to restart the relationship. Halevy, who was close with Zvi Zamir, suggested that Zamir join Dubi for the next meeting with Marwan. Zamir agreed, but Marwan, for whatever reason, did not. So instead, Dubi was given a miniature tape recorder, which he carried in the front pocket of his jeans. The recorder worked fine until it reached the end of the cassette—when it suddenly, inexplicably, began playing back their conversation at full volume. Dubi and Marwan sat uncomfortably for a few moments, not saying a word.

If Marwan understood what had just happened, he didn't show it. He had insisted that their conversations never be taped, for fear that the Mossad could later use the recordings to extort his continued cooperation even after he no longer wanted to give it. Dubi promised he wouldn't record them, and, with the exception of a single case early on, he kept his promise. Now Marwan discovered that the man to whom he had given his complete trust all those years had set some sort of a trap. And Dubi understood that he had just blasted a hole through the fabric of faith that had held them together. In that mortifying moment, Dubi excused himself, walked to the bathroom, and turned off the tape recorder. When he came back, Marwan acted as though nothing had happened, and they soon ended the conversation.

It was Marwan's last meeting with the Mossad.

This was how one of the most successful espionage operations in history came to an abrupt end. But all in all, it was a mutually acceptable end. Marwan, now in his mid-fifties, really had little need for the stimulation of spying, and he hadn't needed the money for nearly two decades. He no longer needed to feed his ego this way, and his importance to the Mossad clearly had dwindled. Danny Yatom's decision to cut ties with Marwan, and Halevy's attempt to reestablish them, were all the indication he needed that he was no longer nearly as important to the Mossad as he had once been. The incident with the tape recorder was really just the last straw.

By this point the Mossad was not terribly upset at the loss of Marwan's services. Leaving aside the problem of continuing with only one handler despite the Yehuda Gil affair, there were other reasons why calling it quits made sense. Efraim Halevy chafed at the thought of spying on Egypt at so high a level, now that the two states were at peace: Any revelation could deal a major blow to relations. As Marwan's ability to provide high-value intelligence dwindled, the cost-benefit analysis kept shifting in favor of cutting ties. Halevy himself enjoyed good personal relationships with a number of Arab leaders, including Mubarak, with whom he had met in secret meetings at Mubarak's residence. That kind of scandal could ruin Halevy's career. So it was not a hard call to make.

In the years that followed, Dubi worked to stay in touch with Marwan by telephone; in practice, most of the contact was with Marwan's secretary, Azza. She knew him only as "Dr. Lord," a friend of Marwan's who showed an abiding interested in her boss's health and well-being, and who joked with her about his bad habits like his habitual tardiness. Azza obliged Dr. Lord, telling him that Marwan's health was in fact not so good, about his bypass surgery and his cancer and the exhausting treatments he had undergone. Dubi understood that she was telling him all this with Marwan's full knowledge—and that Marwan preferred it this way. But even this limited connection came to an end. Late in 2002, when more and more details were coming out in the Israeli media about the mysterious Egyptian spy who warned Israel before the Yom Kippur War, and his identity was becoming clearer and clearer, Dubi called Marwan's office. Azza sounded very cold and was suddenly unwilling to speak to "Dr. Lord" about her boss. Dubi understood that Marwan had decided to break off contact once and for all. This was the end.

MARWAN'S DECISION TO cut the tie with Dubi reflected not just a natural desire of an aging man to bring an end to the secret, dangerous liaison he had built with the Mossad, but also a sense of disappointment at the priest in whom he had confided for so very long. If the debacle with the tape recorder were not proof enough, a second issue loomed much larger: the gradual publication of his

identity in the Israeli press. He didn't care, nor even necessarily
know about, who might have leaked his name or the battles between the Mossad and Military Intelligence. As far as he was concerned, it was a real threat to his life, and the confluence of events
may well have convinced Marwan that the Mossad had decided
to kill him. This was probably the reason he rebuffed repeated attempts by Dubi and even Zamir to contact him—attempts whose
real aim was to try to protect him from the very real threats to his
life that were, it turns out, coming from somewhere else entirely.

ASHRAF MARWAN LIVED in a fifth-floor apartment on 24 Carlton
House Terrace, a gorgeous cul-de-sac in Westminster, London. The
limited traffic on the street, and its central location between Pall
Mall and St. James Park, a five-minute walk from Piccadilly Circus,
made it an ideal place to wind down a successful career in the City.
When the weather was clear, Ashraf Marwan could take a fifteen-
minute stroll to his office on Hill Street. But his health declined,
and his heart weakened, and he could no longer make the walk.
Instead, his limousine took him anywhere he needed to go.

The apartment itself included a large living room and three bed-
rooms, one of which—his own—opened onto a wide balcony. He
also had a study and two full baths. The apartment was decorated
with innumerable knickknacks and works of art, including a portrait of Mona's father, the great Egyptian leader, in profile against a
backdrop of gold. The apartment was not large, but it was assessed
at around £4.5 million because of its superb location. The balcony
looked out over a wide private garden with its lush lawn and tall
trees; in the late spring, yellow roses would bloom. The garden
was restricted to the residents of the building only, and it is hard
to imagine a better place in London to clear one's head. Marwan,
whose declining health forced him to cut back his work hours,
took full advantage of that garden. In 2004, when he was just sixty,

he began to consider retirement. According to Mona, he began spending more time with his grandchildren and other extracurriculars. Just a few years after he ended his espionage career, his business career drew to a close as well.

BUT HISTORY DID NOT let Marwan retire in peace.

On December 21, 2002, the Egyptian newspaper *Al-Ahram* published an interview with the London-based Israeli historian Ahron Bregman, in which the latter was asked, point-blank, whether the "son-in-law" about whom he had written in his new book, also known by the code name Babel, was in fact Ashraf Marwan. Bregman answered in the affirmative. It was the first time that the identity of the Mossad's greatest spy was revealed in public.

This revelation was quite damaging to Marwan, very likely resulting in his death. But the damage to the Mossad was sweeping as well. In an instant, the agency's ability to keep its agents secret and safe was called into question. And if the Israelis couldn't protect a man who had risked his life and that of his family to serve them, then one may imagine how much harder it would now become to recruit new agents. For a small and embattled country like Israel, the revelation was nothing less than a national security catastrophe.

So it is somewhat surprising to discover that in the aftermath of the leak, no immediate formal inquiry was conducted to find out who was responsible. It's even more surprising when it turns out that discovering the guilty party would have been very easy.

All the signs, after all, pointed to Eli Zeira.

The man whose entire legacy was marred by accusations that as Military Intelligence chief during the Yom Kippur War, he failed to abandon the *kontzeptzia* and to pay attention to the overwhelming intelligence predicting a surprise attack in October 1973, the man whose only defense was that Ashraf Marwan, the greatest source of that intelligence, was in fact a "double agent"—he was definitively the man who, beginning in the early 1990s, made sure that people knew the agent's identity.

We can speculate as to the reasons why a career intelligence officer like Zeira would deliberately "out" the greatest spy in the last half century. But the evidence that he did it is overwhelming.

In the early 1990s, historians began publishing hints that twenty-four hours before the attack on October 6, 1973, Zvi Zamir received a warning of what was coming. Three different books appeared describing the history of Israeli intelligence, and all three made mention of a high-level source the Israelis had. Yossi Melman and Dan Raviv said that a "Mossad agent in Cairo" had warned Zamir, without giving any further details.[13] Benny Morris and Ian Black expanded a bit when they described him, quoting a senior Israeli intelligence official, as "the best agent any country had during war-time, a miraculous source."[14] And Shmuel Katz, in his history of the IDF's military intelligence, described the source as "one of the Mossad's most valuable and secretive agents." Katz did a bit of an end run around the military censor when he wrote in a footnote that although he was prohibited from disclosing the agent's nationality, "Yossi Melman and Dan Raviv indicate that the 'valued' Mossad source originated in Cairo, suggesting that the agent was a high-ranking member of the Egyptian leadership."[15]

Yet in spite of these hints, it would not have been possible to deduce the identity of Ashraf Marwan were it not for Zeira's own book, which appeared in 1993.[16] Even before it came out, a few people would have already seen Marwan's name on page 114 of the book's pre-censorship first draft—where he appeared explicitly as the only person who had been present at the August 1973 summit meeting besides Sadat and the Saudi king. The journalist Amnon Dankner, who in the early 1990s carried out research on the Yom Kippur War, laid his hands on that first draft through a member of the government committee who was supposed to approve its publication. According to Dankner, from the context in which his name appeared, it was clear that Marwan was the Mossad's "miraculous source." Dankner showed it to Brig. Gen. (res.) Yoel Ben-Porat, the commander of MI's Sigint unit during the war who had just published his own version of events, and he was furious.[17] What was obvious to Dankner would have been relatively simple for anyone else who came into contact with that manuscript—typists, editors, and others—to deduce as well.

Senior Mossad officials warned against publishing Zeira's book because of the risk that the Angel's identity would be revealed. The military censor instead chose to allow it with only minor modifications. Marwan's actual name did not appear. Yet anyone familiar with the cast of characters could figure it out. In discussing a book by Jeffrey Robinson about the Saudi oil minister Sheikh Yamani, Zeira wrote that "the author of the book, Robinson, interviewed the only person who was present in the meeting between the Egyptian President and the Saudi King. According to that person's testimony, the purpose of Anwar Sadat's visit to Saudi Arabia was to let the king in on the secret and inform him that Egypt and Syria were about to launch a war against Israel in the very near future."[18] Anyone genuinely interested could have gotten a copy of Robinson's book and found that elsewhere he had explicitly mentioned that "Dr. Ashraf Marwan, President Nasser's son-in-law and now a London-based businessman, was head of Egyptian intelligence and the only other person in that meeting with Sadat and Faisal."[19] Given that two pages later in his own book, Zeira blamed the "informant" for keeping the Mossad in the dark about the purpose of the Saudi-Egyptian summit—which, he contended, was the crowning achievement in the Egyptian ruse[20]—it is clear that the "informant" who should have told the Mossad about the meeting, and the person whom Robinson cited as being the only one present at the meeting other

than the leaders, were the same person. This, too, was the conclusion arrived at by Israeli Supreme Court Justice Theodor Orr
who examined the materials later on.[21] Zeira's claim that Marwan
neglected to tell the Mossad about the summit meeting, upon
which Zeira's entire "double agent" hypothesis turns, is simply
false; Marwan reported on the meeting in full. Zeira's book was
also the first published account that authoritatively pointed to
the incredible quality of the materials given by the source, and
the damage he did to Egypt and other Arab states.[22]

The next publication, which revealed Marwan's identity in other
ways, was an article penned by Ronen Bergman in the *Haaretz*
weekend supplement of September 17, 1999, titled "Tomorrow
War Will Break." The piece described, for the first time, how contact was first made with the agent in 1969 (though it was actually
1970), when he showed up at an Israeli embassy in Europe and
offered his services. Bergman, too, detailed the source's activities
and the high quality of the materials he provided, and raised the
question of whether he was really a double agent. Seemingly without any connection to the subject at hand, Bergman then went on
to describe the foiled terror attack in September 1973, mentioning
only that the details appear in the memoir of the Egyptian military attaché in Libya at the time. Anyone who tracked down that
memoir would discover Ashraf Marwan's central role in that plot.
Both Zeira and Bergman used the same tactic to lead perspicacious
researchers to Marwan's identity, by injecting a seemingly irrelevant
external reference into a story and allowing intrepid professionals
to put two and two together themselves.

The question of who was the key source in Bergman's article
was answered by no other than Zvi Zamir, who said that Bergman
showed him the draft of the article before it was published, and
Marwan's name had appeared explicitly. Zamir, who was very surprised, asked Bergman where he'd gotten the idea that the source

was Marwan, and Bergman had responded that he got it "from Eli." Both men knew whom he was talking about.

Nor was Bergman the only writer to whom Zeira apparently exposed Marwan's identity. About nine months before the *Haaretz* piece appeared, Zeira told a scholar named Ephraim Kahana that the Mossad's source was a double agent. Zeira also gave Kahana "identifying details, including the source's approximate age, and biographical details."[23] In his article, which appeared in the summer 2002 issue of the journal *Intelligence and National Security*, Kahana refrained from publishing the key details of the source's identity and in a footnote added that they could not legally be revealed. But despite this, he still allowed himself to write that "the top source was a young Egyptian, who in 1969 was in his late twenties or early thirties. He was the right-hand man of President Nasser and, after his death, continued in the same position under President Sadat." As to the source of his information, Kahana cited an interview he held with Eli Zeira in January 1999.[24] Kahana was, in many respects, unfortunate that he published his piece in an academic journal, with its very long lead times. Had it appeared two years earlier, he would have had the dubious honor of having outed Israel's top spy.

Another writer who covered the Yom Kippur War was Howard Blum, who investigated the double agent theory in detail. He, too, based everything he knew about Marwan on information he received from Zeira. On a personal note, Blum contacted me after my own book on the Yom Kippur War came out, as he was visiting Israel. It was May 6, 2002. We met for dinner in Tel Aviv, and he had just come from a meeting with Zeira at his home. According to Blum, Zeira was interested in one thing and one thing only: the "double agent" who tricked the Mossad. When he asked Zeira who that source was, he said that while he couldn't divulge the name, Blum should know that the source took part in the meeting between Sadat and King Faisal in August 1973 and did not report it to the Mossad. Zeira further said that if Blum were to look on page 148 of the English edition of the memoir of the Egyptian army chief of staff, Shazly, he would find the name of the agent.

When Blum returned to the United States, he checked Shazly's book and found two different names on the page that could be relevant. He called Zeira in Israel. Zeira told him that he still couldn't say who it was, but recommended that he contact the historian Ahron Bregman in London, who knew the relevant details. Blum called Bregman, told him that he'd been referred by Zeira, and that he knew that the source was one of the two names he found in Shazly's book. He wanted to pin Bregman down as to which it was. Bregman, in an act of generosity rare for the field, risked losing his scoop and told him which one it was. Now Blum knew the name of the source, and he published it in his book that came out in 2003.

But by then, Marwan's name had already appeared in public as the greatest spy Israel had ever recruited. Ahron Bregman had broken the story.

BACK IN 1998, Ahron Bregman published a book, together with Jihan el-Tahri, an Arab researcher and a director of documentary movies, surveying the fifty years of the Arab-Israeli conflict.[25] One of the book's key sources was Eli Zeira, who was interviewed by Bregman and described the war as he had personally experienced it. The book dealt heavily with Israel's intelligence failure preceding the war, but made no mention, explicit or implicit, of Ashraf Marwan. Two years later, Bregman published a new book, titled *Israel's Wars, 1947–93*. This time the story about the double agent played a central role in the plot. The book described the episode in some detail and revealed for the first time that the recruitment of the agent had taken place in London. Bregman also touched on specific pieces of intelligence that the source had delivered, such as the minutes of the meeting that Nasser held with the Soviet leaders in Moscow in January 1970, and Sadat's letter to Leonid Brezhnev in August 1972, and he pointed out for the first time that the Mossad's source had been present in the Sadat-Faisal summit but had not told the Mossad about it. Finally, he revealed that Zamir's meeting with the source on the eve of the Yom Kippur War took place not just in any European capital, but in London.[26]

Two years after that, Bregman published an article in the Israeli daily *Yedioth Ahronot* that was based on a chapter of his next book, *History of Israel*, which was about to appear in English. Although the article didn't draw much attention, it gently lay the noose fully around Marwan's neck. For the first time, the story included two details that clearly connected Marwan with the story: one, that the source was a family member of Nasser's; and the other, that he was known as the "In-Law" or the "Doctor." In fact, he was not known in Israel by either of these monikers. But this was enough to get Azza, Marwan's secretary, to stop taking Dubi's calls.

When his book came out that October, Bregman revealed additional details, including the source's close relation to Nasser, his specific job under Sadat, and a detailed account of his role in the foiled terror attack in Rome in September 1973.[27] No doubts remained as to the source's identity. A process that had begun with the publication in Hebrew of Zeira's book, nearly a decade earlier, now had reached its moment of truth. An Egyptian paper called Marwan and asked if he had spied for Israel. Marwan replied that it was a "stupid detective story." Bregman then met with a reporter for *Al-Ahram* and confirmed that Marwan was the spy. He also asserted that Marwan had been a double agent and had fooled the Israelis. A few days later, on December 22, the interview was published.

In 2004, Eli Zeira published a new edition of his book. It had not gone through major revisions from the first edition, despite the passage of nearly a decade. But Zeira did go out of his way to explicitly name the source as Ashraf Marwan.

THE PUBLICATION OF a new edition of Zeira's account of the intelligence failure of 1973 was a perfect opportunity for an hour-long television interview with one of Israel's most esteemed television journalists, Dan Margalit. Margalit gave Zeira free rein to plead his innocence for the intelligence failure. And then, in the second half of the interview, Zeira spelled out his theory that Marwan was a double agent—repeatedly mentioning him by name.

The following week, Margalit hosted Zvi Zamir on his show to offer his side of the story. On the subject of Zeira's exposure of Marwan, Zamir was explicit in his accusation—triggering an intense court battle in the years that followed. Zeira, he said, "needs to stand trial for having revealed sources . . . the man who was in a position to know was the head of military intelligence, and when *he* reveals a source, he breaks the first of the Ten Commandments of the Intelligence Corps."[28]

In response to this interview, Zeira sued Zamir for defamation. The two agreed to submit the suit to arbitration with retired Supreme Court Justice Theodor Orr, who ended up siding fully with Zamir—that, indeed, Zeira had leaked the identity of Ashraf Marwan:

> The picture that emerges on the basis of everything cited above suggests that on different occasions, the plaintiff [Zeira] revealed the agent's identity. In the first edition of his book, in 1993, that revelation took the form of scattering details that could lead researchers and people in the know, including journalists and writers, to the agent's identity. In 1999, he revealed the name to Kahana and Ronen [Bergman]. In

May 2002 he revealed the agent's identity to Howard Blum as described in paragraphs 23–28 above. Dr. [Ahron] Bregman revealed the name of the agent explicitly in an interview with an Egyptian newspaper in December 2002. In the book he [Bregman] published in October 2002, he published clear hints as to the agent's identity. In this revelation, Dr. Bregman relied, *inter alia*, on the first edition of the plaintiff's book, as well as the response of Rami Tal to a conversation he had with him, in which the name of the agent was discussed. Rami Tal, it should be recalled, is the editor of both editions of the plaintiff's book. In 2004, in a television interview, and in the second edition of his book, the plaintiff evoked the agent's name explicitly.[29]

The ruling that exonerated Zamir was handed down on March 27, 2007, and released for publication on June 7.

Less than three weeks later, Ashraf Marwan's body was found at the base of his apartment building in London.

Chapter 13

FALLEN ANGEL

June 27, 2007, was another overcast day in London. Summer had just begun, but a patient drizzle had soaked the city over the course of the past week, with temperatures never breaking out of the seventies. On that day, all eyes were on Prime Minister Tony Blair, who was scheduled to present his resignation to Queen Elizabeth at noon.

Neither the weather nor even the prime minister's resignation was of much interest to four men seated in a room on the third floor of the opulent Institute of Directors building at 116 Pall Mall in St. James's.

From where they sat, they had a clear view of the apartment building where Ashraf Marwan lived.

They were talking about the future of Ubichem, a small chemical company based in Southampton. It was no coincidence that they held the meeting next to Marwan's home; since the 1990s, Marwan had owned Ubichem, holding more than 80 percent of its stock. The location of the meeting was meant to make it easy for Marwan to take part. Neither was it a coincidence that Marwan owned the company. Ubichem's chief executive, Azzam Shweiki, was an Egyptian in his mid-fifties who was married to Azza, the daughter of Fawzi Abdel Hafez, the private secretary of Sadat, and someone who had worked closely with Marwan when the latter had served in the President's Office. This is the same Azza who worked in Marwan's office for years as his assistant and press secretary.

Shweiki was upset. For about a year now, Marwan had been breathing down his neck. Not only had he threatened to fire his wife, but he had also started pressing for Shweiki himself to be replaced by the director of their Budapest branch, Jozsef Repasi. This pressure, which had started mild, had now increased to the point that it was nothing short of brutal. Some of the people who saw the process called it an obsession. Employees at Ubichem more than once saw Marwan's long black limousine arrive at the company's headquarters in Southampton, nearly a two-hour drive from his home in central London, and saw Marwan, whose failing health had become apparent, walk slowly, sometimes with a stick and always with a bag of medications, to a meeting of the board of which he was the chairman. During the meetings, he would repeatedly berate Azzam Shweiki to show how unfit he was for the job and why he had to be fired. Shweiki knew his career was in danger and that his replacement by Repasi would not be long in coming.

Everyone familiar with the story says that the criticism was not professional. The company was a small piece of Marwan's empire, and Marwan did not tend to intervene in the management of his companies even when his investment had been much greater. It was clearly personal—though exactly what it was about remains a mystery. His wife, Mona, claimed for years that Marwan had discovered that Shweiki had embezzled millions from the company. This, however, seems unlikely—not just because Shweiki's denials were so adamant, nor because Scotland Yard was so unimpressed with the charge that they refused even to open an investigation.

Rather the biggest proof that the charges were unfounded was the fact that the Egyptian weekly *Al-Ahram*, which published Mona Marwan's accusations in September 2007, published an apology about it a month later.

Whatever the reasons may have been for Marwan's antipathy for Shweiki, one thing is clear. Marwan's deep involvement in the management of the company's affairs, combined with his intention to fly that same evening to the United States, created a situation in which it was decided to hold a meeting of the board of directors, for the first time ever, right next to his residence, renting an office at the Institute of Directors building. Previous meetings had been held at the Southampton headquarters or at Heathrow Airport to make it easier for Repasi to fly in and out from Budapest. The unusual location of the meeting made it possible for several of the participants to witness the final moments in the life of Ashraf Marwan.

The four men in the room were Shweiki, Repasi, Ubichem founder John Roberts, and Michael Parkhurst, a representative of the Marwan family on the board who was not especially admired by the rest of the directors. It was already past noon, and Parkhurst informed the others that he had spoken to Marwan in the morning and that the chairman had sent word that he would be about an hour late because of various errands. Marwan also asked that they not begin the meeting without him. Now the hour had passed, and the busy executives in the room were getting edgy.

From the bay window in the meeting room, one could see the balcony of Marwan's fifth-floor apartment, not more than twenty yards away. Shweiki and Parkhurst were standing by the window when they saw Marwan walk out onto the balcony. According to Shweiki, they called to him and waved. Marwan waved back. Then they called him on the phone to ask if he was really planning on showing up. At first he answered that he was not but then immediately changed his mind and said he would be there within half an hour, once he had changed his clothes. Shweiki and Parkhurst kept looking out toward the balcony. They saw him turn around in a way that appeared to the two of them, who knew him well, as unnatural. He lurched to the left and right, looking repeatedly over the guardrail, down to the ground below. He then went back into the apartment for the last time.

Shweiki called him again to hurry him along. Marwan answered, annoyed at the pestering, and promised he was coming. But then he went back to the balcony and looked down again. When Shweiki called again, Marwan shouted at him that he'd changed his mind and wasn't coming after all. According to the witnesses, he looked behind him into the bedroom, and then, to the utter horror of Shweiki and Parkhurst, he climbed up onto the rail and threw himself over.

It was 1:40 p.m. when Marwan landed on the ground-floor veranda, half his body in a bed of yellow roses in full bloom. A woman who stood nearby screamed. Shweiki and Parkhurst ran to the scene. According to Shweiki, he found Marwan lying on the ground, with no pulse. Several minutes later, an ambulance arrived.

Only four witnesses—the men in the room at the Institute of Directors—saw Marwan fall. Shweiki, whose testimony received the greatest coverage, said that Marwan, who had been wandering about on his balcony for many minutes, looked behind him and then climbed up onto some objects on the balcony, climbed onto the rail, looked forward, stepped out into the air, and fell to his death. He said he saw no one else on the balcony. Parkhurst testified that he was standing next to Shweiki when Marwan fell. In his initial testimony, he backed up Shweiki's account, saying that he saw Marwan go to the railing. In a later testimony, however, he said all he saw was someone falling from the balcony. Parkhurst, like Shweiki, claimed he saw no one else on the balcony.

The two other participants of the meeting, Repasi and Roberts, saw nothing that happened prior to Marwan's fall. As soon as Repasi heard Shweiki and Parkhurst yelling, he ran over to the window just in time to see Marwan fall. Immediately afterward, when the other two ran to the courtyard, he saw in a flash what looked like a person moving inside Marwan's apartment. "I saw," he later testified, "two men standing on the balcony. They did nothing, just looked down. Their calm was most unusual. A woman in the yard screamed, people ran to try and help out, or to call for help. But these two men just stood there." He added that the men "wore suits and were of Middle Eastern appearance." They looked down at Marwan's body from the balcony, then disappeared, and reappeared later on a different balcony, looking down again. Roberts said he saw them as well. Yet Repasi could not say with certainty whether they were in fact standing on Marwan's balcony, because he had only started watching after Marwan had fallen and didn't know which balcony was his. The police, for some reason, did not immediately take his statement or try to bring him back to the room where they watched, so that he could show them on which balcony the men had been standing. When they finally did take his statement, some two months after the event, they traveled to Budapest to speak with him. Repasi expressed his shock that they never asked him to come back to London and point out which balcony it was. This, it would turn out, was only one of many examples of frightful negligence on the part of Scotland Yard.

The investigators took Repasi's statement, and a short time later it was reported that two men had in fact been seen on a balcony, though there was no official word whether it was Marwan's. As far as is known, the identities of the two men have never been determined, and therefore the investigators were unable to draw any conclusions from the fact—even though it did increase the suspicion that foul play had been involved. In an interview he gave in the *Sunday Times*, Repasi said that in his opinion, Marwan may not have been physically pushed, but it was clear that he was pressured into jumping to his death by someone else on the balcony or inside his apartment. Scotland Yard affirmed, several months later, that they could not rule out any of three possibilities: an accident, a suicide, or a murder. This indeterminate result signaled, more or less, the end of the inquiry.

Three years later, in July 2010, a three-day-long public investigation was launched in London to try to determine the cause of Marwan's death. This is a common procedure in cases where there is a suspicion of criminal behavior without sufficient evidence to warrant an indictment. The investigation was undertaken at the request of Marwan's family, and many witnesses were called to testify. Astonishingly, Jozsef Repasi, whose statement had been the clearest proof that Marwan died at someone else's hand, was not asked to participate. Neither was John Roberts, who may have never given a statement at all. At the end of three days of testimony, the special homicide investigator who had been appointed to handle the inquiry concluded that he could not rule out the possibility that Marwan had either committed suicide or been murdered. The possibility of an accident was, finally, abandoned.[1]

THE RIDDLE OF Marwan's death remains only one of the many unsolved mysteries that shrouded his whole life. Part of it has to do with what looks an awful lot like incompetence on the part of Scotland Yard. Not only was the key statement of Repasi taken just two months after the event, and not at all during the public inquiry, but it was also entirely unclear whether a statement from Roberts, who had been with Repasi when Marwan fell, was ever taken. These, however, are not the only parts of the investigation that were bungled. The shoes Marwan was wearing when he died were never found. If Shweiki and Parkhurst were telling the truth, that he climbed up on the planter, and then on the air-conditioning unit, in order to get to the guardrail before jumping, then his shoes would have picked up dust, soil, or paint. The disappearance of the shoes leaves open the possibility that he never deliberately climbed onto the rail at all but was rather pushed over it.[2] Some people familiar with the investigation, who requested anonymity, raised the possibility that the repeated police failures in the investigation were quite deliberate. In their view, it is entirely possible that Her Majesty's Government had no desire at all to resolve the violent death of a high-ranking foreign citizen, which, though it took place on British soil, was far removed from British interests.

Another explanation, of course, has to do with the natural limitations of police investigations. The investigators used the means at their disposal, which do not necessarily include building an entire historical profile of the victim as we have done here. From their standpoint, so long as there were no clear indicators that Marwan committed suicide—such as a suicide note—they couldn't rule it out as such. Similarly, so long as there was no compelling evidence of a homicide, or even a suicide under duress, they couldn't go that way, either.

Historians, however, are not limited by the legal procedures of criminal investigations or the laws of admissible evidence. Naturally, whatever answers suggested by the evidence in this case are quite speculative, and probably wouldn't stand up in court. Little more than an educated guess, really.

The first question to be addressed is whether it was a suicide. Once it has become clear why such a suggestion seems highly unlikely, we will then turn to the question of who may have killed him: business rivals? the Mossad? the Egyptians?

IMMEDIATELY AFTER MARWAN's death, a number of speculations were raised about a possible suicide. From everything known about the way he lived his life, however, it is hard to find any of the hallmarks of a man seriously considering taking his own life. He had no family history of suicides and did not suffer from depression, isolation, or a trauma such as losing his job or the death of a loved one. He did not use drugs, either, which is correlated with a higher suicide rate. The same is true for indicators of suicidal intentions. In the days preceding his death, no one ever reported hearing a word from him that he might harm himself—nor is there any indication that he looked for a means of carrying it out, such as accumulating sleeping pills or acquiring a weapon. Marwan exhibited no behaviors at all associated with someone suicidal, such as loss of hope, anger or vengeance, wanton carelessness, a feeling of entrapment, abuse of alcohol or drugs, distancing from family and friends, antisocial behavior, panic attacks, sleepless nights or oversleeping, mood swings, or extreme apathy.[3]

From all accounts of the final days of Marwan's life, he behaved completely normally, even if he was under a certain amount of stress. Michael Parkhurst, with whom he was close, said that the day Marwan died, he met him in the late morning, and Marwan behaved utterly normally, chatting with him and asking after his children. The building's superintendent, who also saw him that morning, said that he seemed "completely normal," even chipper. His friend Sharif Salah spoke to him by telephone the day before he died and testified that there was nothing in the conversation that suggested he had planned on harming himself. Marwan's sister Azza, who lived in the same apartment, told her friends that she had seen him two hours before his death, and he hadn't shown any worrisome signs. And his wife, Mona, testified that Marwan "was always sociable and expressed a joy of living despite his medical problems," implying that she, too, had seen no suspicious signs in his behavior. In a conversation between them that morning, Marwan told her that he was packing for his trip, later that day, to the United States.

A more detailed account comes from the historian Ahron Bregman, who first revealed Marwan's identity as a spy to the general
public but managed to stay in touch with him afterward nonetheless. According to Bregman, less than twenty-four hours before
his death, Marwan left him a recorded message in which he identified himself according to an agreed-upon code name, saying he
was calling "about the book." He asked Bregman to call him back
on his cell phone. Fifty-nine minutes later, he left another, similar message—and another one twenty minutes after that. In all
the years of their contact, Marwan had never before left recorded
messages. This fact, combined with the number of calls, suggests
that he was in serious straits. When Bregman called him back, the
two spoke about the report released by Justice Orr. A week earlier,
Bregman had sent Marwan a collection of media items that had
appeared in Israel following the Orr Report's publication, and had
begun explaining what they were about. Marwan wanted to know
the bottom line, and Bregman answered that the report had been
printed, and his name had appeared in it. Marwan suggested they
meet the following day, and they discussed when and where they
would meet. They agreed that Marwan would call again to finalize.
At the end of the conversation, Bregman asked Marwan, "Other
than that, how are you?" Marwan answered, "Other than this headache?" Bregman understood that Marwan was saying he was fine,
besides the current mess involving the publication of his identity as
an Israeli spy. They ended their conversation. It was their last.

"It is clear to me, from my knowledge of him," Bregman concluded in an interview with the Israeli newspaper *Haaretz*, "that
the fact that he called me three times in an hour and a half can
be said to reflect a crisis. His tone was not as it had been. It didn't
sound like the Ashraf Marwan I knew." And yet, their conversation
itself didn't strike Bregman as all that unusual—Marwan was char-
acteristically curt and impatient, but polite. He also didn't strike

Bregman as having been under a lot of pressure during the conversation. In his opinion, which he expressed both immediately after
Marwan's death and again three years later, Marwan was under
pressure because of Justice Orr's report being seen by journalists—
though he was not yet aware that the report had been published in
its entirety on the Internet. In any event, according to Bregman, he
had not detected anything in Marwan's behavior to suggest suicidal
intentions.[4]

From the weight of the evidence it seems that Marwan, who
from the outset lacked any of the classic characteristics of the suicidal type, showed very little in the final twenty-four hours of
his life to suggest that he had resolved to kill himself. Based on
the circumstantial evidence, the British homicide investigator who
conducted the public inquiry ruled that his behavior prior to his
death was "normal and full of life," and that "there is no evidence
of mental or psychiatric disorder . . . no evidence of any intention
to commit suicide." He then added, "It is clear that Dr. Marwan
had a great deal to be worried about and was stressed."[5]

Suicide, therefore, seems logically possible, but not more than
that. If we rule out the possibility of suicide, however, then we are
left with the unavoidable conclusion that someone else caused him
to fall. Then we face the same questions common to all unsolved
murders: Who did it, and why? All of our evidence here, it should
be stressed again, is circumstantial. But it is evidence all the same.

THREE POSSIBILITIES HAVE been raised as to who might have caused
the death of Ashraf Marwan: He was murdered by business rivals;
he was murdered by Israelis in retribution for his having deceived
them in 1973; or he was murdered by Egyptians who wanted to
bring the saga to an end in such a way as to avoid his revealing
what happened.

The possibility that Marwan was murdered by business rivals

seems nearly impossible. In 2007, his biggest battles were far behind him. It is true that Mohamed al-Fayed, his nemesis ever since the Harrods affair, was still prospering in London. But he had no reason to strike back at Marwan just now; and Marwan was no longer in a position to harm Al-Fayed. Moreover, Al-Fayed's business methods, which were sometimes very creative, did not include violence. Others have suggested that his death had something to do with his past as an arms dealer. Indeed, according to a sensational exposé by the Egyptian weekly *Rose al-Yusuf* in March 2012, President Hosni Mubarak allegedly dictated memoirs, in which he claimed that Muammar Gaddafi ordered Marwan's assassination because of disagreements concerning the sale of arms to an African nation. After the publication in *Rose al-Yusuf*, which is not known for its reliability, sources close to Mubarak denied that he ever wrote or dictated his memoirs. The Scotland-based Canongate Books, the purported publisher of the memoirs, denied that they even existed—although Canongate is scheduled to publish the memoirs of Mubarak's wife, Suzanne. Nor is there any evidence whatsoever that any of Marwan's former arms-dealing contacts, whether in business or in government, had any interest in his elimination. Marwan himself had been long out of the arms-dealing business by 2007.

The possibility that the Israelis killed him also seems without serious evidentiary grounding. The people who have led the charge on this theory have been members of his family, especially his widow, Mona. They have their reasons. Several months after his death, Mona asserted in an interview with the weekly *Al-Ahram* that "the Israelis definitely had a hand in the cold-blooded murder of my husband." In response to the testimony of Azzam Shweiki, according to which no one else was on the balcony when Marwan fell to his death, she said: "That man—Azzam Shweiki—embezzled millions from my husband's company, and I have decided to fire him from the company. . . . I am sure that the courts will send him to prison. He is a liar who gave false testimony when he said my husband threw himself off the balcony. . . . Israelis were the ones who made up the story about my husband killing himself. They paid off people like Azzam Shweiki in order to back up the story."[6] Three years later, just as the public investigation was getting started, Mona told the *Observer* that Marwan had said his life was in danger no fewer than three times during the final four years of his life, the last being just nine days before he died, when they were alone together in their London apartment. "He turned to me and said: 'My life is in danger. I might be killed. I have a lot of different enemies.' He knew they were coming after him. He was killed by Mossad." Later she said that on the day of the murder, the front door of the apartment had been left unlocked, and the housekeeper, who was present at the time, heard nothing. "I believe that the intruders took him to the bedroom, they hit him and they threw him out of the window over the balcony. Someone on a fourth-floor balcony who gave evidence to the police heard him scream before he fell. Do people committing suicide scream before they fall?"[7]

Mona Marwan's unequivocal assertion that the Mossad murdered her husband has the advantage of serving both her interests and those of her family—for it makes him out as an Egyptian patriot who managed to pull one over on the all-powerful Mossad. Implicating the Mossad, of course, uses the same who-benefits logic that has been behind every conspiracy theory, without regard to evidence. But the alternative narrative—that Marwan was killed by the Egyptians in the wake of the publication of his role as a spy for the Mossad—is so potentially devastating to both Mona and the family that one cannot blame either her or other family members for doing everything in their power to make sure no one reaches that conclusion.

This does not mean that Mona Marwan is deliberately lying.

The fact is that she was the one who demanded that Scotland Yard carry out an investigation that, she believed, would prove her claim. Had she known the truth about who, most likely, killed Marwan, she would probably not have taken the risk.

Nor should we assume that her faith in her husband's patriotism is purely of her own invention. In all likelihood she heard her husband say more than once that his life was in danger, that the published rumors of his having spied for Israel were only a disinformation campaign by the Mossad aimed at getting him killed. Again, one of the reasons he kept working with the Mossad for so many years was his fear that if he stopped, they might try to kill him. In a conversation with Ahron Bregman in 2003, he said that after reading Howard Blum's book on the Yom Kippur War, he came to the conclusion that Eli Zeira believed that the Mossad would kill him.[8] Two years later, an article appeared in the Israeli daily *Yedioth Ahronot* by Ronen Bergman, claiming that Hosni Mubarak's warm embrace of Marwan on October 1, 2003, was proof that he was a double agent. In a phone call on the following day, Marwan told Ahron Bregman that the fact that the piece was published twenty months after the events described shows that certain Israelis had taken it upon themselves to get him into hot water with the Egyptians.[9]

All this raises the possibility that the volatile Marwan really believed that the Mossad had an interest in divulging his identity and either killing him themselves or getting him killed. As far as he was concerned, this was the true motivation behind all the articles surrounding his involvement as a spy, particularly that of Ahron Bregman himself. Marwan, it should be emphasized, did not have a real understanding of the ins and outs of the Israeli security establishment, and he certainly could not have known anything of the personal motivations that may have stood behind Eli Zeira's leaks of the identity of the man previously known publicly only as

Babel. So from his perspective, the Mossad was out to get him. The distinction between the Mossad and Zeira, who was the former chief of Military Intelligence and the agency's bitter rival, was irrelevant to him. It is not surprising, therefore, that he also rebuffed repeated attempts by the Mossad at around this time to offer him protection.[10]

There is another reason, however, why his wife and sons insist that the Mossad murdered Ashraf Marwan. They are under the impression that Marwan was on the verge of completing his memoir. As they understand it, he was going to describe how he hoodwinked the Israelis just before the war. The idea for the book came after the first revelations about Babel appeared in the Israeli press. Bregman suggested that he write up his memoirs, and "leave them with your children, for the next generation." Marwan, Bregman reports, liked the idea, and fairly soon his writing became a central focus of their conversations—especially after he proposed to take Bregman on as an adviser for the project. Bregman thought the book should begin in 1969, the year he believed Marwan first offered his services to the Israelis, but Marwan wanted to start the story after May 1971, when he became Sadat's close adviser and began, as he would have it, the incredibly complex counterespionage operation that only he and Sadat knew about. Despite his direct involvement in the project, Bregman has not ruled out the possibility that behind all of Marwan's conversations with him—which were all via telephone except for a single meeting they held at London's InterContinental Hotel on Park Lane—lurked a very different motivation. In an interview with the weekly *Spectator*, he suggested that Marwan's real aim was to get information about what was being said and written about him in Israel, information that he desperately needed in order to plan his next moves.[11]

Did Marwan really write a book? The evidence is contradictory and inconclusive. According to some witnesses, he was nearly done with it. The *Sunday Times* reported that three manuscript volumes, each about two hundred pages long, were removed from his apartment the day he died. In addition, cassette tapes with his dictations of the text went missing that day as well. According to the paper's sources, which included police who investigated his death and received details from family members and friends of Marwan, on the day he died Marwan was scheduled to fly to New York in order to begin writing the final chapter. The book itself, according to this claim, was scheduled to hit bookstores in October 2007, on the thirty-fourth anniversary of the Yom Kippur War.[12] According to another source, during an academic conference in 2006 in London commemorating the fiftieth anniversary of the Suez Crisis, Ashraf Marwan was seen in the audience with a thumb drive hanging on a lanyard around his neck. When asked about it, he had said it held a draft of his book, in which he would reveal the truth about his role in the Yom Kippur War, and that the book would be "explosive."[13] There were also further indications that Marwan was engaged in a research project. About a year before he died, he paid at least two visits to George Washington University's National Security Archive in Washington, D.C., which specializes in declassified materials under the Freedom of Information Act, in order to learn more about the 1973 war. Marwan also hired a research assistant who collected materials about the war, including the translation of articles in Hebrew concerning his role in it.[14]

At the same time, however, there is one salient fact that raises serious doubts about whether he ever actually wrote a book: To this day, not a single page of the manuscript has been found. In a digital age, it is hard to imagine that Marwan kept only one printed copy (the volumes taken from his apartment) and one digital copy (the thumb drive on the lanyard). And if Marwan was really so afraid his book would be stolen, why did he wear it so openly on his person, and why did he tell people what it was? No copies were found in his safe, on his computer, with his family or close friends, or in any of the myriad places that were already available in what is today known as the "cloud." There are other reasons to be suspicious of the claim as well. If he really had made recordings of himself dictating the text, that would suggest some kind of typist or other assistant who turned the recordings into written words. Why has no one come forward saying they worked on the project? Presumably such a person was loyal to Marwan and would have every reason to support the family's claim that he had written his memoirs. Another question: Where is all the research material, the photocopies of documents or other collected sources without which no author can actually write a book of this sort? And why, if it was near completion, is there nobody willing to say what exactly was in the book? If there really was an "explosive" book nearing completion, he would surely have told people what was in it, especially if it really supported the claim that most Egyptians anyway wanted to believe about him—namely, that he was a double agent.

Only one fact about this book is clear. Other than a few very vague, one-sentence assertions, nobody on earth has said a word about what the three volumes contained or knows anything about the thumb drive other than what Marwan is alleged to have said. As for the undeniable facts of his visiting the archives in Washington or hiring a research assistant, these prove nothing about his writing. After all, from the moment he had been revealed as the Mossad's top spy in Egypt, Marwan had an enormous interest in knowing everything that had been written or published about him, because every item that appeared meant the noose was tightening just a little bit more around his neck. For a man of Marwan's means, no price was too much to pay for accurate information about the threats he faced.

But beyond all these, it is also hard to follow the rationale that would have motivated Marwan to write his side of the story in the first place. As we have seen, the information he gave Israel over a period of years was consistently precise, true, and potentially devastating to the Egyptian war effort. Every time IDF Military Intelligence or the Mossad tried to verify his intelligence, it checked out—and not just at the time of its delivery but also years later, when Egyptian sources retold their preparations for the war, and it was possible to compare their testimony with the information that Marwan had supplied. Regarding Marwan's allegedly deliberate failure to provide Israel with the precise date and time of the attack, our own reconstruction of the events provides an entirely plausible explanation. He genuinely did not know when it would happen until the day before the attack (Friday), and then he immediately let his Mossad handlers in on it when he met them that same night—a fact that is backed up not only by the Mossad but by Egyptian sources as well. It is hard to imagine how he would have overcome all that evidence in a book. The only thing he could have written would be that the real secret was known only to himself and Sadat—with the latter conveniently unavailable to confirm or deny.

But even then, he would have had to show precisely how and when the plan was hatched and carried out. In so complex an intelligence world, a plan so impossible and unprecedented must have had others in the loop. If so, where are they? Nobody has yet turned up claiming to have been in on the secret—even though the Egyptians insist they are endlessly proud of having caught Israel by surprise.

Marwan was asked repeatedly to address the question of his double agency and often had difficulty answering. Howard Blum had a conversation with him after his identity had become known. Marwan repeatedly dismissed Ahron Bregman's claim that he had been a spy for Israel, saying that "people can write or say whatever they want. . . . As far as I'm concerned, it all looks like something out of a detective story." Blum pressed the point, asking if Marwan had been a double agent. Marwan asked for Blum's fax number. Later that day, Blum received a fax with a copy of a piece from *Al-Ahram* dated March 22, 1976, which described the ceremony marking Marwan's departure from his job at the President's Office, in which Sadat gave him a medal for his special contribution to the war effort.[15] The point, apparently, was to show Blum that he had in fact tricked Israel at the start of the war. But as we know today, that whole ceremony was meant as a sop to Marwan to make up for his being fired, and his "contribution to the war effort" was his successful procurement of the Mirages from France via Libya despite the weapons embargo. Even what he told Ahron Bregman in their telephone conversation in 2006 showed just how weak Marwan's story really was. He cited the crisis facing the IDF, and the emotional crisis of Golda Meir who, he claimed, had considered killing herself when the war broke out, as proof that the Israelis had been tricked, adding that he had made his contribution as part of a team of forty people whose job it was "to feed the Israelis the *kontzeptzia* . . . it wasn't just one double agent . . . it was Egypt."[16] This is a far cry from definitively asserting that he was a double agent, and certainly does not constitute hard evidence that he played a hand in fooling the Israelis. If this was the best he could do, it is no wonder he never wrote that book.

Three conclusions arise from the evidence at hand. First, it is fair to assume that Ashraf Marwan never wrote a memoir depicting his side of the story in the Yom Kippur War, because doing so would have forced him to deal with a contradictory, undeniable reality, one that would have falsified his claims and showed him to be a charlatan and, most definitively, a Mossad spy after all. Marwan had no real interest in putting his life in the hands of the judging public in this way.

A second conclusion has to do with the image Marwan crafted

for himself as someone writing a book that would unveil the secrets of Egypt's trickery, with himself as protagonist. This allowed
him to rebuff demands, both in Egypt and elsewhere, that he respond to claims that he was a spy for the Mossad. At first Marwan
tried to ignore them, but as time went on, the Israeli press published report after report revealing more and more details. Suddenly writers like Ahron Bregman, Ronen Bergman, and Howard
Blum began calling Marwan for his side of the story. He retorted,
conveniently, that he was about to tell all in a book.

Finally, a conclusion may be drawn about the family. The myth
of the memoir serves them well, since it makes it easier to claim
that Marwan was an Egyptian patriot who fooled the Israelis, and
that the most decisive proof was lost when the Israelis not only
killed him but also destroyed all existing copies of the book. Journalists eat up this sort of convoluted conspirational story. Nothing
sells like murder and missing memoirs.

BUT THERE ARE far more compelling reasons to dismiss the theory
that the Mossad killed Ashraf Marwan—reasons that only come to
light when looking at the Israeli side of the events. A careful look
at the internal dynamics of the Israeli intelligence community and
its response to the revelation of Marwan's identity will show that
not only was the Mossad consistently and intensely interested in
keeping him alive, but that after the fact, the agency saw his death
as nothing less than a fiasco for the organization.

Soon after his identity was revealed, a public debate emerged in
Israel about how to deal with the person responsible for the leak—
and it was widely known who that was. Inside the Mossad, the
debate went as follows. On one side was the Mossad chief, Meir
Dagan, who believed that opening an investigation against Eli Zeira,
or even making him stand trial, would constitute a formal acknowl-
edgment that Marwan had spied for Israel, putting Marwan's life at
serious risk and, by extension, making the Mossad look incapable

of protecting its spies. And so, until June 2007, Dagan opposed any action being taken against Zeira. On the other side were many of the senior officers who had built their careers in the Mossad, especially the man who had been the head of the Tzomet branch and was now Dagan's deputy, who argued that by allowing Marwan's name to reach the public, Zeira had violated the First Commandment of intelligence, profaning its holy of holies as it were, and had to stand trial.[17] Dagan won that battle, and on his recommendation, the Israeli attorney general's office declined to investigate.

Regardless of which side was right, the important point for our purposes is that this internal debate—with one side actively trying to keep Marwan alive, the other wanting to punish the man who risked his life—could not have happened if the Mossad had wanted him dead. On the contrary, both the Mossad and the Israeli government saw his death as a disaster. Zamir was the first to admit it. Interviewed on Israeli television, he said, "We have lost the greatest source in our history . . . and we lost him because of criminal negligence . . . and I failed to protect him."[18] In his memoirs published in late 2011, Zamir devoted a full chapter to Marwan, called "The Best of All Agents: Between Myself and Ashraf Marwan." "Not a single day passes," he writes, "without my torturing myself over the question of whether I could have protected him better."[19]

But if the Mossad didn't do it, and Marwan's business rivals didn't do it, the only reasonable option is that the Egyptians did it. Only here do we find both the motives that would have led them to kill Ashraf Marwan and also a clear common thread between his death and similar deaths of others who stood in the way of the Egyptian regime in the past.

ONE OF THE biggest questions arising from Marwan's death was this: How is it possible that between the revelations of his identity as Babel in 2002 and his death in 2007, the Egyptian government made no effort to investigate his treachery or make him stand

trial—that instead it even honored Marwan, inflating his contribution to the war in 1973? One answer is that the Egyptians really
do believe the double agent story. But it is hard to imagine that
Egyptian intelligence officers, who know a good deal about what
went down on their own turf, would accept a version of the facts
in which Marwan and Sadat collaborated on tricking Israel without letting anyone else in on it. It is fair to assume, as well, that
Egyptian intelligence officials read everything that came out about
the agent Babel in the Israeli press and were able to figure out who
Babel was. They, like the rest of the world, discovered that Ashraf
Marwan had been a Mossad agent. And if they read the literature
about the days leading up to the war, they knew that Israel's failures happened largely despite, not because of, Marwan.

The way President Mubarak approached Marwan after his exposure illustrates the complex and cautious way the regime addressed
the problem. The two had known each other at least since the early
1970s, when Marwan ran the project to get the French Mirages for
the Egyptian air force and Mubarak was the air force commander.
They had been on good terms ever since.[20] Their firstborn sons
were close friends and business partners. Publicly, Mubarak embraced Marwan. In 2005, Egyptian media showed the two of them
shaking hands in a public ceremony to mark the anniversary of the
October War. The picture convinced at least one Israeli journalist
that Marwan was indeed a double agent.[21] But, according to *Al-
Ahram*'s Mohamed Hassanein Heikal, Mubarak was surprised to see
Marwan at the ceremony and ordered his men to escort him out
of Egypt immediately. The next morning Marwan was already on a
plane back to London. Following this incident, Mubarak issued an
order barring Marwan from returning to Egypt.[22]

The Egyptian media also praised Marwan after his death.
Mubarak called him "a true patriot," and members of the political,
military, and intelligence elites attended his funeral. But in Septem-

ber 2011, after the fall of the Mubarak regime, *Rose al-Yusuf*, the same weekly that would, six months later, claim that Mubarak had accused Gaddafi of having Marwan killed, reported that Mubarak personally ordered the assassination of Marwan. Given the magazine's dubious record, the claim attracted little attention.

Whether any of these claims is true or false is not known. But it is clear that Mubarak and his men wanted to bury this embarrassing episode deep in the ground. No wonder that when Egypt's most respected journalist, Mohamed Hassanein Heikal, asked him to open a formal investigation into the Marwan case, Mubarak refused.[23]

Three complementary explanations account for the kid glove treatment that Marwan received after his identity as a Mossad spy became known. One is the centrality of the issue of shame in Arab society. Whereas in Western culture, much of a person's worth in society turns on the question of guilt versus innocence, in Arab culture the question is much more one of shame versus honor. Shame reflects not just on the individual but also on the groups he associates with, including nuclear and extended families, tribes, and nations. If it were to turn out that a member of the upper elites of Egypt, no less the son-in-law of Nasser himself, the personal adviser and confidant to Sadat, one of whose sons is Jimmy Mubarak's best friend and another married to the daughter of the former foreign minister and secretary-general of the Arab League, Amr Moussa—that this man was the greatest traitor in Egyptian history, it would bring shame not just on Marwan but also on Mubarak and the entire ruling elite, as well as deal a massive blow to the national pride of the whole country.

Closely related to the burden of shame is the powerful circling of wagons that characterizes the upper strata of Arab societies in general and Egypt in particular—the "one of us" factor. For the strongest men in the regime Marwan may have been a traitor, but he was also a friend and a respected member of their closed circles. As such, he merited protection.

The combination of the "one of us" factor and considerations of shame was powerful enough to drive a far more legalistic culture than Egypt's to actively avoid bringing a similar traitor to justice. When, in the early 1960s, British MI6 received undeniable proof that one of its senior members, Kim Philby, now a journalist in Beirut, had in fact been a Soviet spy, the agency avoided formally charging him in London. Instead, his old friends in the service seem to have given him a way out, by allowing him to defect to the USSR and thus prevent the embarrassment involved in a judicial process that would reveal in detail how "one of us" had betrayed them.[24] The Egyptian way of dealing with the problem was deadlier but not less effective.

Finally, there was also the fear of the damage that Marwan could cause had the regime initiated a legal process against him. More than forty years of being an integral part of the Egyptian elite and learning the intimate secrets of the most powerful men in Egypt had turned him into a real threat. Marwan himself was aware of it and made it clear that he would not hesitate to use his power. In a talk with Heikal in London in September 2006, he denied that Mubarak prohibited him from visiting Egypt and added: "He cannot do it. I can destroy him." He also said he can destroy others, including Omar Sulciman, the strongman of the Egyptian Mukhabarat.[25]

For all these reasons, the public admission by Eli Zeira, both in his book and in subsequent television interviews in 2004, to the effect that Marwan worked for the Mossad, created for Egypt a new reality: there's a big difference when such a claim comes from a journalist or historian and when it comes from the man who headed IDF Military Intelligence during the Yom Kippur War. And all the more so when a former Israeli Supreme Court justice issues a ruling on the subject, which could easily be interpreted as formal judicial affirmation of Marwan's treachery.

In June 2007, the awareness that this affair could threaten the foundations of Egyptian rule, and of the need to neutralize that threat, were becoming more and more acute for the regime in Cairo. Something had to be done.

ALL OF THIS, however, only explains the motive—why in the immediate aftermath of the Orr ruling, the Egyptians had every reason in the world to have Ashraf Marwan killed. But motive alone is not enough. Are there other indicators suggesting that the Egyptians had a hand in his death?

There are—specifically, the method of his execution. By tossing him off the balcony and finding a way to make his shoes vanish, one can maximize the likelihood that suicide or an accident will never be ruled out. After Marwan's death, Egyptian journalists raised a number of parallels, two of which bear a striking resemblance.

The first happened in 1973, when Gen. El-Leithy Nassif, whom Nasser had chosen to command the Revolutionary Guard, and who, under Sadat's orders, had jailed leading opposition figures in May 1971, was murdered in London. The general, who had a reputation for being honest and ethical, had been reassigned out of the Guard in 1972. Sadat promoted him in rank and appointed him to a meaningless "advisory" position in the army. A year later, he was made ambassador to Greece, but before moving to Athens he stopped in London for a medical procedure. He stayed on the eleventh floor of the Stuart Tower, a residence in Westminster frequented by Middle Eastern visitors. On August 15, 1973, his body was found at the base of the tower, having fallen from the balcony of his suite. An autopsy revealed nothing suspicious, but his wife repeatedly claimed he had been murdered by Sadat's men, who shoved him out of the shower and off the balcony, because he had been a secret Nasser man. In particular, she blamed a senior Egyptian intelligence officer who lived in the same building at the time. The officer owned the apartment where Nassif was staying and had a key to the front door. In Nassif's home in Cairo, it was later learned, surveillance devices had been planted, and Nassif knew

about them. Though it is far from clear why Sadat would have
wanted him killed after he had been loyal during the Corrective
Revolution, the general sense in Egypt was that this was no accident but an execution on the orders of the government.[26]

Twenty-eight years later, on June 21, 2001, an Egyptian movie
actress, Soad Hosny, met a very similar death. Hosny, who had appeared in eighty Egyptian films and was dubbed the "Cinderella of
Egyptian Cinema," was found dead at the base of Stuart Tower, after
falling from her balcony on the seventh floor. Hosny had suffered
from chronic pain and was being treated for weight gain, but people
who were close to her in her four years in London claimed that
she showed no suicidal signs. Her personal physician also knew her
closely; he testified that he had spoken with her a day before her
death, and she had sounded optimistic, promising to see him soon.
Another close friend, her personal assistant, testified that when she
had entered the apartment, Hosny had been on the balcony, but
then once the assistant was inside, she could no longer find Hosny.
She walked out onto the balcony and saw Hosny's body on the
grounds below. But because the assistant had contradictions in her
story, the British judge attempting to establish the cause of death
concluded that she was an unreliable witness.

The mysterious death of Soad Hosny, one of the most revered
movie stars in the Arab world, triggered a wave of rumors, some
of which pointed fingers at Egyptian intelligence. According to
what became the established narrative, she was planning on writing a memoir in which she would reveal how she had worked
for Egyptian intelligence in the 1980s. Her story of her work as
an agent—which likely included acts of seduction by the beautiful actress—got a boost when the head of the Mukhabarat at the
time, Gen. Fuad Nasser, claimed in an interview for an Egyptian
paper that Hosny had been murdered. No wonder, then, that many
around the Arab world believe that she was killed by Egyptian

government officials who feared the embarrassment that would be caused by the publication of her memoir.[27] No wonder that according to the sensational *Rose al-Yusuf* weekly, Scotland Yard's investigators of Marwan's death concluded that the same team of three Egyptians—two men and a woman—committed the murder of both the movie actress and the Mossad spy.[28] Probably a false story, it received no confirmation from Scotland Yard or any other knowledgeable source.

THE IMPRESSIVE FUNERAL and President Mubarak's statement, according to which he did "not doubt at all the patriotism of Dr. Ashraf Marwan" and that Marwan "was not a spy for any organization at all,"[29] convinced quite a few Western journalists and analysts that maybe the double agent hypothesis was right after all. Others, familiar with the tiniest details of the story of Ashraf Marwan during the war, remained skeptical. Israeli Brig. Gen. (res.) Amos Gilboa, himself a former head of MI-Research who went through all the material that Marwan had provided, gave his own take on the behavior of official Egypt. The pictures of the funeral in which senior government officials are shown comforting his bereaved widow and their sons, he said, reminded him "of a mafia film. The mafia takes somebody out. Then, when the widow and children are crying on his grave, the killers come and kiss her."[30]

In any event, it was Mubarak's speech, more than anything else, that set the tone about how Marwan should be seen in Egypt. Independent journalists and bloggers continued talking about Marwan in a way that contradicted the official line, but all of the spokespeople to whom the journalists turned for official commentary emphasized that Marwan had served Egypt faithfully, adding that since the subject at hand was a sensitive security issue, it was imperative to maintain secrecy. The producers at *60 Minutes* who prepared a segment on Marwan tried for many weeks to solicit a response to questions about his having worked for the Mossad, in vain. In early questioning, Egyptian officials just repeated different versions of the double agent theory, saying that Marwan had tricked the Israelis—but they were unwilling to say even that on camera, for reasons of secrecy. In the end, the Egyptian position was presented on camera by Dr. Abdel Moneim Said, the head of the Al-Ahram Center for Political and Strategic Studies, who claimed that Marwan was a central axis of the Egyptian effort to fool the Israelis, without which the Egyptian army would have had no chance of defeating the IDF. He provided no compelling details to back up his claim, however.[31]

Said's comments, which aired in May 2009, were the closest approximation of an official Egyptian statement about Marwan since Mubarak had declared that he "did not spy for any agency." More than anything, they reflected the severe discomfort on the part of the Mubarak regime under pressure to say something about Ashraf Marwan. The implication, it seems, is that they themselves did not really know what he had done. If Nasser's son-in-law was really a double agent who fooled Israel, then it should be one of the most incredible stories of counterespionage in history, proving Egyptian cleverness over that of the Israelis to a fantastic degree. One would think that the Egyptians would see this as an endless source of pride.

So why were there no Egyptians willing to tell the whole story? Why the secrecy, more than forty years after the war, more than thirty years after Sadat's death, and close to a decade after Marwan's death? If the Egyptians were so clever as to have outsmarted even the Mossad, why has this not become a central part of the Egyptian account of the October War, with books and documentaries and all the rest? Why not milk the story for all the national-pride-enhancing and regime-propping value it was worth, just as they did for their military accomplishments in the war, building a whole museum in Cairo to celebrate them? Clearly, they have an interest in providing all the details of the whole affair. Don't they?

Apparently not. The Egyptians refuse to provide a compelling, detailed account of the double agent narrative because they cannot. The only shred of evidence they actually have to back up their claim is the fact of Israel's failure to prepare adequately for the Egyptian attack on October 6, 1973.

IT HAS BEEN more than four decades since Israel's official commission of inquiry, the Agranat Commission, published its findings about the Israeli debacle in the Yom Kippur War. In it, the world learned that Israel's failures in the opening days of the war had nothing to do with Egyptian cleverness and everything to do with Israeli refusal to abandon their outdated *kontzeptzia*. In the meantime, the Egyptian double agent hypothesis about Ashraf Marwan remains a baseless fantasy. And so it will continue to remain, until and unless someone produces hard evidence to support it—such as, for example, descriptions of when and where Marwan met with his handlers, and what was said at the meetings. If he really was working for Egypt, there has to be some record, somewhere, of how he handled his handlers, how he pulled the wool over the eyes of the Mossad chief. As long as they cannot produce a single document from the Egyptian side of his work, as long as every single statement is little more than a reflexive reaction to Israeli publications or articles that come from Israeli sources, there is no avoiding the conclusion that, despite all their protestations, they still have no idea at all what Ashraf Marwan was doing before and during the war.

And as long as that is the case, there is no avoiding the conclusion that Ashraf Marwan was no double agent at all, but rather one of the most important spies the world has seen in the last half century.

Acknowledgments

The surprise of the Yom Kippur War in 1973 and the war itself are the most traumatic events in Israel's history. That the surprise was not complete, however, and that Israel was able to avert a far more grievous outcome, was due to a last-minute warning from the Mossad's "miraculous" source in Egypt—a dramatic story that started to become publicly known in the early 1990s.

My personal involvement in this story started in 1998, when I was tasked by the IDF Military Intelligence's Research Department, where I served as a reserve officer, to conduct a top-secret study into the causes of the 1973 intelligence debacle. Among the documents I had access to was a large file comprising hundreds of intelligence reports collected in the months before the war via all the methods of intelligence—signal, visual, and human. It provided a clear and comprehensive picture of the imminent threat. Among this secret treasure, the reports by the Mossad source, codenamed "Khotel," were the jewel in the crown.

While conducting my research at the time, I never asked about his real identity. Everyone I interviewed continued to view it as a supremely guarded secret—as did I. Within five years, however, the secret had been revealed, and Ashraf Marwan's identity was known. His death in June 2007 removed the main obstacle to an in-depth investigation into his life as a spy. Following a request by the team from CBS's *60 Minutes* to advise them on the production of an episode on Marwan (which aired May 2009), I decided to throw myself more deeply into his story.

In exploring it, I used my earlier expertise as a student of Israel's 1973 intelligence failure, which produced a book (*The Watchman Fell Asleep*, 2005) as well as a number of academic articles. In writing these I developed relationships of trust with a number of people who played key roles in the dramatic events that led to the war. The result was the Hebrew-language publication of *The Angel* in 2010 and an updated edition in 2011. This was the basis for the current book.

While investigating Marwan's story, I enjoyed the support of many. Most important among them were the intelligence officers who were directly involved in his handling. I conducted numerous talks with Zvi Zamir, the Mossad chief in 1973, as well as other intelligence officers who asked that their names be withheld. These interviews constituted the foundations for this book. The names of the interviewees who did not request anonymity appear in the list of sources. I thank them all.

Others who deserve my gratitude are Professors Shimon Shamir and Yoram Meital, who helped me understand the complexity of Egyptian politics; Khadir Sawaed and Barak Rubinstein, who served as my research assistants; Drs. Ahron Bregman and Nadav Zeevi, who allowed me to use their unpublished materials; Drs. Dima Adamsky and Nehemia Burgin, who were always there when I needed their help; Dr. Hagai Tsoref of the Israeli Archives; and many other friends and family members who provided support throughout the process.

The origins of the book's English edition go back to 2009 and to the coffeehouses of San Francisco, where I discussed it again and again with my good friend Michael Lavigne. To a large extent the idea materialized through the translation made by David Hazony, who proved to be not only an excellent translator but also a good partner in turning the manuscript into a book. Peter Bernstein, my agent, was always supportive, committed, effective, and patient. Claire Wachtel, the veteran senior editor at HarperCollins, contributed her vast experience and talent to the making of this book; in the final editing stage, Hannah Wood took charge, bringing it to a safe harbor.

This English edition corrects a number of mistakes and adds new information to the earlier Hebrew editions. Nevertheless, although I had access to some Israeli archives, the same could not be said for those of the Mossad, which are likely to remain closed to the public for many more years, and I am aware of my limitations in providing the most complete and error-free account of Ashraf Marwan's service as the best source the Mossad ever had. I believe that the story I am telling here is accurate. My hope is that it will prove to be so also in the years to come.

NOTES

Chapter: Cairo, 1944–1970

1. Muhammad Tharwat, *Ashraf Marwan: Fact and Illusion* (Cairo: Madbuli, 2008), pp. 19–20; unknown author, "Al-Souhagh: Birthplace of Ashraf Marwan," from the website of Mallawi in the Al-Manya Province.

2. Tharwat, *Ashraf Marwan: Fact and Illusion*, pp. 19–20.

3. Anne Alexander, *Nasser* (London: Haus Publishing, 2005), p. 104; Anthony Nutting, *Nasser* (New York: E. P. Dutton, 1972), p. 306.

4. Tahia Gamal Abdel Nasser, *Nasser: My Husband* (Cairo and New York: American University in Cairo Press, 2013), p. 94.

5. Opportunist, "The Bright Side of the Moon," *Egyptian Chronicles*, June 28, 2007, http://egyptianchronicles.blogspot.com/2007/06/opportunist-well-bright-dark-side-of.html.

6. Tahia Gamal Abdel Nasser, *Nasser: My Husband*, p. 94.

7. Amru al-Laithi interview with Mona Abdel Nasser, *Ahathraq* Egyptian Television, March 10, 2009.

8. Mohamed Fawzi, *Secrets of the Assassination of Ashraf Marwan* (Beirut: Al-Watan Lel Nasher, 2007), p. 18.

9. Kemal Halef al-Tawil, "Ashraf Marwan: The Dilemma Child," *Al-Akhbar al-Lobnaniya*, February 7, 2007.

10. Mohamed Jam'a, *I Knew Sadat: Half a Century of Secrets About Sadat and the [Muslim] Brotherhood* (Cairo: Al-Maktab al-Masry al-Hadeth, 1999), p. 182.

11. Tahia Gamal Abdel Nasser, *Nasser: My Husband*, p. 93.

12. Amru al-Laithi interview with Mona Abdel Nasser.

13. Nadav Zeevi, *Life of an Agent* (unpublished manuscript in Hebrew). The contradiction between the way Mona's parents accepted Ashraf Marwan and

Hoda's husband is evident in Tahia Nasser's memoirs. She described in detail Hoda's engagement process and marriage (Tahia Gamal Abdel Nasser, *Nasser: My Husband*, pp. 92–93) and summarized in only six lines Mona's marriage to Ashraf (ibid., p. 94).

14. Al-Tawil, "Ashraf Marwan: The Dilemma Child."
15. Tharwat, *Ashraf Marwan: Fact and Illusion*, pp. 20–21.
16. Assam Abdel Fatah, *The Agent Babel: The Man Who Shocked the Command of the Mossad* (Cairo: Dar el-Katab el-Arabi, 2008), p. 26; Amru el-Laithi interview with Mona Abdel Nasser.
17. Mohammad Zara, "Reliving a Piece of History," *Egypt Daily News*, September 22, 2006.
18. Selim Nassib, *Umm* (Tel Aviv: Asia, 1999), p. 159.
19. Amru al-Laithi interview with Mona Abdel Nasser.
20. Mohamed Salmawy, *Al-Ahram Weekly*, July 5–11, 2007.
21. Said K. Aburish, *Nasser: The Last Arab* (New York: Thomas Dunn, 2004), p. 234.
22. Tharwat, *Ashraf Marwan: Fact and Illusion*, pp. 20–23.
23. Opportunist, "The Bright Side of the Moon," *Egyptian Chronicles* (see n. 5 above).
24. Al-Tawil, "Ashraf Marwan: The Dilemma Child."
25. Nutting, *Nasser*, p. 306.
26. Gamal Nkrumah, "Sami Sharaf: Shadows of the Revolution," *Al-Ahram Weekly Online*, August 9–15, 2001, http://weekly.ahram.org.eg/2001/546/profile.htm; Nutting, *Nasser*, pp. 306–8.
27. Assam Abdel Fatah, *Who Killed Ashraf Marwan?: The File of Agent Babel* (Cairo: El-Eiman, 2007), p. 14; Musa Sabri, *Sadat: The Truth and the Legend* (Cairo: Al-Maktab al-Masry al-Hadeth, 1985), p. 651.
28. Abdel Majid Farid interview with the Egyptian television program *Ahatraq*, broadcast November–December 2008.
29. Fatah, *Agent Babel*, pp. 15–18.
30. Panayiotis J. Vatikiotis, *The Modern History of Egypt* (New York: Praeger, 1969), p. 432.
31. Souad al-Sabah, *Falcon of the Gulf: Abdullah Mubarak al-Sabah* (Kuwait: Kadhma, 1995), pp. 259–68.
32. Ibid., pp. 263–64.
33. Al-Tawil, "Ashraf Marwan."
34. Zeevi, *Life of an Agent*.
35. Saad el-Shazly, *The Crossing of the Suez: Revised Edition* (San Francisco: American Mideast Research, 2003), pp. 184–85.
36. Scott Shane, "A Spy's Motivation: For Love of Another Country," *New York Times*, April 20, 2008; Yuri Modin, *My Five Cambridge Friends: Burgess, Mac-*

lean, Philby, Blunt, and Cairncross (New York: Farrar, Straus, and Giroux, 1994);
Victor Cherkashin and Gregory Feiger, *Spy Handler: Memoirs of a KGB Officer: The True Story of the Man Who Recruited Robert Hanssen and Aldrich Ames* (New York: Basic Books, 2005); David Wise, *Nightmover: How Aldrich Ames Sold the CIA to the KGB for $4.6 Million* (New York: HarperCollins, 1995); Jerrold L. Schecter and Peter S. Deriabin, *The Spy Who Saved the World: How a Soviet Colonel Changed the Course of the Cold War* (New York: Charles Scribner's Sons, 1992); Dusko Doder, "Of Moles and Men," *Nation*, February 18, 2002, pp. 25–32.

Chapter 2: London, 1970

1. Unless noted otherwise, this chapter is based on interviews with Zvi Zamir, Meir Meir, Nahik Navot, Freddy Eini, Amos Gilboa, and other sources who requested anonymity, as well as: Zvi Zamir and Efrat Mass, *With Open Eyes* (Or Yehuda: Zmora-Bitan, 2011), pp. 129–64.
2. Tom Mangold, *Cold Warrior: James Jesus Angleton: The CIA's Master Spy Hunter* (New York: Touchstone Books, 1992), pp. 183–226.
3. Meron Medzini, *Golda: A Political Biography* (Tel Aviv: Yedioth Ahronot, 2008), p. 511.
4. Thomas Harris, *Garbo: The Spy Who Saved D-Day* (Richmond, VA: Public Record Office, 2000); Stephan Talty, *Agent Garbo: The Brilliant, Eccentric Secret Agent Who Tricked Hitler and Saved D-Day* (Boston: Houghton Mifflin Harcourt, 2012).
5. John le Carré, *The Secret Pilgrim* (New York: Alfred A. Knopf, 1990), p. 9.

Chapter 3: April 1971

This chapter is based on interviews with Zvi Zamir, Meir Meir, Nahik Navot, Freddy Eini, Amos Gilboa, and other sources who requested anonymity.

Chapter 4: May 1971

1. Anwar el-Sadat, *In Search of Identity: An Autobiography* (New York: Harper-Collins, 1978), p. 139.
2. Said K. Aburish, *Nasser: The Last Arab,* pp. 242, 286; Tahia Gamal Abdel Nasser, *Nasser: My Husband,* pp. 103–17.
3. Arieh Shalev, "Intelligence Estimates in Advance of the War," in *National Trauma: The Yom Kippur War After Thirty Years and Another War,* ed. Moshe Shemesh and Ze'ev Drori (Sdeh Boker: Ben-Gurion University Press, 2008), pp. 125–83, 106;

Arieh Shalev, *Failure and Success in the Warning: Intelligence Assessments on the Eve of the Yom Kippur War* (Tel Aviv: Maarachot, 2006), p. 167.

4. Sources for this exchange: Shimon Shamir, *Egypt Under Sadat's Leadership: The Search for a New Orientation* (Tel Aviv: Dvir, 1978); Vatikiotis, *Modern History of Egypt*, n. 28 of ch. 1; Sadat, *In Search of Identity*; Jehan Sadat, *A Woman of Egypt* (New York: Simon & Schuster, 2002); interview with Prof. Shimon Shamir at Tel Aviv University, December 31, 2009; Nutting, *Nasser*; Kirk J. Beattie, *Egypt During the Sadat Years* (New York: Palgrave Macmillan, 1980); "The Underrated Heir," *Time*, May 17, 1971; "A Preemptive Purge in Cairo," *Time*, May 24, 1971.

5. Sadat, *In Search of Identity*, p. 170.

6. Beattie, *Egypt During the Sadat Years*, p. 291.

7. Fatah, *Who Killed Ashraf Marwan?*, p. 21. Fatah's source is Salah al-Shahed, a senior officer in the President's Office who had gone to school with Sadat; Tharwat, *Ashraf Marwan: Fact and Illusion*, n. 1 in ch. 1, p. 184. Tharwat relies, among others, on: Mahmud Jamaa, *I Knew Sadat: Fifty Years of Secrets About Sadat and the Muslim Brotherhood* (Cairo: al Maktab al Misri, 1999).

8. Fatah, *Who Killed Ashraf Marwan?*, n. 14 of ch. 1, p. 21.

9. Owen L. Sirrs, *A History of the Egyptian Intelligence Service: A History of the Mukhabarat, 1910–2009* (New York: Routledge, 2010), p. 120.

10. Joseph J. Trento, *Prelude to Terror: The Rogue CIA and the Legacy of America's Private Intelligence Network* (New York: Carroll & Graf, 2005), pp. 261–62.

11. Fatah, *Who Killed Ashraf Marwan?*, n. 14 of ch. 1, p. 23.

12. Tharwat, *Ashraf Marwan: Fact and Illusion*, n. 1 of ch. 1, p. 184.

13. Zamir and Mass, *With Open Eyes*, p. 135.

14. "Sadat in the Saddle," *Time*, May 31, 1971.

15. Tharwat, *Ashraf Marwan: Fact and Illusion*, n. 8 of ch. 1.

Chapter 5: The Dream of Every Spy Agency on Earth

1. Interview with Meir Meir.

2. This affair served as the basis for Michael Frayn's play *Democracy*, which premiered at Britain's Royal National Theatre in September 2003.

3. Interview with Yonah Bandman.

4. Interview with Meir Meir.

5. Interviews with Meir Meir, Yonah Bandman, and Yaakov Rosenfeld, who in 1971 served as an MI expert on the Egyptian army.

6. Gad Yaacobi, *By a Hair's Breadth: How an Agreement Between Israel and Egypt Was Missed, and the Yom Kippur War Was Not Prevented* (Tel Aviv: Edanim, 1989), p. 157.

7. Interview with Yaakov Rosenfeld.

8. Yaacobi, *By a Hair's Breadth*, p. 157.

9. Interviews with Freddy Eini and Zvi Zamir.

10. Shalev, *Failure and Success in the Warning*, n. 3 of ch. 4, p. 63.

11. Yitzhak Rabin, *Record of Service* (Tel Aviv: Maariv, 1978), pp. 345–46.

12. Military Intelligence document from June 1971; Shalev, *Failure and Success in the Warning*, n. 3 of ch. 4, p. 63.

13. It should be said, however, that the roots of the Concept could be found as early as 1968, two years before Marwan offered his services. In a meeting of the IDF General Staff about the possibility of war with Egypt that fall, the chiefs of the Israeli Air Force expressed their opinion that any Egyptian effort to cross the Suez Canal without first neutralizing Israel's air superiority would necessarily fail. The IDF chief of operations, Maj. Gen. Ezer Weizman, who had been the commander of the IAF, said of such an Egyptian move, "If only they would make such a mistake." Uri Bar-Joseph, *The Watchman Fell Asleep: The Surprise of Yom Kippur and Its Sources* (Albany: SUNY Press, 2005), p. 45.

14. Shazly, *Crossing the Suez*, p. 128.

15. See: Ibid., p. 18; Sadat, *In Search of Identity*, p.178; Mohamed Abdel Ghani el-Gamasy, *The October War: Memoirs of Field Marshall El-Gamasy of Egypt* (Cairo: American University of Cairo Press, 1993), p. 205; Mohamed Heikal, *Autumn of Fury: The Assassination of Sadat* (New York: Random House, 1983), p. 50.

16. Sadat, *In Search of Identity*, p. 244.

17. Bar-Joseph, *The Watchman Fell Asleep*, pp. 84–85.

18. Shalev, *Failure and Success in the Warning*, n. 3 of ch. 4, p. 81, where he quotes from an MI document from May 1969.

19. "Intelligence Summary from Operation Dovecote," December 17, 1972; Shalev, *Failure and Success in the Warning*, n. 3 of ch. 4, pp. 80–81; Eli Zeira, *Myth Versus Reality: Yom Kippur War—Failures and Lessons* (Tel Aviv: Yedioth Ahronot, 2004), pp. 89–90. The first edition of Zeira's book came out in 1993.

20. Zvi Zamir interviewed on the Israeli television program *Fact (Uvda)*, Channel 2, "The Last Spy," December 27, 2007.

21. Interview with Zvi Zamir, July 8, 2008.

22. Conversation with Amos Gilboa.

23. Shalev, *Failure and Success in the Warning*, n. 3 of ch. 4, p. 186.

24. Interview with Aharon Levran.

25. Moshe Dayan interview with Rami Tal, in Ronen Bergman and Gil Meltser, *The Yom Kippur War: Real Time* (Tel Aviv: Yedioth Ahronot, 2003), p. 180.

26. Interview with Yonah Bandman.

27. Zeira, *Myth Versus Reality*, pp. 155–56.

28. Ibid., pp. 151–63.

29. "Supplement of Supplements," Israel Television Channel 1, interviewed by Dan Margalit, September 23–24, 2004.

30. Interview with Arieh Shalev.
31. Interview with Aharon Levran.
32. Bergman and Meltser, *The Yom Kippur War*, p. 175.
33. Zamir and Mass, *With Open Eyes*, p. 133.
34. Ibid., pp. 132–35.
35. Interviews with Zvi Zamir and Freddy Eini.

Chapter 6: Sadat's Emissary for Special Affairs

1. Nadav Safran, *Saudi Arabia: Ceaseless Quest for Security* (Ithaca, NY: Cornell University Press, 1988), p. 145; Robert Dreyfuss, *Devil's Game: How the United States Helped Unleash Fundamentalist Islam* (New York: Henry Holt, 2006), p. 151; Gerald Posner, *Secrets of the Kingdom* (New York: Random House, 2005), pp. 80–82; Said K. Aburish, *The Rise, Corruption, and Coming Fall of the House of Saud* (London: Bloomsbury, 2005), p. 301; Bob Woodward, *Veil: The Secret Wars of the CIA, 1981–1987* (New York: Simon & Schuster, 2005), p. 347; Mohamed Heikal, *The Sphinx and the Commissar: The Rise and Fall of Soviet Influence in the Middle East* (New York: Harper & Row, 1978), p. 226.
2. Mohamed Hassanein Heikal interview with Al Jazeera Television, December 17, 2009.
3. Fawzi, *Secrets of the Assassination of Ashraf Marwan*, p. 31. Other sources about the deal include: Jamaa, *I Knew Sadat*, pp. 216–18; Sabri, *Sadat: The Truth and the Legend*, p. 653; Tharwat, *Ashraf Marwan: Fact and Illusion*, pp. 27–36.
4. Jeffrey Robinson, *The Risk Takers* (New York: HarperCollins, 1985), p. 122.
5. Avi Shlaim, *Lion of Jordan: The Life of King Hussein in War and Peace* (New York: Alfred A. Knopf, 2008), pp. 346–47.
6. Gideon Gera, *Gaddafi's Way in Libya* (Tel Aviv: Hakibutz Hameuhad, 1983), pp. 118–19.
7. John K. Cooley, *Libyan Sandstorm* (New York: Holt, Reinhart and Winston, 1982), pp. 6–7, 68.
8. Mohamed Hamad, "Egypt-Libya Relations from Revolution to War: Recollections of Salah al-Din al-Saadani, Egypt's First Ambassador to Libya After the Revolution," part 13, *Al-Rei al-A'am* (Kuwait), October 15, 1997, p. 12.
9. Sabri, *Sadat: The Truth and the Legend*, pp. 652–53.
10. Tharwat, *Ashraf Marwan: Fact and Illusion*, p. 34.
11. Ibid.; Sabri, *Sadat: The Truth and the Legend*, pp. 652–53.
12. "For 100,000 dollars a month . . . the 'prophetic,' one of the great weapons dealers of Egypt," *Al-Shaab*, December 2, 2009.
13. Sabri, *Sadat: The Truth and the Legend*, p. 652.
14. Fawzi, *Secrets of the Assassination of Ashraf Marwan*, p. 29.

15. Jamaa, *I Knew Sadat*, pp. 217–18; Sabri, *Sadat: The Truth and the Legend*, p. 652; Fatah, *Who Killed Ashraf Marwan?*, p. 26.

16. Fatah, *Who Killed Ashraf Marwan?*, p. 31.

17. Jamaa, *I Knew Sadat*, pp. 184–85; Tharwat, *Ashraf Marwan: Fact and Illusion*, pp. 27–36.

18. Jamaa, *I Knew Sadat*, pp. 184–85; Tharwat, *Ashraf Marwan: Fact and Illusion*, pp. 35–36.

19. Jeffrey Robinson, *Yamani: The Inside Story* (London: Simon & Schuster, 1988), pp. 85–86.

20. Shazly, *Crossing the Suez*, pp. 148–49.

21. Conversation with Howard Blum, September 1, 2010.

22. Ronen Bergman, "The 'Khotel' Code," *Yediot Ahronot (7 Days Supplement)*, September 7, 2007, pp. 29–30.

Chapter 7: Egypt Girds for War

1. Eyal Zisser, "Syria and the October War: The Missed Opportunity," in *The October 1973 War: Politics, Diplomacy, Legacy*, ed. Asaf Siniver (London: Hurst, 2013), pp. 67–83.

2. Uri Bar-Joseph and Amr Yossef, "The Hidden Factors That Turned the Tide: Strategic Decision-Making and Operational Intelligence in the 1973 War," *Journal of Strategic Studies* 37, no. 4, pp. 584–608.

3. Arieh Braun, *Moshe Dayan in the Yom Kippur War* (Tel Aviv: Edanim, 1992), p. 17.

4. Ibid., p. 18.

5. Ibid., pp. 17–18.

6. Rabin, *Record of Service*, p. 380.

7. Braun, *Moshe Dayan in the Yom Kippur War*, p. 18.

8. Ibid., p. 19.

9. Interview with Avner Shalev, Tel Aviv, August 29, 1998. In 1973 Shalev served as the Chief of Staff's aide-de-camp.

10. Branch 6, *Intelligence Survey 15/73*, January 24, 1973.

11. Lon Norden and David Nicole, *Phoenix Over the Nile: A History of Egyptian Air Power, 1932–1994* (Washington, DC,: Smithsonian Institute Press, 1996), pp. 269–70.

12. Arieh Shalev, "Intelligence Assessment Before the War," in *National Trauma: The Yom Kippur War After Thirty Years and Another War*, ed. Moshe Shemesh and Zeev Drori (Sdeh Boker: Ben-Gurion University, 2008), p. 117.

13. *Commission of Inquiry—The Yom Kippur War, Additional Partial Report: Justifications and Additions to the Partial Report of 9 Nissan 5734 (January 4, 1974)*, vol. 1, Jerusalem (1974), p. 93 (hereafter: Agranat Commission, Third and Final Report).

14. Shalev, "Intelligence Assessment," pp. 118–19.
15. Interview with Yonah Bandman.
16. For a detailed description of this discussion, see: Bar-Joseph, *The Watchman Fell Asleep*, 2005, pp. 69–70.
17. Ibid., pp. 71–73.
18. Shmuel Gordon, *Thirty Hours in October, Fateful Decisions: The Air Force at the Start of the Yom Kippur War* (Tel Aviv: Maariv, 2008), p. 193.

Chapter 8: Final Preparations and an Intermezzo in Rome

1. Braun, *Moshe Dayan in the Yom Kippur War*, p. 28.
2. *Time*, July 30, 1973, p. 13.
3. Robinson, *Yamani*, pp. 84–86.
4. Hanoch Bartov, *Dado: 48 Years and Another 20 Days* (Or Yehuda: Dvir, 2002), pp. 237–39.
5. John K. Cooley, *Libyan Sandstorm* (New York: Holt, Reinhart, and Winston, 1982), pp. 106–09.
6. Aaron J. Klein, *The Master of Operations: The Story of Mike Harari* (Jerusalem: Keter, 2014), pp. 16–20; Zamir and Mass, *With Open Eyes*, pp. 142–46; Mohamad Hamad, *El-Rai el-A'am* (Kuwait), October 15, 1997, p. 12; interview with Zvi Zamir, September 1, 2009; Oded Granot, "How Gaddafi and Sadat Conspired to Shoot Down an El Al Plane," *Maariv* Sabbath Supplement, December 2, 1994; Nadav Zeevi, "The Betrayed: Senior Mossad and MI Officials Talk for the First Time About the Handling and Abandonment of Ashraf Marwan, Israel's Number One Agent," *Maariv*, December 28, 2007; Ilana Dayan, "The Last Spy: The Life and Death of Dr. Ashraf Marwan," *Fact (Uvda)*, Israel Television Channel 2, December 27, 2007; *Maariv*, September 6, 1973.
7. See, for example, Shalev, *Failure and Success in the Warning*, p. 133.
8. Agranat Commission, Third and Final Report, vol. 1.

Chapter 9: Signing at Sundown on Saturday

1. Mohamed Heikal, *Mubarak and His Time . . . From the Podium to the Square* (Cairo: Dar al-Shorouq, 2013), p. 257.
2. In a personal interview conducted with Zamir on August 19, 1998, Zamir rejected the commission's report that he had used the word "imminent." That, he claimed, is a word he never uses.
3. Transcripts of telephone conversations among Freddy Eini, Zvi Zamir, and Eli Zeira, in *The Commission of Inquiry—Yom Kippur War: Additional Interim Report:*

Reasoning and Addenda for the Interim Report of April 1, 1974, vol. 1, Appendix A, "Actions of the Mossad in Early October," pp. 51–52.

4. Braun, *Moshe Dayan in the Yom Kippur War*, pp. 58–59, 61.

5. Shazly, *Crossing the Suez*, p. 213; El-Gamasy, *The October War*, p. 197.

6. "Mohammad Nusseir to the TV Show 'Ahatraq': Ashraf Marwan Didn't Know When the October War Would Begin, and His Relations with Arab Intelligence Were Strong," *Al-Mizri Al-Yum*, November 7, 2008, quotes from television interview given November 6, 2008. "So He Was in London on the 5th of October 1973!!" *Egyptian Chronicles*, October 23, 2008, http://egyptian chronicles.blogspot.com/2008/10/so-he-was-in-london-on-5th-of-october.html.

7. Mohamed Heikal, *The Road to Ramadan* (New York: Quadrangle/New York Times Books, 1975), pp. 15–16.

8. Howard Blum, *The Eve of Destruction: The Untold Story of the Yom Kippur War* (New York: HarperCollins, 2003), p. 120.

9. Yigal Kipnis, *1973: The Road to War* (Charlottesville, VA.: Just World Books, 2013), pp. 46-47.

10. Bar-Joseph, *The Watchman Fell Asleep*, pp. 116–17, 148–49, 248–50. True, Zeira tried to claim on a number of occasions that he gave the order to deploy the special equipment forty hours before the war was launched (that is, Thursday night at 10:00 p.m. Israel time). However, Col. Yossi Langotsky, who at the time commanded the unit responsible for deploying them, stated that forty hours before the start of war, Zeira approved conducting a check of the equipment's readiness ("tool check") and insisted that they be turned off again on Friday at 6:00 a.m. The commander of the 848th Intelligence Unit, Col. Yoel Ben-Porat, told him personally that the equipment had been shut down at that time. Langotsky, who also checked with the soldiers who were physically involved (that is, who actually pushed the button), said that they were deployed operationally only "on the morning of Yom Kippur, a couple of hours before the war." Yossi Langotsky, "The Truth About the 'Special Means,'" *Haaretz*, December 20, 2005; personal correspondence with Yossi Langotsky.

11. Account of the events of Friday, October 6, according to Bar-Joseph, *The Watchman Fell Asleep*, pp. 141–86.

12. Zamir and Mass, *With Open Eyes*, p. 150.

Chapter 10: Dovecote

1. Personal interviews with Freddy Eini, Arieh Shalev, Avner Shalev, and Zvi Zamir.

2. Quoted from the transcript of the conversation, as it was recorded by Maj. Gen. Shlomo Gazit, coordinator of the territories, who was present at the meeting. *Haaretz* Weekend Supplement, January 1, 1999.

3. Bar-Joseph, *The Watchman Fell Asleep*, p. 199.

4. Prime Minister's Office, National Archive, *Summary of Consultations with the Prime Minister, October 6, 1973, 8:05* (recorded by Eli Mizrahi), http://www.archives.gov.il/NR/rdonlyres/66FC5A72-27F7-41A6-9969-7ED71A097F57/0/yk6_10_0805.pdf.

5. For example: *Prime Minister's Office, National Archive, Meeting with the Prime Minister, October 7, 1973, 1450 hours* (recorded by Eli Mizrahi), http://www.archives.gov.il/NR/rdonlyres/0FC0ABE9-C023-466D-9B65-2502586EE0AF/0/yk7_10_1450.pdf.

6. Elchanan Oren, *The History of the Yom Kippur War* (Tel Aviv: IDF-History Department, 2013), pp. 112–13; Maj. Gen. (ret.) Amnon Reshef, *We Will Never Cease! Brigade 14 in the War of Yom Kippur* (Ot Yehuda: Dvir, 2013), pp. 94–95.

7. Motti Ashkenazi with Baruch Nevo and Nurit Ashkenazi, *Tonight at Six There Will Be War* (Tel Aviv: Hakibutz Hameuhad, 2003), pp. 61–67.

8. Braun, *Moshe Dayan in the Yom Kippur War*, p. 82.

9. Telephone conversation with Eitan Karmi, August 27, 2010. "In the Middle of Yom Kippur, the IDF Spokesman Announced: 'At approximately 2:00 p.m., the forces of Egypt and Syria launched an attack in Sinai and the Golan Heights. Our forces are working to fight the attackers,'" IAF website, http://iaf.org.il/843-13277-he/IAF.aspx.

10. Shimon Golan, *Decision-Making of the Israeli High Command in the Yom Kippur War* (Ben Shemen: Modan and IDF History Department, 2013), pp. 318–19, 328–29, 341–42, 369–70; Amiram Ezov, "'Ministerial Recommendation': The Southern Command During the Yom Kippur War—October 7, 1973—Thwarted the Counter-Attack," in *War Today: Studies of the Yom Kippur War*, ed. Hagai Golan and Shaul Shai (Tel Aviv: Maarachot, 2003), pp. 204–58, 208.

11. Ibid., p. 227.

12. Prime Minister's Office, National Archive, *Meeting with the Prime Minister, October 7, 1973, 2350 Hours* (recorded by Eli Mizrahi), http://www.archives.gov.il/NR/rdonlyres/FD8B4764-23C7-4D0B-8466-EA5FDB1C507B/0/yk7_10_2350.pdf; Prime Minister's Office, National Archive, *Meeting with the Prime Minister, October 8, 1973, 1950 Hours. Report of M-G Bar-Lev and Minister Alon After Surveying the Front* (recorded by Eli Mizrahi), http://www.archives.gov.il/NR/rdonlyres/A6A68F84-86A8-488D-8A3C-216644051639/0/yk8_10_1950.pdf.

13. Personal interview with Zvi Zamir, August 13, 1998.

Chapter 11: The Rise and Fall of Ashraf Marwan

1. "Sekretarijat za informacije," *Yugoslav Survey*, vol. 17, 1976, p. 68.

2. Interview with Zvi Zamir, July 8, 2008; telephone conversation with Freddy Eini, October 1, 2010; Shimon Golan, "The Yom Kippur War: The Debate About Crossing the Canal on October 12, 1973," in *State Army Relations in Israel, 1948–1974*, ed. Yehudit Ronen and Avraham Zohar (Tel Aviv: Golda Meir Memorial Association and the Israeli Society for Military History, 2004), pp. 128–45; Uri Bar-Joseph, "When the Gates Were Locked: MI in the Yom Kippur War," in *Mlechet Machshevet: 60 Years of Israeli Intelligence—A View from Within*, ed. Amos Gilboa and Efraim Lapid (Tel Aviv: Yedioth Ahronot, 2008), pp. 70–77; Zeira, *Myth Versus Reality*, p. 162.

3. Hagai Tzoref, "The Director of the Mossad, Zvi Zamir, and Israel's Leadership During the War of Yom Kippur." An unpublished paper. Dr. Tzoref is a senior archivist in Israel's National Archives, in charge of the archive's collection of documents during Golda Meir's tenure as prime minister (1969–1974).

4. Victor Israelyan, *Inside the Kremlin During the Yom Kippur War* (University Park: Pennsylvania State University Press, 1995), 103–14.

5. Tzoref, "The Director of the Mossad."

6. *Maariv*, November 9, 1973; *Maariv*, December 4, 1973; Bahgat Korany and Ali E. Hillal Dessouki, *The Foreign Policies of Arab States: The Challenge of Globalization* (Cairo: American University of Cairo Press, 2008), p. 184.

7. *Maariv*, December 19, 1973.

8. Henry Kissinger, *Years of Upheaval* (Boston: Little, Brown, 1982), p. 1061.

9. *Maariv*, May 7, 1974.

10. Kissinger, *Years of Upheaval*, p. 844.

11. Le Carré, *The Secret Pilgrim*, p. 193.

12. Fawzi, *Secrets of the Assassination of Ashraf Marwan*, p. 17; *Maariv*, August 23, 1974.

13. Gerard Chaliand, ed., *People Without a Country: Kurds and Kurdistan* (London: Zed Books, 1984), p. 170; Asadollah Alam, *The Shah and I: The Confidential Diary of Iran's Royal Court, 1969–1977* (London: I.B. Tauris, 1991), p. 185.

14. "Memorandum of conversation between: Mr. Ismail Fahmy, Minister of Foreign Affairs of the Arab Republic of Egypt, Dr. Ashraf Marwan, Presidential Secretary for Foreign Contacts, and Dr. Henry Kissinger, Secretary of State and Assistant to the President for National Security Affairs, and Mr. Peter W. Rodman, NSC Staff, August 13, 1974, Madison Room, 8th Floor, Department of State," National Security Archives, Washington, D.C., pp. 10–11.

15. "After the Jehan Sadat Interview: Shocking Secrets Revealed by Her Husband's Friend," Al-Arabiya Network, March 4, 2007.

16. Christopher Andrew and Vasili Mitrokhin, *The World Was Going Our Way: The KGB and the Battle for the Third World* (New York: Basic Books, 2005), pp. 161, 167.

17. John Cooley, *Unholy Wars* (London: Pluto Press, 2002), p. 17; "Saudi Ambassador to the United States Prince Turki Al-Faisal Interview with the Saudi-US

Relations Information Service (SUSRIS)," March 2, 2006, http://www.saudi embassy.net/archive/2006/transcript/Page19.aspx.

18. Joseph J. Trento, *Prelude to Terror: The Rogue CIA and the Legacy of America's Private Intelligence Network and the Compromising of American Intelligence* (New York: Carroll & Graf, 2005), p. 5; Peter Dale Scott, *The Road to 9/11: Wealth, Empire, and the Future of America* (Berkeley: University of California Press, 2007), p. 111.

19. Heikal, *Mubarak and His Time*, p. 248.

20. Tharwat, *Ashraf Marwan: Fact and Illusion*, pp. 38–40.

21. J. C. Louis and Harvey Z. Yazikian, *The Cola Wars: The Story of the Global Battle Between the Coca-Cola Company and PepsiCo, Inc.* (New York: Everest House, 1980), pp. 177–178.

22. Jamaa, *I Knew Sadat:*, p. 181.

23. Sabri, *Sadat: The Truth and the Legend*, p. 653.

24. Jamaa, *I Knew Sadat*, pp. 216–18.

25. *Maariv*, October 15, 1975.

26. *Al-Ahram*, March 22, 1976.

27. Sabri, *Sadat: The Truth and the Legend*, p. 655; Fawzi, *Secrets of the Assassination of Ashraf Marwan*, p. 32.

28. "The Arabs Diversify into the Arms Business," *Business Week*, October 31, 1977, pp. 31–32; Thomas Lippman, "The Arab Organization for Industry Signs Secret Agreements with France and Britain for Joint Production of Modern Weaponry," *Maariv*, September 11, 1978.

29. Sabri, *Sadat: The Truth and the Legend*, pp. 654–55; Fatah, *Who Killed Ashraf Marwan?*, pp. 33–34.

30. Fawzi, *Secrets of the Assassination of Ashraf Marwan*, p. 29; Sabri, *Sadat: The Truth and the Legend*, p. 656.

31. Sabri, *Sadat: The Truth and the Legend*, pp. 656–57.

32. Ibid., pp. 657–59; Tharwat, *Ashraf Marwan: Fact and Illusion*, pp. 36–38.

33. *Al-Akhbar*, October 12, 1978.

34. Sabri, *Sadat: The Truth and the Legend*, pp. 656–57; Fatah, *Who Killed Ashraf Marwan?*, p. 43.

35. Fatah, *Who Killed Ashraf Marwan?* p. 44.

36. *Maariv*, October 17, 1978.

37. "Statement from Ashraf Marwan, Responding to Claims in the Book by (The Engineer) Osman Ahmed Osman," *Al-Akhbar al-Youm* and *Al-Ahram*, April 16, 1981; Sabri, *Sadat: The Truth and the Legend*, p. 665.

38. Sabri, *Sadat: The Truth and the Legend*, pp. 662–65.

Chapter 12: An Angel in the City, a Son-in-Law Exposed

1. Interview with Tom Bower; *New York Times*, December 28, 2004.

2. A report on the Proposed Merger, *Lonrho Limited and House of Fraser Limited*, Presented to Parliament in Pursuance of Section 83 of the Fair Trading Act 1973 (London: Her Majesty's Printing Office, December 9, 1981), p. 27 (hereafter: Griffiths Report, 1981).

3. Pinkindustry, "The House of Fraser," *Atlantic Semantic*, http://pinkindustry .wordpress.com/the-house-of-fraser.

4. Tom Bower, *Fayad: The Unauthorized Biography* (London: Macmillan, 1998), p. 151; Tom Bower, *Tiny Rowland: A Rebel Tycoon* (London: Mandarin, 1994), pp. 499–500.

5. Chris Blackhurst, "As Mysterious in Life as in Death," *Timeout* London, July 2, 2007.

6. Chris Blackhurst, "The Shadowy World of Ashraf Marwan," *Business*, May 5, 1987.

7. Interview with Tom Bower.

8. Quotations from Griffiths Report, 1981; statement of Member of Parliament Charles Wardle, June 4, 1997, http://hansard.millbanksystems.com/com mons/1997/jun/04/dti-inquiries#column_318; commentary on Griffiths's choice of words; interview with Tom Bower, June 28, 2010.

9. Letter from Sir Andrew Bowden MBE, MP, to the Parliamentary Commissioner for Standards, February 13, 1997 (hereafter: Bowden Letter).

10. Interviews with Bower and Blackhurst; Robinson, *Yamani*, pp. 130–35.

11. Simon Parkin, "Who Killed the 20th Century's Greatest Spy?" *Guardian*, September 15, 2015: http://www.theguardian.com/world/2015/sep/15/ who-killed-20th-centurys-greatest-spy-ashraf-marwan.

12. Graham Greene, *Our Man in Havana* (New York: Penguin, 1969); John le Carré, *The Tailor of Panama* (New York: Knopf, 1996).

13. Yossi Melman and Dan Raviv, *Imperfect Spies* (Tel Aviv: Maariv, 1990), p. 176.

14. Ian Black and Benny Morris, *Israel's Secret Wars* (New York: Grove Weidenfeld, 1991), p. 286.

15. Shmuel Katz, *Soldier Spies: Israeli Military Intelligence* (Novato, CA: Presidio, 1992), p. 246.

16. Eli Zeira, *Myth versus Reality: The Yom Kippur War—Failures and Lessons* (Tel Aviv: Eidanim, 1993).

17. Telephone conversation with Amnon Dankner, May 13, 2010.

18. Zeira, *Myth versus Reality*, p. 124.

19. Robinson, *Yamani*, p. 85.

20. Zeira, *Myth versus Reality: The Yom Kippur War—Failures and Lessons*, p.126.

21. Ruling of Arbitration, before Justice (ret.) Theodor Orr. Plaintiff: Eliahu (Eli) Zeira, represented by Adv. B. Mozer et al.; v. Defendant: Zvi Zamir, represented by Adv. Danziger, Klegsbald et al., March 25, 2007, pp. 15–17 (hereafter: Orr Ruling).

22. Zeira, *Myth versus Reality: The Yom Kippur War—Failures and Lessons*, pp. 85, 123.
23. Orr Ruling, pp. 16–17.
24. Ephraim Kahana, "Early Warning Against Concept: The Case of the Yom Kippur War 1973," *Intelligence and National Security* 7, no. 2 (2002): 81–104, 99.
25. Ahron Bregman and Jihan el-Tahri, *The Fifty Years War: Israel and the Arabs* (London: Penguin, 1998).
26. Ahron Bregman, *Israel's Wars, 1947–93* (London: Routledge, 2000).
27. Ahron Bregman, *A History of Israel* (Houndmills, UK: Palgrave Macmillan, 2002).
28. Israel Television Channel One, *Supplement of Supplements*, September 23, 2004.
29. Orr Ruling, p. 34.

Chapter 13: Fallen Angel

1. In addition to the sources cited below, the current description of the events surrounding Marwan's death relies on interviews with two of the people most closely associated with the affair but who preferred to remain anonymous. Other sources include: Private electronic correspondence with Dr. Ahron Bregman, June 28, 2010; Yossi Melman, "It Doesn't Sound Like the Ashraf Marwan I Know"; Majdi al-Jallad, "*Al-Masry al-Youm* Publishes Important Details on the Death of Ashraf Marwan," *Al-Masry al-Youm*, July 7, 2007; "Mona Abdel Nasser Interviews with *Al-Ahram Weekly*: The Israelis Murdered My Husband and Paid Money to Distort the Truth," *El-Araby*, September 24, 2007; "Apology," *Al-Ahram Weekly*, November 2007, Issue 872, pp. 22–28; Rajiv Syal, "'Double Agent' Billionaire's Death in Fall from Balcony Was Murder, Says Friend," *Sunday Times*, October 13, 2007; "An Egyptian Riddle," *Private Eye*, August 4, 2010; Parkin, "Who Killed the 20th Century's Greatest Spy?"
2. Rajiv Syal, "Evidence Missing in 'Spy' Death-Fall Mystery," *Times Online*, August 29, 2007.
3. Rick E. Ingram, ed., *The International Encyclopedia of Depression* (New York: Springer, 2009), pp. 546–47.
4. Yossi Melman, "It Doesn't Sound Like the Ashraf Marwan I Know"; electronic correspondence with Dr. Ahron Bregman, June 28, 2010; Parkin, "Who Killed the 20th Century's Greatest Spy?"
5. Andrew Hosken, "Billionaire's 'Spy' Death Remains a Mystery," BBC Radio, July 15, 2010.
6. *Al-Araby*, September 24, 2007.
7. "Mossad Agents Murdered My Husband, Says Widow of Billionaire Arms Dealer," *Observer*, July 11, 2010.

8. Telephone conversation between Ahron Bregman and Ashraf Marwan, October 14, 2003, in Dr. Bregman's private collection.

9. Transcript of telephone conversation between Ahron Bregman and Ashraf Marwan, May 7, 2005.

10. Zamir and Mass, *With Open Eyes*, pp. 151–53.

11. James Forsyth, "Did He Fall or Was He Pushed?," *Spectator*, August 15, 2007.

12. Rajiv Syal, "Missing Memoirs Fuel Spy Death Mystery," *Sunday Times*, August 13, 2007.

13. Ronen Bergman, "The 'Khotel' Code."

14. Electronic correspondence with the librarian at the archive in Washington and with Dr. Ahron Bregman, August 10 and 29, 2010.

15. Howard Blum, "The Double Agent Who Fooled Israel," early draft of "Another Operative Is Outed—But in Israel This Time," *Los Angeles Times*, October 5, 2003.

16. Telephone conversation between Ahron Bregman and Ashraf Marwan, October 6, 2006.

17. Yossi Melman, "What Is Known About the Mysterious Death of Ashraf Marwan, the Agent Who Warned Israel of the Yom Kippur War," *Haaretz*, May 28, 2010.

18. Ilana Dayan, "The Last Spy."

19. Zamir and Mass, *With Open Eyes*, p. 129.

20. Heikal, *Mubarak and His Time*, p. 246.

21. Ronen Bergman, "Their Man in Cairo," *Yediot Ahronot*, May 6, 2005.

22. Heikal, *Mubarak and His Time*, p. 252.

23. Ibid., p. 256.

24. Ben Macintyre, *A Spy Among Friends* (New York: Crown, 2014), pp. 265–67.

25. Heikal, *Mubarak and His Time*, p. 260.

26. Dr. Moustafa al-Fiqi, "On El-Leithy Nassif, the Egyptian General Who Died in a Manner Similar to Ashraf in London," *Al-Masry al-Youm*, October 9, 2008; "Egyptian X-File: Stuart Tower, the Beginning," *Egyptian Chronicles*, May 21, 2010, http://egyptianchronicles.blogspot.com/2010/05/egyptian-x-file-stuart-tower-beginning.html.

27. Kris Kenway, "Searching for Cinderella," *Egypt Today* 25, no. 6 (June 2004): pp. 22-30; "Egyptian X-File: Cinderella's Rank," *Egyptian Chronicles*, July 14, 2009, http://egyptianchronicles.blogspot.com/2009/07/egyptian-x-file-cinderella-rank.html.

28. *Rose al-Yusuf*, June 29, 2011.

29. Reuters, July 2, 2007.

30. Ilana Dayan, "The Last Spy."

31. Steve Kroft, "Was the Perfect Spy a Double Agent?" *60 Minutes*, May 10, 2009.

Bibliography

Books

Arabic

Fatah, Assam Abdel. *Who Killed Ashraf Marwan? The File of Agent Babel.* Cairo: El-Eiman, 2007.

Fawzi, Mohamed. *Secrets of the Assassination of Ashraf Marwan.* Beirut: Al-Watan Lel Nasher, 2007.

Heikal, Mohamed Hassanin. *Mubarak and His Time . . . From the Podium to the Square.* Cairo: Dar al-Shorouq, 2013.

Jam'a, Mohamed. *I Knew Sadat: Half a Century of Secrets About Sadat and the [Muslim] Brotherhood.* Cairo: Al-Maktab al-Masry al-Hadeth, 1999.

Sabah, Souad al. *Falcon of the Gulf: Abdullah Mubarak al-Sabah.* Kuwait: Kadhma, 1995.

Sabri, Musa. *Sadat: The Truth and the Legend.* Cairo: Al-Maktab al-Masry al-Hadeth, 1985.

Tharwat, Muhammad. *Ashraf Marwan: Fact and Illusion.* Cairo: Madbuli, 2008.

Hebrew

Ashkenazi, Motti, with Baruch Nevo and Nurit Ashkenazi. *Tonight at Six There Will Be War.* Tel Aviv: Hakibutz Hameuhad, 2003.

Barto, Hanoch. *Dado: 48 Years and Another 20 Days.* Or Yehuda: Dvir, 2002.

Bergman, Ronen, and Gil Meltser. *The Yom Kippur War: Real Time.* Tel Aviv: Yedioth Ahronot, 2003.

Braun, Arieh. *Moshe Dayan in the Yom Kippur War.* Tel Aviv: Edanim, 1992.

Gera, Gideon. *Gaddafi's Way in Libya.* Tel Aviv: Hakibutz Hameuhad, 1983.

Golan, Shimon. *Decision-Making of the Israeli High-Command in the Yom Kippur War.* Ben Shemen: Modan and IDF History Department, 2013.

Gordon, Shmuel. *Thirty Hours in October, Fateful Decisions: The Air Force at the Start of the Yom Kippur War.* Tel Aviv: Maariv, 2008.

Klein, Aaron J. *The Master of Operations: The Story of Mike Harari*. Jerusalem: Keter, 2014.

Medzini, Meron. *Golda: A Political Biography*. Tel Aviv: Yedioth Ahronot, 2008.

Melman, Yossi, and Dan Raviv. *Imperfect Spies*. Tel Aviv: Maariv, 1990.

Nassib, Selim, *Umm*. Tel Aviv: Asia, 1999.

Oren, Elchanan. *The History of the Yom Kippur War*. Tel Aviv: IDF-History Department, 2013.

Rabin, Yitzhak. *Record of Service*. Tel Aviv: Maariv, 1978.

Reshef, Amnon. *We Will Never Cease! Brigade 14 in the War of Yom Kippur*. Or Yehuda: Dvir, 2013.

Shalev, Arieh. *Failure and Success in the Warning: Intelligence Assessments on the Eve of the Yom Kippur War*. Tel Aviv: Maarachot, 2006.

Shamir, Shimon. *Egypt under Sadat's Leadership: The Search for a New Orientation*. Tel Aviv: Dvir, 1978.

Yaacobi, Gad. *By a Hair's Breadth: How an Agreement between Israel and Egypt Was Missed, and the Yom Kippur War Was Not Prevented*. Tel Aviv: Edanim, 1989.

Zamir, Zvi, and Efrat Mass. *With Open Eyes*. Or Yehuda: Zmora-Bitan, 2011.

Zeira, Eli. *Myth versus Reality, The October '73 War: Failures and Lessons*. Tel Aviv: Yedioth Ahronot, 2004.

English

Aburish, Said K. *Nasser: The Last Arab*. New York: Macmillan Publishers, 2004.

———. *The Rise, Corruption, and Coming Fall of the House of Saud*. London: Bloomsbury, 2005.

Alam, Asadollah. *The Shah and I: The Confidential Diary of Iran's Royal Court, 1969–1977*. London: I. B. Tauris, 1991.

Alexander, Anne. *Nasser*. London: Haus Publishing, 2005.

Andrew, Christopher, and Vasili Mitrokhin. *The World Was Going Our Way: The KGB and the Battle for the Third World*. New York: Basic Books, 2005.

Bar-Joseph, Uri. *The Watchman Fell Asleep: The Surprise of Yom Kippur and Its Sources*. Albany: SUNY Press, 2005.

Beattie, Kirk J. *Egypt during the Sadat Years*. New York: Palgrave Macmillan, 1980.

Black, Ian, and Benny Morris. *Israel's Secret Wars*. New York: Grove Weidenfeld, 1991.

———. *A History of Israel*. Houndmills, UK: Palgrave Macmillan, 2002.

Blum, Howard. *The Eve of Destruction: The Untold Story of the Yom Kippur War*. New York: HarperCollins, 2003.

Bower, Tom. *Fayad: The Unauthorized Biography*. London: Macmillan Publishers, 1998.

———. *Tiny Rowland: A Rebel Tycoon*. London: Mandarin, 1994.

Bregman, Ahron, and Jihan el-Tahri. *The Fifty Years War: Israel and the Arabs*. London: Penguin, 1998.

———. *Israel's Wars, 1947–93*. London: Routledge, 2000.

Chaliand, Gerard, ed. *People without a Country: Kurds and Kurdistan*. London: Zed Books, 1984.

Cherkashin, Victor, and Gregory Feiger. *Spy Handler: Memoirs of a KGB Officer: The True Story of the Man Who Recruited Robert Hanssen and Aldrich Ames*. New York: Basic Books, 2005.

Cooley, John K. *Libyan Sandstorm*. New York: Holt, Rinehart and Winston, 1982.

———. *Unholy Wars*. London: Pluto Press, 2002.

Dreyfuss, Robert. *Devil's Game: How the United States Helped Unleash Fundamentalist Islam*. New York: Henry Holt, 2006.

Gamasy, Mohamed Abdel Ghani el. *The October War: Memoirs of Field Marshal El-Gamasy of Egypt*. Cairo: The American University of Cairo Press, 1993.

Greene, Graham. *Our Man in Havana*. New York: Penguin, 1969.

Harris, Tomás. *Garbo: The Spy Who Saved D-Day*. Tonawanda, NY: Dundurn Press, 2000.

Heikal, Mohamed. *The Road to Ramadan*. New York: Quadrangle/New York Times Book Co., 1975.

———. *The Sphinx and the Commissar: The Rise and Fall of Soviet Influence in the Middle East*. New York: Harper & Row, 1978.

———. *Autumn of Fury: The Assassination of Sadat*. New York: Random House, 1983.

Ingram, Rick E., ed. *The International Encyclopedia of Depression*. New York: Springer, 2009.

Israelyan, Victor. *Inside the Kremlin during the Yom Kippur War*. University Park: Pennsylvania State University Press, 1995.

Katz, Shmuel. *Soldier Spies: Israeli Military Intelligence*. Novato, CA: Presidio, 1992.

Kipnis, Yigal. *1973: The Road to War*. Charlottesville, VA: Just World Books, 2013.

Kissinger, Henry. *Years of Upheaval*. Boston: Little, Brown, 1982.

Korany, Bahgat, and Ali E. Hillal Dessouki. *The Foreign Policies of Arab States: The Challenge of Globalization*. Cairo: American University of Cairo Press, 2008.

Le Carré, John. *The Secret Pilgrim*. New York: Alfred A. Knopf, 1990.

———. *The Tailor of Panama*. New York: Alfred A. Knopf, 1996.

Louis, J. C., and Harvey Z. Yazikian. *The Cola Wars: The Story of the Global Battle Between the Coca-Cola Company and PepsiCo, Inc.* New York: Everest House, 1980.

Macintyre, Ben. *Double Cross: The True Story of the D-Day Spies*. New York: Broadway Books, 2013.

———. *A Spy Among Friends: Kim Philby and the Great Betrayal*. New York: Broadway Books, 2014.

Mangold, Tom. *Cold Warrior: James Jesus Angleton: The CIA's Master Spy Hunter*. New York: Touchstone Books, 1992.

Modin, Yuri. *My Five Cambridge Friends: Burgess, Maclean, Philby, Blunt, and Cairncross*. New York: Farrar, Straus and Giroux, 1994.

Nasser, Tahia Gamal Abdel. *Nasser: My Husband*. Cairo and New York: American University in Cairo Press, 2013.

Nordeen, Lon, and David Nicole. *Phoenix over the Nile: A History of Egyptian Air Power, 1932–1994.* Washington, DC: Smithonian Institute Press, 1996.

Nutting, Anthony. *Nasser.* New York: E. P. Dutton, 1972.

Posner, Gerald. *Secrets of the Kingdom.* New York: Random House, 2005.

Robinson, Jeffrey. *The Risk Takers.* New York: HarperCollins, 1985.

———. *Yamani: The Inside Story.* London: Simon & Schuster, 1988.

Sadat, Anwar el. *In Search of Identity: An Autobiography.* New York: HarperCollins, 1978.

Sadat, Jehan. *A Woman of Egypt.* New York: Simon & Schuster, 2002.

Safran, Nadav. *Saudi Arabia: Ceaseless Quest for Security.* Ithaca, NY: Cornell University Press, 1988.

Schecter, Jerrold L. and Peter S. Deriabin. *The Spy Who Saved the World: How a Soviet Colonel Changed the Course of the Cold War.* New York: Charles Scribner's Sons, 1992.

Scott, Peter Dale. *The Road to 9/11: Wealth, Empire, and the Future of America.* Berkeley: University of California Press, 2007.

Shazly, Saad el. *The Crossing of the Suez: Revised Edition.* San Francisco: American Mideast Research, 2003.

Shlaim, Avi. *Lion of Jordan: The Life of King Hussein in War and Peace.* New York: Alfred A. Knopf, 2008.

Sirrs, Owen L. *A History of the Egyptian Intelligence Service: A History of the Mukhabarat, 1910–2009.* New York: Routledge, 2010.

Talty, Stephan. *Agent Garbo: The Brilliant, Eccentric Secret Agent Who Tricked Hitler and Saved D-Day.* Boston: Houghton Mifflin Harcourt, 2012.

Trento, Joseph J. *Prelude to Terror: The Rogue CIA and the Legacy of America's Private Intelligence Network.* New York: Carroll & Graf, 2005.

Vatikiotis, Panayiotis J. *The Modern History of Egypt.* New York: Praeger, 1969.

Wise, David. *Nightmover: How Aldrich Ames Sold the CIA to the KGB for $4.6 Million.* New York: HarperCollins, 1995.

Woodward, Bob. *Veil: The Secret Wars of the CIA, 1981–1987.* New York: Simon & Schuster, 2005.

Academic Articles and Chapters

Zisser, Eyal. "Syrian and the October War: The Missed Opportunity." In *The October 1973 War: Politics, Diplomacy, Legacy*, edited by Asaf Siniver, pp. 67–83. London: Hurst, 2013.

Bar-Joseph, Uri, and Amr Yossef. "The Hidden Factors that Turned the Tide: Strategic Decision-Making and Operational Intelligence in the 1973 War." *Journal of Strategic Studies* 37, no. 4 (2014): pp. 584–608.

Ezov, Amiram. "'Ministerial Recommendation': The Southern Command during the Yom Kippur War—October 7, 1973—Thwarted the Counter-Attack." In *War Today: Studies of the Yom Kippur War*, edited by Hagai Golan and Shaul Shai, 204–58. Tel Aviv: Maarachot, 2003.

Shalev, Arieh. "Intelligence Estimates in Advance of the War." In *National Trauma: The Yom Kippur War After Thirty Years and Another War*, edited by Moshe Shemesh and Ze'ev Drori, pp. 125–83. Sdeh Boker: Ben-Gurion University Press, 2008.

Kahana, Ephraim. "Early Warning against Concept: The Case of the Yom Kippur War 1973." *Intelligence and National Security* 17, no. 2 (2002): pp. 81–104.

Websites and Blogs

"Egyptian X-File: Cinderella's Rank," Egyptian Chronicles, July 14, 2009, http:// egyptianchronicles.blogspot.com/2009/07/egyptian-x-file-cinderella-rank .html. Accessed January 20, 2016.

"Egyptian X-File: Stuart Tower, the Beginning." *Egyptian Chronicles*, May 21, 2010, http://egyptianchronicles.blogspot.com/2010/05/egyptian-x-file-stuart-tower-beginning.html. Accessed January 20, 2016.

In the Middle of Yom Kippur, the IDF Spokesman Announced: 'At approximately 2:00 p.m., the forces of Egypt and Syria launched an attack in Sinai and the Golan Heights. Our forces are working to fight the attackers,'" IAF website, http://iaf.org.il/843-13277-he/IAF.aspx. Accessed January 20, 2016.

"The Opportunist: 'The Bright Side of the Moon.'" *Egyptian Chronicles*, June 28, 2007, http://egyptianchronicles.blogspot.com/2007/06/opportunist-well-bright-dark-side-of.html. Accessed January 20, 2016.

Pinkindustry, "The House of Fraser," *Atlantic Semantic*, http://pinkindustry.word-press.com/the-house-of-fraser. Accessed January 20, 2016.

"Saudi Ambassador to the United States Prince Turki Al-Faisal Interview with the Saudi-US Relations Information Service (SUSRIS)," March 2, 2006, http://www .saudiembassy.net/archive/2006/transcript/Page19.aspx. Accessed January 20, 2016.

"So He Was in London on the 5th of October 1973!!" *Egyptian Chronicles*, October 23, 2008. http://egyptianchronicles.blogspot.com/2008/10/so-he-was-in-london-on-5th-of-october.html. Accessed January 20, 2016.

Newspapers, Magazines, and Electronic Media

Al Arabiya Network. "After the Jehan Sadat Interview: Shocking Secrets Revealed by Her Husband's Friend." March 4, 2007.

Al Jazeera television. "An Interview with Mohamed Hassanein Heikal." December 17, 2009.

Al-Ahram Weekly. "Apology." 872 (November 2007), pp. 22–28.

Al-Akhbar al-Youm and Al-Ahram. "Statement from Ashraf Marwan, Responding to Claims in the Book by (The Engineer) Osman Ahmed Osman." April 16, 1981.

al-Fiqi, Moustafa. "On El-Leithy Nassif, the Egyptian General Who Died in a Manner Similar to Ashraf in London." *Al-Masry al-Youm* (Egypt), October 9, 2008.

al-Laithi, Amru. "Intervuew with Mona Abdel Nasser," *Ahathraq* (Egyptian television program), March 10, 2009.

Al-Mizri Al-Youm (Egypt). "Mohammad Nosseir, to the TV Show 'Ahatraq': Ashraf Marwan Didn't Know When the October War Would Begin, and His Relations with Arab Intelligence Were Strong." November 7, 2008.

Al-Shaab (Egypt). "For 100,000 Dollars a Month . . . the 'Prophetic,' One of the Great Weapons Dealers of Egypt." December 2, 2009.

Bergman, Ronen. "The 'Khotel' Code." *Yediot Ahronot,* September 7, 2007.

———. "Their Man in Cairo." *Yediot Ahronot,* May 6, 2005.

———. "Tomorrow War Will Break Out." *Haaretz,* September 17, 1999.

Blackhurst, Chris. "As Mysterious in Life as in Death." *Timeout London,* July 2, 2007.

———. "The Shadowy World of Ashraf Marwan," *Business,* May 5, 1987.

Business Week. "The Arabs Diversify into the Arms Business." October 31, 1977.

Dayan, Ilana. "The Last Spy: The Life and Death of Dr. Ashraf Marwan." *Fact (Uvda),* Israel Television Channel 2. December 27, 2007. http://www.mako.co.il/tv-ilana_dayan/d0a2066bd9686110-94fdba003aa7c110/Article-a1156ce47951911004.htm. Accessed January 20, 2016.

Doder, Dusko. "Of Moles and Men." *Nation,* February 18, 2002, pp. 25–32.

El-Araby. "Mona Abdel Nasser Interviews with Al-Ahram Weekly: The Israelis Murdered My Husband and Paid Money to Distort the Truth." September 24, 2007.

Farid, Abdel Majid. "Interview," *Ahatraq* (Egyptian television program), November–December 2008.

Forsyth, James. "Did He Fall or Was He Pushed?" *Spectator,* August 15, 2007.

Granot, Oded. "How Gaddafi and Sadat Conspired to Shoot Down an El Al Plane." *Maariv* (Israel), December 2, 1994.

Hamad, Mohamed. "Egypt-Libya Relations from Revolution to War: Recollections of Salah al-Din al-Saadani, Egypt's First Ambassador to Libya After the Revolution." *Al-Rei al-A'am* (Kuwait), October 15, 1997.

Hosken, Andrew. "Billionaire's 'Spy' Death Remains a Mystery." *BBC Radio,* July 15, 2010.

Kemal, Halef al-Tawil. "Ashraf Marwan: The Dilemma Child." *Al-Akhbar al-Lebnaniya* (Lebanon), February 7, 2007.

Kenway, Kris. "Searching for Cinderella." *Egypt Today* 25, no. 6 (June 2004), pp. 22-30.

Kroft, Steve. "Was the Perfect Spy a Double Agent?" *60 Minutes,* CBS, May 10, 2009. http://www.cbsnews.com/news/was-the-perfect-spy-a-double-agent/. Accessed January 20, 2016.

Langotsky, Yossi. "The Truth about the 'Special Means.'" *Haaretz*, December 20, 2005.

Lippman, Thomas. "The Arab Organization for Industry Signs Secret Agreements with France and Britain for Joint Production of Modern Weaponry." *Maariv*, September 11, 1978.

Margalit, Dan. "Supplement of Supplements." Israel Television Channel 1, September 23–24, 2004.

Melman, Yossi. "It Doesn't Sound Like the Ashraf Marwan I Know." *Haaretz*, July 6, 2007.

———. "What Is Known about the Mysterious Death of Ashraf Marwan, the Agent Who Warned Israel of the Yom Kippur War." *Haaretz*, May 28, 2010.

Mohammad, Zara. "Reliving a Piece of History." *Egypt Daily News*, September 22, 2006.

Nkrumah, Gamal. "Sami Sharaf: Shadows of the Revolution," *Al-Ahram Weekly*, August 9–15, 2001.

Parkin, Simon. "Who Killed the 20th Century's Greatest Spy?" *Guardian*, September 15, 2015. http://www.theguardian.com/world/2015/sep/15/who-killed-20th-centurys-greatest-spy-ashraf-marwan. Accessed January 20, 2016.

Private Eye. "An Egyptian Riddle." August 4, 2010.

Shane, Scott. "A Spy's Motivation: For Love of Another Country." *New York Times*, April 20, 2008.

Syal, Rajiv. "'Double Agent' Billionaire's Death in Fall from Balcony Was Murder, Says Friend." *Sunday Times*, October 13, 2007.

———. "Evidence Missing in 'Spy' Death-Fall Mystery." *Sunday Times Online*, August 29, 2007.

———. "Missing Memoirs Fuel Spy Death Mystery." *Sunday Times*, August 13, 2007.

Time. "A Preemptive Purge in Cairo." May 24, 1971.

———. "Interview with Moshe Dayan." July 30, 1973.

———. "Sadat in the Saddle." May 31, 1971.

———. "The Underrated Heir." May 17, 1971.

Yugoslav Survey. "Sekretarijat za informacije." 1976.

Zeevi, Nadav. "The Betrayed: Senior Mossad and MI Officials Talk for the First Time about the Handling and Abandonment of Ashraf Marwan, Israel's Number One Agent." *Maariv* (Israel), December 28, 2007.

Documents

Israel. Commission of Inquiry—Yom Kippur War. *Additional Interim Report: Reasoning and Addenda for the Interim Report of April 1, 1974*, vol. 1, Jerusalem, 1974.

Israel. Commission of Inquiry—Yom Kippur War. *Additional Partial Report: Justifications and Additions to the Partial Report of 9 Nissan 5734* (January 4, 1974), vol. 1., Jerusalem, 1974.

Israel. IDF Military Intelligence, Branch 6. *Intelligence Survey 15/73.* January 24, 1973.

Israel. IDF Military Intelligence. *Intelligence Summary from Operation Dovecote.* December 17, 1972.

Israel. Prime Minister's Office. Meeting with the Prime Minister, October 7, 1973, 1450 hours (recorded by Mr. Eli Mizrahi). National Archive. http://www.archives. gov.il/NR/rdonlyres/0FC0ABE9-C023-466D-9B65-2502586EE0AF/0/ yk7_10_1450.pdf. Accessed January 20, 2016.

Israel. Prime Minister's Office. Meeting with the Prime Minister, October 7, 1973, 2350 hours (recorded by Eli Mizrahi). National Archive. http://www.archives. gov.il/NR/rdonlyres/FD8B4764-23C7-4D0B-8466-EA5FDB1C507B/0/ yk7_10_2350.pdf. Accessed January 20, 2016.

Israel. Prime Minister's Office. Meeting with the Prime Minister, October 8, 1973, 1950 hours. *Report of M-G Bar-Lev and Minister Alon after Surveying the Front* (recorded by Eli Mizrahi). National Archive. http://www.archives.gov.il/NR/ rdonlyres/A6A68F84-86A8-488D-8A3C-216644051639/0/yk8_10_1950.pdf. Accessed January 20, 2016.

Israel. Prime Minister's Office. Summary of Consultations with the Prime Minister, October 6, 1973, 8:05 (recorded by Eli Mizrahi). National Archive. http://www.archives.gov.il/NR/rdonlyres/66FC5A72-27F7-41A6-9969- 7ED71A097F57/0/yk6_10_0805.pdf. Accessed January 20, 2016.

Israel. Ruling of arbitration, before Justice (ret.) Theodor Orr. Plaintiff: Eliahu (Eli) Zeira, represented by Adv. B. Mozer et al.; v. Defendant: Zvi Zamir, represented by Adv. Danziger, Klegsbald et al. Tel Aviv: March 25, 2007.

United Kingdom. *A Report on the Proposed Merger, Lonrho Limited and House of Fraser Limited, Presented to Parliament in Pursuance of Section 83 of the Fair Trading Act 1973.* London: Her Majesty's Printing Office, December 9, 1981.

United Kingdom. Statement of Member of Parliament Charles Wardle. London: June 4, 1997, http://hansard.millbanksystems.com/commons/1997/jun/04/ dti-inquiries#column_318. Accessed January 20, 2016.

United States. "Memorandum of Conversation between: Mr. Ismail Fahmy, Minister of Foreign Affairs of the Arab Republic of Egypt, Dr. Ashraf Marwan, Presidential Secretary for Foreign Contacts, and Dr. Henry Kissinger, Secretary of State and Assistant to the President for National Security Affairs, and Mr. Peter W. Rodman, NSC Staff, August 13, 1974, Madison Room, 8th Floor, Department of State." National Security Archives, Washington, DC.

Unpublished Sources

Blum, Howard. "The Double Agent Who Fooled Israel," early draft of "Another Operative Is Outed—But in Israel This Time," *Los Angeles Times*, October 5, 2003.

Telephone conversation between Ahron Bregman and Ashraf Marwan, October 14, 2003, in Dr. Bregman's private collection.
Telephone conversation between Ahron Bregman and Ashraf Marwan, May 7, 2005. Dr. Bregman's private collection.
Telephone conversation between Ahron Bregman and Ashraf Marwan, October 6, 2006. Dr. Bregman's private collection.
Tzoref, Hagai. "The Director of the Mossad, Zvi Zamir, and Israel's Leadership During the War of Yom Kippur" (an unpublished paper).
Zeevi, Nadav. Life of an Agent (unpublished manuscript in Hebrew).

Interviews (partial list)

Adan, Avraham "Bren," Ramat Hasharon, October 28, 2010.
Bandman, Yonah, Tel Aviv, August 17, 1998.
Blackhurst, Chris, London, June 27, 2010.
Blum, Howard, private electronic correspondence, 2003–2007.
Bower, Tom, London, June 28, 2010.
Bregman, Dr. Ahron. Private electronic correspondence with June 28, 2010.
Eini, Freddy, Kfar Shmaryahu, Israel, July 22, 2008; August 14, 2009.
Gera, Gideon, Tel Aviv, May 3, 2010.
Gilboa, Amos, Tel Aviv, July 20, 2008.
Halevy, Efraim, Tel Aviv, March 21, 2011.
Levran Aharon, Kfar Saba, March 8, 1999.
Meir, Meir, Holon, Israel, June 25, 2008; August 19, 2009.
Navot, Menahem "Nahik," Ramat Hasharon, Israel, February 8, 2010.
Orr, Ori, Beit Yanai, Israel, October 14, 2009.
Porat, Yehuda, Shefayim, Israel, July 25, 1998.
Rosenfeld, Yaacov, Tel Aviv, September 14, 1998.
Shalev, Arieh, Tel Aviv, August 27, 1998.
Shalev, Avner, Neve Magen, Israel, May 4, 1999; October 29, 1999.
Shimon, Shamir, Tel Aviv, December 31, 2009.
Zamir, Zvi, Tel Aviv, August 13, 1998, August 19, 1998; Rishon Lezion, Israel, July 8, 2008, September 1, 2009; Tel Aviv, August 7, 2013, April 18, 2014.

Index